Colloquial Spanish

The Colloquial 2 Series

Series Adviser: Gary King

The following languages are available in the Colloquial 2 series:

French
Italian
Russian
Spanish

Accompanying cassettes and CDs are available for the above titles. They can be ordered through your bookseller, or send payment with order to Taylor & Francis/ Routledge Ltd, ITPS, Cheriton House, North Way, Andover, Hants SP10 5BE, UK, or to Routledge Inc, 29 West 35th Street, New York NY 10001, USA.

Colloquial Spanish

The next step in language learning

Untza Otaola Alday

Routledge
Taylor & Francis Group

LONDON AND NEW YORK

First published 2004
by Routledge
11 New Fetter Lane, London EC4P 4EE

Simultaneously published in the USA and Canada
by Routledge
29 West 35th Street, New York, NY 10001

Routledge is an imprint of the Taylor & Francis Group

© 2004 Untza Otaola Alday

Typeset in Sabon and Helvetica by
Florence Production Ltd, Stoodleigh, Devon

Printed and bound in Great Britain by
TJ International Ltd, Padstow, Cornwall

British Library Cataloguing in Publication Data
A catalogue record for this book is available from the British Library

Library of Congress Cataloging in Publication Data
Alday, Untza Otaola.
  Colloquial Spanish 2: the next step in language learning / Untza Otaola
  Alday.
  p. cm – (The colloquial 2 series)
1. Spanish language – Textbooks for foreign speakers – English.
I. Title. II. Series.
  PC4129.E5A4482 2003
  468.2'421–dc21
                                                        2003005219

ISBN 0–415–27337–4 (book)
ISBN 0–415–27338–2 (audio cassette)
ISBN 0–415–30262–5 (audio CD)
ISBN 0–415–27339–0 (pack)

A mis aitas quienes me
han enseñado lo que es importante en la vida

A todos mis estudiantes por toda la ayuda que me han ofrecido,
en especial a Amanda. A Susana, mi querida prima, por todo

Contents

Acknowledgements

We acknowledge the permission from *Mía* magazine for the use of their article on work permits, in Unit 9. Our thanks also to Liri Andersson for the use of her photo of the Guggenheim Museum in Unit 13.

How to use this book

First of all, congratulations for having come this far! You are obviously very serious about learning Spanish. This book will help you to consolidate what you have already learned, discover new structures/functions and gain a better understanding of some of the more complex differences between English and Spanish. You will also learn more about Spain and its culture.

Colloquial Spanish 2 can be used by adult learners working with or without a teacher. Each unit begins with a list of things that you should be able to understand and use by the time you finish the unit. This is followed by a Dialogue with a short introduction in English. You will find a list of new words you will hear in the dialogue on the CD. Before you listen to the dialogue, look at the words closely. They will help you to understand the gist of the conversation. Also before listening to the dialogue, have a look at the comprehension exercise/s given for each dialogue; they will also give you clues about what you are about to hear and will help you to concentrate on that particular information. Remember that it is perfectly normal not to understand everything said at first. The more you practise, the easier it will become.

The Dialogues are followed by Language points where you will find explanations of many of the functional and grammar points that you have come across in the dialogue. You will find a number of examples that will clarify each language point covered. All the examples have been translated, some of them literally. These literal translations will help you to see the differences between both languages. Each language point is followed by an exercise or two that focus your attention on the item explained. There are a variety of exercises, some of them will to help you understand the language point you have just learnt, others will be testing your knowledge of other points in Spanish.

Each unit, except for the first one, also has one or two reading texts followed by more language points and exercises. You may find that you will not know all the words used in the text but, before you look up the word in the dictionary, try to see if you can guess the meaning of the words from the context. You will be pleasantly surprised to find that you have guessed many words correctly! The dialogues and the written texts will help you to see how the language is used in two different mediums: spoken and written, and both the dialogues and the written texts will give you an insight into the Spanish culture.

Before you start, decide how much time you are going to spend studying the language. Give yourself realistic targets; it is better to do a little often than try to do a lot occasionally. The more often you think about the language, the easier it will be to remember new vocabulary and structures.

Don't forget that if you'd like more practice material, click onto the *Colloquial Spanish 2* website at www.routledge.com/colloquials/ spanish. There you'll find more exercises plus links to useful Spanish language sites.

1 El País Vasco

In this unit you can learn about:

▶ asking and giving personal information
▶ some uses of **ser** / **estar** / **hay**
▶ using reflexive verbs: **llamarse**, **encontrarse**
▶ talking about the weather
▶ talking about past events: **pretérito perfecto, indefinido e imperfecto**
▶ prepositions

Dialogue 1

A journalist is interviewing a number of Spanish authors living in England. He is interviewing Untza Sale, author of this book. Listen to the interview in which Untza Sale speaks about her life. When you listen to the interview, look out for the information needed to answer the following questions.

Exercise 1

1 What are her surnames and why?
2 Where is she from?
3 Does she miss Spain much? What does she miss?
4 What are the similarities between England and the north of Spain?
5 What does she like about London?

Vocabulary ♦

euskera	the name of the Basque language (*in Basque*)
un montón de	many (*colloquial expression*)

echar de menos /   to miss a person / something
   echar en falta
pincho   bite-size snack found in the Basque bars

PETER Bueno, ¿cómo te llamas realmente? El nombre que aparece en tu primer libro es Untza Otaola Alday y el que me han dicho al presentarnos es Untza Sale. ¿Por qué los apellidos son diferentes?

UNTZA Es que Sale es el apellido de mi marido que es inglés. Otaola Alday son mis apellidos españoles, dos porque como ya sabrás, en España usamos dos apellidos, el del padre y el de la madre.

PETER ¡Ah sí!, y ¿de dónde eres?

UNTZA Soy de un pueblo muy pequeño, de unos 800 habitantes, que se llama Okondo en euskera, Oquendo en castellano. Está a unos 22 km de Bilbao aunque pertenece a la provincia de Álava.

PETER ¡Ah! Eres vasca. Y, ¿hablas euskera?

UNTZA No, sólo sé unas palabras.

PETER Me imagino que te gusta Inglaterra, pero ¿no echas de menos España?

UNTZA ¡Claro!, pero no tanto como la gente piensa. Todo el mundo me dice que cómo puedo vivir aquí, que qué hago en Londres con el frío que hace . . . pero la verdad es que me gusta mucho y además el tiempo se parece bastante al del norte de España. Es verdad que hace más calor y que hay más luz pero también llueve, hiela, nieva . . . Además, llevo ya mucho tiempo en Inglaterra y tengo un montón de amigos ingleses. Aparte de todo esto Londres es una ciudad muy cosmopolita, donde hay gente de todas las partes del mundo y las ciudades españolas no son así aunque es cierto que están cambiando. La verdad es que lo que más echo en falta de España, aparte de mi familia y mis amigos, es el poder ir a un bar a cualquier hora del día, encontrarme con un amigo y tomarme un vino, comerme un pincho.

Language points ◆

How to give and ask details about a person

Remember that in Spanish there is no need to use the personal pronoun (**yo, tú, él / ella, usted, nosotros/as, vosotros/as, ellos/as**). The ending of the verb tells you who does the action.

EUSKAL HERRIA

¿De dónde eres?	Where are you from?
Soy de Oquendo.	I am from Oquendo.
Mi marido es inglés.	My husband is English.
¿Eres inglesa?	Are you English? (*talking to a woman*)
¿Es tu mujer española?	Is your wife Spanish?

¿Cómo te llamas realmente?
What is your real name?

Me llamo Untza Otaola Alday.
My name is Untza Otaola Alday.

El director de la película se llama Carlos Saura.
The director of the film is Carlos Saura.

Mis hermanos se llaman Pablo y Carlos.
My brothers' names are Pablo and Carlos.

In order to express the idea of how long you have been in a place, job, etc., you do not need to use the past tense, just use the verb **Llevar** in the present tense:

Llevo mucho tiempo aquí en Londres.
I've been in London for a long time.

¿Cuánto tiempo llevas en esta empresa?
How long have you been with this company?

To talk about likes and dislikes, you can use the verb **gustar**, which only has two possible endings in the present tense: **gusta / gustan** according to the number, i.e. singular or plural of the object/person that is liked. Also remember that this verb needs an indirect pronoun (**me, te, le, nos, os, les**).

Me gusta el último libro de Isabel Allende.
I like Isabel Allende's last book.
(*Literally*: The last book of Isabel Allende pleases me.)

Me imagino que te gusta Londres.
I presume you like London.

¿Te gustan los cuadros de Picasso?
Do you like Picasso's paintings?

A Sofía no le gusta el chorizo.
Sofía doesn't like chorizo.

A los españoles les gusta salir mucho.
Spanish people like going out a lot.

Exercise 2

You have been asked to find out about Spanish actors. Listen to the information on the recording on one particular actor and fill in the worksheet.

Name: _____

Place of birth: _____

Residence: _____

Marital status: _____

Spouse: _____

Children: _____

Hobbies: _____

Talking about the weather

Spanish uses the verb **hacer** in the third person to construct expressions to do with the weather:

¿Qué tiempo hace en el norte de España?
What is the weather like in the north of Spain?

En las Canarias no hace mucho frío en invierno.
It is not very cold in the Canary Islands in winter.

En la Costa de la Luz hace mucho viento.
It is very windy in the Costa de la Luz.

Hace frío.	It's cold.
Hace calor.	It's hot.
Hace viento.	It's windy.
Hace buen tiempo.	The weather is fine.
Hace mal tiempo.	The weather is bad.

Remember that if you want to specify how cold/hot/windy it is, you need to use the adjective **mucho** instead of the adverb **muy**:

En el centro de España hace mucho frío en invierno y mucho calor en verano.
In the centre of Spain it's very cold in winter and very hot in summer.

En las Canarias hace buen tiempo.
The weather is good in the Canary Islands.

The verbs **llover** (to rain), **helar** (to freeze), **nevar** (to snow) exhibit changes in vowel. In the present tense you only need to learn the third person singular:

No llueve mucho en el sur.
It doesn't rain very much in the south.

Llueve mucho en Galicia.
It rains a lot in Galicia.

En invierno hiela bastante.
It freezes quite a lot in winter.

Nieva bastante en invierno.
It snows quite a bit in winter.

Exercise 3

Read the following statements and say whether they are true or false:

	Verdadero	Falso
1 En el centro de España hace mucho frío en invierno.		
2 No llueve nunca en el sur.		
3 Nunca nieva en España.		
4 No hace mucho frío en Las Palmas.		
5 Normalmente hace mucho viento en la Costa de la Luz.		
6 Llueve más en el norte que en el sur.		

Some uses of *ser / estar / hay*

Ser is used in the following ways:

To talk about where people are from:

¿De dónde eres?	Where are you from?
Soy de Oquendo.	I am from Oquendo.

To express nationality:

mi marido que es inglés	my husband who is English
¡Ah! Eres vasca.	Ah! You are Basque.

To describe a place, to talk about facts:

Londres es una ciudad muy cosmopolita.
London is a cosmopolitan city.

Las ciudades españolas no son así.
Spanish cities are not like that.

Estar is used in the following ways:

To talk about where people and things are located:

Está a unos 22 km de Bilbao.
It's about 22 km from Bilbao.

To form the present continuous:

aunque es cierto que están cambiando
even though it is true they are changing

Hay is used in the following ways:

To express the existence of people or things. It does not change regardless of the number of things or people it refers to:

donde hay gente de todas las partes del mundo
where there are people from all over the world

¿Hay muchos inmigrantes en España?
Are there many immigrants in Spain?

¿Hay una farmacia por aquí?
Is there a chemist round here?

Exercise 4

Fill in the gaps with the appropriate verb (**ser, estar, hay**) in the appropriate person:

1 Madonna _____ estadounidense y su marido _____ inglés.
2 ¿Dónde _____ Toledo? ¿_____ en el centro de España?
3 _____ muchos vinos diferentes en España.
4 El museo de Guggenheim _____ en Bilbao y _____ un museo impresionante.
5 ¿A cuántos kilómetros _____ Cuenca? ¿ _____ lejos de aquí?
6 Chillida _____ un escultor muy famoso, _____ del País Vasco.
7 ¿ _____ algún hotel en tu pueblo?
8 Las Meninas _____ un cuadro de Velázquez.
9 Raúl _____ un jugador de fútbol del Real Madrid.
10 ¿_____ restaurantes vegetarianos en Bilbao?

Prepositions

Some basic uses of the prepositions you can see in the dialogue.

En means 'in / on / at':

en tu primer libro	in your first book
en España	in Spain

A is used to express distance:

Está a unos 22 km de Bilbao.
It's about 22 km from Bilbao.

It is also used to express direction:

Quiero ir a un bar.
I want to go to a bar.

Remember that **a** plus the article **el** becomes **al**:

Se parece bastante al (tiempo) del norte de España.
It is very similar to the weather in the north of Spain.

De is normally used to express origin and possession, normally 'from' or 'of' in English:

Soy de un pueblo.	I'm from a village.
el apellido de la madre	the mother's surname

Remember that **de** plus the article **el** becomes **del**:

el apellido del padre	the father's surname
todas las partes del mundo	everywhere in the world (*Literally*, all the parts of the world)

Con means 'with':

encontrarme con un amigo	to meet up with a friend

Exercise 5

Fill in the gaps with the appropriate preposition. Remember, **a** plus the article **el** becomes **al**:

1 ¿ _____ cuántos km está Vitoria?
2 Oquendo está _____ la provincia de Álava.
3 ¿ _____ dónde es el presidente de España?
4 El domingo voy _____ el teatro.
5 El apellido _____ mi madre es Alday.
6 Voy a Córdoba _____ mi marido.
7 ¿Qué haces _____ España?
8 Mañana voy _____ la playa.

Reflexive verbs

Reflexive verbs are verbs used with a reflexive pronoun (**me, te, se, nos, os, se**) because the subject also receives the action. You don't normally translate these pronouns when you translate them into English:

¿Cómo <u>te llamas</u> realmente?
What is your real name?

Soy de un pueblo que <u>se llama</u> Oquendo.
I'm from a village called Oquendo.

<u>Me imagino</u> que te gusta Londres.
I presume you like London.

el tiempo <u>se parece</u> bastante al del norte de España
the weather is quite similar to the weather in the north of Spain

Remember that the pronoun is added to the end of the infinitive:

encontrar<u>me</u> con un amigo, y tomar<u>me</u> un vino, comer<u>me</u> un pincho

Note that the verbs **tomar** and **comer** are not normally reflexive verbs. Spanish people tend to use them as reflexive verbs when they think they have eaten / drunk too much:

Me comí todo el pollo.	I ate the whole chicken.
Se bebió toda la botella.	S/he drank the whole bottle.

Exercise 6

A student from your class has been asked by the teacher to do a study of the group's habits. She is now asking you some questions. Reply to her questions in Spanish with your own information:

prepararse   to get ready   **tardar**   to take (a) long (time)

1 ¿A qué hora te levantas entre semana?
2 ¿A qué hora te levantas los domingos?
3 ¿Te duchas o te bañas?
4 ¿Cuándo prefieres ducharte, por la noche o por la mañana?
5 ¿Tardas mucho en prepararte?

Dialogue 2

Listen to the second part of the interview during which Untza Sale talks about her knowledge of languages, her studies and her reason for coming to England. Cover up the dialogue and listen first, then try to answer the questions before looking at it. Before listening to the dialogue, read the questions below as it will help you to select the necessary information. Focus on selecting the information that answers the questions rather than trying to understand the entire recording.

Vocabulary ♦

acabar de (*plus an infinitive*)	to have just done something
ir bien / mal	to go well / badly
volver a (*plus an infinitive*)	to do something again
apetecer (*plus an infinitive*)	to feel like doing something
arrepentirse de (*plus an infinitive*)	to regret
tiempo parcial	part-time
licenciatura (f)	degree
pasar de (*plus an infinitive, or a noun*)	to ignore / not to be interested (*colloquial*)

Exercise 7

1 Untza sabe
   (a) portugués
   (b) portugués y francés
   (c) portugués, alemán y francés
2 Untza vino a Londres en
   (a) el año 77
   (b) el año 87
   (c) el año 78
3 Untza vino a Londres porque
   (a) quería vivir sola
   (b) quería estudiar inglés y conocer a gente inglesa
   (c) quería estudiar inglés y salir del pueblo
4 Es más fácil trabajar y estudiar en Inglaterra porque
   (a) hay más trabajos a tiempo completo
   (b) hay más trabajos a tiempo parcial
   (c) hay muchas universidades
5 Una diferencia grande entre las universidades en Inglaterra y España es que
   (a) hay más gente en las universidades españolas
   (b) hay más gente en las universidades inglesas
   (c) hay más universidades en España

Now listen to the interview again and check your answers.

PETER ¿Hablas otros idiomas aparte del inglés?
UNTZA Sé portugués porque lo estudié en la universidad pero no lo hablo muy bien. Cuando estudiaba pasé un mes en la universidad de Lisboa pero ya hace mucho tiempo de eso. Acabo de volver de

Brasil donde he podido practicar lo que sabía y bueno, no me ha ido tan mal. Además del portugués estudié francés hace unos años, hice el examen de GCSE pero desde entonces no he vuelto a estudiarlo.

PETER ¿Cuándo viniste a Inglaterra y por qué?

UNTZA ¡No sé cuántas veces he tenido que contestar esa pregunta! Vine a Londres por primera vez en el 77 cuando sólo tenía 18 años. Para decirte la verdad no sé exactamente por qué vine a Londres, creo que porque quería aprender inglés y porque me apetecía salir del pueblo y ver otras cosas. Pero ha pasado tanto tiempo que ya no estoy segura.

PETER ¿Y no te has arrepentido nunca de haberte quedado?

UNTZA Para nada, aquí he podido hacer un montón de cosas . . .

PETER ¿Cómo qué?

UNTZA Bueno, pues, por ejemplo, en Londres es bastante fácil estudiar y trabajar a la vez. Tuve la suerte de poder estudiar en la universidad de Londres, en UCL, mientras que trabajaba en bares, restaurantes, etc. Hay muchos más trabajos a tiempo parcial que en España en general.

PETER ¿Qué estudiaste?

UNTZA Hice historia y literatura de España y de América Latina. Fue un curso estupendo, no sólo aprendí muchísimo sino que fueron unos de los mejores años de mi vida. Quizás una diferencia bastante grande entre las universidades españolas e inglesas es que cuando yo hice la licenciatura sólo éramos 15 en el curso mientras que en España hay tanta gente en las clases que los jóvenes pasan de ir. El número de personas que va a la universidad en España es mucho mayor que en Inglaterra así que las clases están llenísimas.

Language points ♦

Talking about things that have already happened

Here is a reminder of how to use some of the most common past tenses in Spanish: **pretérito perfecto, indefinido** and **imperfecto**. We will look at them in more detail in other units.

- The present perfect tense (**pretérito perfecto**) is used when the action is finished but the period of time in which the action took place has not finished. You could almost say 'up to now' I've done this or that.

- This tense is normally used with the following time expressions: **esta semana, este mes, este año, hoy,** etc.

Pero ha pasado tanto tiempo.
It's been so long.

¿Y no te has arrepentido nunca?
Haven't you ever regretted it? (*up to now*)

Aquí he podido hacer un montón de cosas.
I've been able to do lots of things here. (*up to now*)

Exercise 8

Fill in the following gaps with the appropriate person of the present perfect tense. If you want to revise the formation of the present perfect, see the Grammar reference at the end of the book.

1 Mi familia sólo _____ _____ dos veces a Inglaterra (venir).
2 (Yo) _____ _____ todo el día en el hospital (estar).
3 ¿Por qué (tú) _____ _____ tan pronto? (llegar)
4 ¿(ellos) _____ _____ todas las cartas? (leer)
5 ¿Quién _____ _____ la cena? (preparar)
6 Ya (nosotras) _____ _____ con ellos (hablar).

The simple past or preterite (**indefinido**) is used to express an action completed at a definite period in the past. This tense is normally used with time expressions such as **ayer, anoche, la semana pasada, el otro día, en 1997, en octubre, hace un año,** etc.

Los estudié en la universidad.
I studied them [languages] at university.

Aparte del portugués estudié francés hace unos años.
In addition to Portuguese, I studied French a few years ago.

Hice el examen de GCSE. I took the GCSE exam.
¿Cuándo viniste a Inglaterra? When did you come to England?
Vine a Londres en el 77. I came to London in 1977.

Remember the useful phrase **hace** ... '... ago':

Fui a Madrid hace un año.   I went to Madrid a year ago.
La vimos hace una semana.   We saw her a week ago.

Note that **hace** goes just before the time expression.

Exercise 9

Fill in the following gaps with the appropriate part of the simple past:

1 (Yo) _____ a tu casa el otro día (ir).
2 (Nosotros) la _____ el domingo (ver).
3 ¿Quién _____ el sábado pasado? (cocinar)
4 ¿Dónde (tú) _____ inglés? (estudiar)
5 Mis padres me _____ el año pasado (visitar).
6 ¿Vosotros _____ con la profesora ayer? (hablar)

The imperfect tense (**imperfecto**) is used mainly to talk about events that used to happen repeatedly, for descriptions in the past, and to express continuance and duration (in English normally the continuous form, e.g. 'I was working in restaurants', or the expression 'used to', e.g. 'I used to live in a village', is used). This tense is normally used with time expressions such as: **cada día, con frecuencia, a menudo, siempre**, etc.

porque quería aprender inglés
because I wanted to learn English

porque me apetecía salir del pueblo
because I felt like leaving my village

mientras que trabajaba en restaurantes
while I worked / was working in restaurants

Cuando era pequeña llevaba gafas.
When I was small I used to wear glasses.

Fumaba mucho.
I used to smoke a lot.

Siempre iba en autobús.
I always went by bus.

Remember that when you are talking about the age of someone in the past tense, you always need to use the imperfect tense of the verb **tener**:

> **cuando sólo tenía 18 años**
> when I was only 18 years old

> **¿Cúantos años tenías cuando fuiste a la universidad?**
> How old were you when you went to university?

Look at the following example from the dialogue:

> **Cuando estudiaba pasé un mes en la universidad de Lisboa.**
> When I was studying I spent a month at Lisbon university.

The first verb (**estudiaba**) is in the imperfect because it was a continuous action in the past and the second verb (**pasé**) is in the simple past because it is an action completed at a definite period in the past. You spent a month in Lisbon and it's finished.

Exercise 10

Fill in the gaps with the appropriate part of the imperfect tense:

1 Cuando (yo) _____ (vivir) en Oquendo _____ (andar) mucho.
2 ¿Cuántos años _____ (tener) tu hermano cuando se fue a Valencia?
3 ¿(Tú) _____ (ser) morena cuando _____ (ser) pequeña?
4 ¿Qué (tú) _____ (querer) ser cuando _____ (tener) 10 años?
5 (Nosotros) No _____ (estar) en casa cuando llamaste.
6 Ellos _____ (venir) todos los años en agosto.

Exercise 11

Learn something about the Spanish royal family. Fill in the gaps with the appropriate forms of **ser / estar / hay**:

S.M.	**Su Majestad**	His Majesty
soler	**Suelo ir al cine.**	I normally go to the cinema.
	Suelo comer en casa.	I normally eat at home.

S.M. el Rey Don Juan Carlos y S.M. la Reina Doña Sofía 1 _____
los Reyes de España. Juan Carlos 2 _____ español y Sofía 3
_____ griega. Viven en el Palacio de la Zarzuela que 4 _____
en Madrid. El palacio 5 _____ grande, 6 _____ muchas
habitaciones pero 7 _____ cómodo. La Zarzuela, además de
vivienda, 8 _____ también lugar de trabajo donde los Reyes
reciben a Jefes de Estado. Juan Carlos 9 _____ muy deportista,
10 _____ alto y delgado pero ahora 11 _____ un poco más
fuerte. Normalmente los Reyes 12 _____ en Madrid pero en
verano suelen 13 _____ en su casa de Mallorca donde 14
_____ posibilidades de hacer deporte naútico. Los Reyes tienen
tres hijos, Elena que 15 _____ casada, Cristina, la segunda, que
también 16 _____ casada y Felipe que 17 _____ soltero.
Felipe 18 _____ más alto que su padre y 19 _____ muy
guapo. El marido de Elena, Jaime de Marichalar 20 _____ de
Pamplona y 21 _____ economista. El marido de Cristina, Iñaki
Urdangarín, 22 _____ vasco y 23 _____ jugador de balon-
mano. Iñaki 24 _____ famoso porque 25 _____ casado con
la infanta y porque 26 _____ un jugador muy bueno.

¿Sabía usted? ♦

Euskal Herria, the land of the Basque men and women, is the name
used when talking about the seven historical provinces belonging to
the Basque Country: **Bizkaia, Gipuzkoa, Araba, Nafarroa, Lapurdi,
Nafarroa Beherea, Zuberoa** (names written in Basque). The first four
are in Spain and the other three in France. **Álava, Vizcaya** and
Guipuzcoa, located in the north of the Iberian Peninsula, constitute
the **Comunidad Autónoma del País Vasco,** also known as **Euskadi.**
Navarra has a separate administration as the **Comunidad Autónoma
de Navarra,** its capital being **Pamplona.** The capital of **Vizcaya** is
Bilbao, Álava's is **Vitoria** and **Guipuzcoa's** is **San Sebastián.** There
are about 2 million people living in **Euskadi,** of which about 20 per
cent speak **Euskera. Castellano** is the other official language spoken
in the Basque Country. The Basque Government, seated in **Vitoria,**
has, among other powers, the power to raise taxes, to administer
schools and the health services. **Euskadi** has its own police force, the
Ertzantza. The president of the Basque government is called **lehen-
dakari** in **Euskera.**

Note the differences between **Euskera** and **Castellano**:

Euskera	Castellano
Bizkaia	Vizcaya
Gipuzkoa	Guipúzcoa
Araba	Álava
Nafarroa	Navarra
Bilbo	Bilbao
Gasteiz	Vitoria
Donostia (also Donosti)	San Sebastián
Iruña	Pamplona

Note that the Basque language does not have the letter v.

2 Viajando

In this unit you can learn about:

▶ how to apologise for something
▶ the verbs **sentir / sentirse**
▶ direct and indirect objects
▶ more about adverbs
▶ expressing frequency
▶ making comparisons
▶ travelling in Spain during Bank and public holidays

Dialogue 1

Andrea has just arrived in Madrid. She cannot find her luggage so she goes to the airline's information desk before going through passport control. Listen to the dialogue between her and the assistant.

Vocabulary ◆

resguardo de facturación (m)	baggage identification tag
megafonía (f)	public address system
por desgracia	unfortunately
neceser (m)	wash bag
boda (f)	wedding

ANDREA Buenos días, acabo de llegar de Londres y no puedo encontrar mi equipaje. Parece que no ha llegado con el vuelo.

SRA. VIDAL Un momento, vamos a ver. ¿Tiene el billete de avión y el resguardo de facturación de las maletas?

ANDREA Sí, claro, aquí están.

SRA. VIDAL Tiene facturadas dos maletas, ¿no? Bueno, si no le importa esperar aquí un momento tengo que mirar en otro ordenador para ver si están todavía en Londres o si las han enviado a otro aeropuerto.

ANDREA   Está bien pero tengo un amigo que está esperándome fuera, ¿puedo salir y volver a entrar?

SRA. VIDAL   No, lo siento mucho pero no es posible. Lo único que podemos hacer es darle un mensaje por megafonía. ¿Cúal es el nombre de su amigo?

ANDREA   Se llama Pedro Álvarez.

SRA. VIDAL   Está bien, ahora mismo mandamos el mensaje. Mientras tanto, espéreme aquí, por favor.

Media hora más tarde.

SRA. VIDAL   Perdone por tardar tanto. Mire, sus maletas, por desgracia, parece ser que están en Marruecos.

ANDREA   ¿En Marruecos? ¿Cómo han ido a parar allí?

SRA. VIDAL   No lo sé todavía, pero lo único que podemos hacer ahora es ponernos en contacto con el aeropuerto de Marrakesh.

ANDREA   ¿Cuánto tiempo cree que tardarán en llegar aquí?

SRA. VIDAL   Dos días, me imagino. Mientras tanto le podemos ofrecer un neceser y . . .

ANDREA   Perdone, pero qué voy a hacer yo con un neceser, ¿eh? ¿Qué es lo que me voy a poner? Sólo tengo lo que llevo puesto. Tengo una boda mañana y el vestido que iba a ponerme está en la maleta.

SRA. VIDAL   Lo siento mucho pero no sé si podremos hacer algo.

ANDREA   Pues yo no me muevo de aquí hasta que no me diga exactamente cuándo voy a recibir las maletas.

Exercise 1

Now listen to the dialogue again and answer the following questions in English:

1 Why does Andrea want to go out and come back? Can she do it?
2 Where are Andrea's suitcases?
3 Why is it so important for Andrea to get her suitcases?

Language points ◆

How to apologise for something

One of the best ways to apologise for something is by using **perdona** (informal), **perdone** (formal), followed by the preposition **por** and an infinitive. Remember that you need to use the infinitive form of the verb when a verb comes after a preposition:

Perdone por tardar tanto.
Excuse me (*formal*) for taking so long.

Perdona por llegar tarde.
Excuse me (*informal*) for arriving late.

Perdona por interrumpirte.
Excuse me for interrupting you.

You can also use a noun but then you do not need the preposition **por**:

Perdone la molestia.
Excuse me (*formal*) for bothering you.

If you do not agree with what has been said and you do not want to hurt the person's feelings, you can start the sentence with **perdona** or **perdone**:

Perdone, pero qué voy a hacer yo con un neceser, ¿eh?
Excuse me, but what I am going to do with a wash bag?

Perdona, pero me parece que no tienes razón.
Excuse me, but I think you are wrong.

Another common way of apologising / excusing oneself is by using the expression **lo siento**, from the verb **sentir**:

Lo siento mucho pero no es posible.
I'm very sorry but that isn't possible.

Lo siento, pero tienes que irte ahora mismo.
I'm sorry but you have to leave immediately.

Lo siento and **perdón** are also used to apologise when you bump into someone.

The verb **sentir**, which is also used to express the feeling of regret, is a regular vowel-changing verb:

Luis lo siente mucho pero no puede estar aquí.
Luis is very sorry but he cannot be here.

Sentí no encontrarte en casa.
I was sorry I did not find you at home.

Exercise 2

Try to match the following excuses:

1 I'm sorry but you need to come back.
2 Excuse me for not going.

3 Excuse me, but I think you have to do it.
4 Excuse me for not calling at eleven.
5 I'm very sorry but I cannot come at eleven.

a Lo siento mucho pero no puedo venir a las once.
b Perdona, pero creo que tienes que hacerlo.
c Lo siento pero tienes que volver.
d Perdona por no ir.
e Perdona por no llamar a las once.

Talking about health

When the verb **sentir** is used as a reflexive verb, it means the same as **encontrarse** when you are talking about health:

Pedro se siente peor hoy.
Pedro feels worse today.

¿Cómo te sientes hoy?
How are you feeling today?

Nosotros nos sentimos mejor pero ella está peor.
We are feeling better but she is worse.

Lola se sintió mejor después de comer.
Lola felt better after eating.

Pedro se encuentra mejor.
Pedro feels better.

Exercise 3

Fill in the appropriate form of the verbs **sentir** and **sentirse** according to the context:

1 Su madre _____ peor hoy.
2 _____ mucho que no puedas venir (ella).
3 Raúl _____ mucho la muerte de su amigo.
4 Lo _____ mucho pero tienes que hacerlo ahora (yo).
5 _____ mejor que ayer (yo).

More about direct and indirect objects and where they go in a sentence

Direct (**me, te, lo / la, nos, os, los / las**) and indirect objects (**me, te, le / se, nos, os, les / se**) normally go before the whole verb.

Before you go on, read the dialogue about Andrea at the beginning of the chapter and see how many direct / indirect objects you can find, then check the sentences below and see whether you have found them all.

Si no le importa esperar aquí un momento.
If you don't mind waiting here for a second.

Las han enviado a otro aeropuerto.
They have sent them to another airport.

un amigo que está esperándome
a friend who is waiting for me

Lo que podemos hacer es pasarle un mensaje.
What we can do is to pass on a message to her/him.

Espéreme aquí.
Wait for me here.

No lo sé todavía.
I don't know yet.

Mientras tanto le podemos ofrecer un neceser.
Meanwhile we can offer you a wash bag.

The pronouns **nos** (pone**nos** en contacto) and **me** (iba a pone**rme**) are neither direct nor indirect objects, they are reflexive pronouns. Both verbs are reflexive in this context: **ponerse**.

Tienes que ponerte en contacto con él.
You must get in touch with him.

¿Qué vas a ponerte para la boda?
What are you going to wear at the wedding?

If you have another look you will see that some direct and indirect objects have been added to the gerund form (**esperándome**); to the infinitive (**pasarle, haberle, perdonarme**); and to the imperative (**espéreme**). Direct and indirect objects as well as reflexive pronouns can go before or after a gerund:

Un amigo que me está esperando and **un amigo que está esperándome** are both correct.

¿Estás haciéndolo ahora?
Are you doing it now?

¿Lo estás haciendo ahora?
Are you doing it now?

Perhaps for an English speaker, it's more natural to put the reflexive pronouns, and direct / indirect objects at the end:

Lola está preparándolo.	Lola is preparing it.
¿Quieres hacerlo ahora?	Do you want to do it now?

With an infinitive, again, the object can go after or before the infinitive, but the safest bet is to put it straight after the infinitive, which again is more natural for English speakers:

¿Puedes hacerlo hoy?	Can you do it today?

Exercise 4

Match the following questions with their correct answers:

1	¿Has enviado ya el dinero?	a	Espérame en el bar del aeropuerto.
2	¿Quiere hacer la reserva hoy?	b	Lo necesito para el lunes de la semana próxima.
3	¿Quién está esperándote?	c	Lo he guardado en el bolso.
4	¿Para cuándo necesita el visado?	d	Sí, lo envié ayer.
5	¿Dónde te espero?	e	Me gustaría comprarlos mañana.
6	¿Dónde has guardado el pasaporte?	f	Sí, me gustaría hacerla ahora.
7	¿Cuándo quieres comprar los billetes?	g	Me está esperando mi hermana.

Exercise 5

Answer the following questions by translating the prompts given. Place the direct or indirect object in the correct position:

Example: **¿Has leído los emilios?**
Yes, I read them this morning.
Sí, los he leído esta mañana.

emilio   colloquial for email

1 ¿Cuándo lees el periódico? (lo)
I read it in the evenings.
2 ¿Cuándo quieres ver la obra de García Lorca? (la)
I want to see it on Saturday.
3 ¿Cúando va a visitarte? (me)
He is going to visit me next month.
4 ¿Cuándo vas a ver a tus padres? (los)
I am going to see them tomorrow.
5 ¿Cuándo vas a terminar el informe? (lo)
I hope to finish it by next week.
6 ¿Estás haciendo los deberes? (los)
Yes, I am doing them, don't worry. (no te preocupes)
7 ¿Para cuándo quiere Lola las revistas? (las)
She wants them for Sunday.

Verbs with infinitives

There are many verbs in the Spanish language which are followed by an infinitive. You have heard a few infinitives in the dialogue at the airport:

Si no le importa esperar.
If you don't mind waiting.

No me importa ir sola.
I don't mind going alone. (*a woman talking*)

Remember that when you use a verb after a preposition (**a, con, de, en, por, para, sin,** etc.), the verb is in the infinitive in Spanish (e.g. to think), but a gerund (thinking) is normally used in English.

Habla sin pensar.
S/he talks without thinking.

Tarda mucho en hacerlo.
S/he takes a long time doing it.

Poder plus an infinitive means 'to be able to':

No puedo encontrar las maletas.
I cannot find the suitcases.

Lo único que podemos hacer . . .
The only thing we can do . . .

Le podemos ofrecer . . .
We can offer you . . . (*formal*)

Acabar de plus an infinitive means 'to have just':

Acabo de llegar.
I have just arrived.

Acaba de verlo.
S/he has just seen it / him.

Note that you use the present tense of the verb **acabar** plus the preposition **de**. In English you use the present perfect.

Tener que plus an infinitive means 'to have to':

Tengo que mirar.
I have to look.

¿Tienes que irte ahora?
Do you have to leave now?

Volver a plus an infinitive means 'to do something again':

¿Puedo salir y volver a entrar?
Can I go out and come back again?

¿Quieres volver a hacerlo?
Do you want to do it again?

Ir a plus an infinitive means 'to be going to':

¿Qué voy a hacer?
What am I going to do?

¿Qué voy a ponerme?
What am I going to wear?

Exercise 6

Fill in the following sentences with the appropriate verb: **tener, volver, ir, acabar, poder:**

1 ¿ _____ que hacerlo ahora? (tú)
2 ¿ _____ Julio venir mañana?
3 El domingo _____ a ir a la playa si hace sol (nosotros).
4 ¿Quieres _____ a ver la película? (tú)
5 _____ de hablar con él (yo).
6 ¿ _____ a venir tus padres en agosto?

Adverbs

There is a tendency in Spanish to substitute the adverbs ending in **-mente** (in English -ly) for an adverbial expression formed with a noun of quality:

con seguridad	seguramente
con claridad	claramente
con facilidad	fácilmente
con alegría	alegremente
con rapidez	rápidamente
con eficacia	eficazmente

If you want to say *very* quickly you would say **con gran rapidez,** and so on.

Habla con gran claridad.   S/he speaks very clearly.

The following three expressions are used as much as or more than their equivalents ending in -**mente:**

por desgracia	desgraciadamente
por suerte	afortunadamente
en serio	seriamente

Exercise 7

Translate the following sentences into Spanish using the adverbial expressions above:

1 He does his work quickly.
2 Unfortunately he is not feeling well.
3 Fortunately he is feeling better.
4 He wrote the document very easily.

Text 1

Exercise 8

A British friend who is thinking of moving to Madrid but who will have to travel frequently between Madrid and Barcelona has asked you to send her information about the different transport possibilities. You have come across the following information on el **puente aéreo** between Madrid and Barcelona and have decided to read it and to make notes for her on:

1 Duration and frequency of flights.
2 Information on passengers.
3 Advice given on bookings.
4 Advice given on parking and travelling to the airport.

Vocabulary ♦

jornada laboral (f)	working day
trayecto (m)	journey, trip
horas punta (fpl)	rush hours, peak hours
con antelación	in advance

El puente aéreo

El puente aéreo que une Madrid con Barcelona empezó en 1974. Muchas personas, la mayoría ejecutivos, utilizan cada día esta ruta en jornada laboral. En general, los ejecutivos van y vuelven en el mismo día. La duración aproximada del trayecto es de 55 minutos. Hay hasta 45 vuelos diarios en cada sentido, 4 vuelos a la hora, cada 15 minutos en horas punta, de 6.45 a 9.15, uno cada hora desde las diez de la mañana hasta las tres de la tarde y dos a la hora a partir de las tres de la tarde. La mayoría vuela sin reserva y compra el billete en el aeropuerto unos minutos antes de embarcar pero si es importante llegar al destino a una cierta hora es aconsejable reservar el billete con antelación. Es también bastante difícil encontrar sitio en el aparcamiento público del aeropuerto y cuando lo encuentras el precio es de unos 14 euros todo el día. También se puede ir al aeropuerto en taxi pero sale mucho más caro, unos 35 euros, ida y vuelta. Se puede ir al aeropuerto en Metro, y con la apertura del nuevo tramo desde Nuevos Ministerios se puede facturar el equipaje en la misma estación de metro, evitando así la incomodidad de viajar con el equipaje en transporte público. Las cosas cambiarán cuando empiece a funcionar el AVE Madrid-Barcelona en el año 2005.

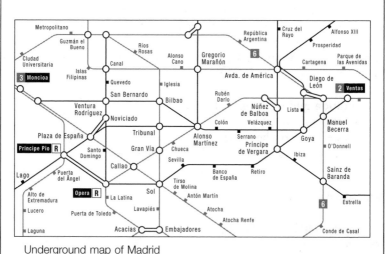

Underground map of Madrid

Language points ♦

How to express frequency

You have probably noticed in the text a number of words or expressions used to express frequency:

Utilizan <u>cada día</u> esta ruta.	They use this route every day.
Hay hasta 45 vuelos <u>diarios</u>.	There are up to 45 flights daily.
4 vuelos <u>a la hora</u>	4 flights an hour
<u>cada</u> 15 minutos	every 15 minutes

Note that in **vuelos diarios, diarios** is an adjective and therefore it changes in gender and number according to the noun it qualifies:

Dan una comida diaria.	They give a daily meal.

Other useful adjectives:

semanal	weekly
mensual	monthly
anual	yearly
bienal	biennial

These adjectives take the number of the noun they qualify:

revista semanal	weekly magazine
revistas semanales	weekly magazines
periódico semanal	weekly newspaper

Note: **Diario** can also be used as a noun meaning a daily newspaper, **un periódico.**

Exercise 9

Complete the following sentences with expressions of frequency:

1 How many flights are there daily?
   ¿Cuántos vuelos _____ hay?
2 This newspaper is a weekly one.
   Este periódico es un periódico _____ .
3 The trains run every half an hour.
   Hay trenes _____ media hora.
4 There are two flights a week.
   Hay dos vuelos _____.

Exercise 10

Listen to the announcements and fill in the gaps.

1   Flight number: IB425
    Message:
    Reason:

2   Flight number:
    Message: The flight has been cancelled.
    Reason:
    Action to be taken: passengers to go to the Information desk to find out about the next flight.

3   Flight number:
    Message:

4   Names: Mrs Gónzalez Martín and Mrs López Isla
    Message:
    Reason: This is the last call.

Text 2

An American friend wants to rent a car in the Canary Islands but she is not sure of the local procedures. She has asked you for information. Before you read the article, have a look at Exercise 11 and find out what your friend needs to know.

Before you read the following information on how to rent a car, see whether you can match the following synonyms:

carnet / carné de conducir (m)	vale la pena
utilitario (m)	andar, viajar
tarifa (f)	encargarse de
hacerse cargo de	automóvil, coche, vehículo
recorrer	permiso de conducir
merece la pena	precio
devolver	por anticipado
por adelantado	entregar

Cómo alquilar un coche

Si quieres alquilar un coche en España necesitas ser mayor de 21 años y haber tenido el carné de conducir por lo menos por un año. Los precios varían según la categoría del utilitario y de dónde se alquile, por ejemplo, es mucho más barato alquilar un coche en las Islas Canarias que en la Península y del tipo de contrato, sin límite de kilometraje o según la distancia que vas a recorrer. Las tarifas siempre incluyen el seguro obligatorio del vehículo y el de responsabilidad civil a terceros. Si quieres tener más protección tendrás que pagar una cantidad extra por día pero merece la pena. No olvides llenar el depósito antes de devolver el coche, si no lo haces te va a resultar más caro. Y ten cuidado con las multas porque tú eres responsable de ellas. La empresa sólo se hace cargo de las multas si son debidas al mal estado del coche como puede ser el estado de las luces. Si vas a alquilar un coche en Baleares o Canarias lo mejor que puedes hacer es reservarlo por adelantado porque aunque hay muchas compañías hay demasiada demanda.

Exercise 11

Tell her about the following:

1 Age and driving experience needed.
2 Type of insurance included in the price.
3 Whether it is worth paying extra for full insurance.
4 What to do about the petrol.
5 Who is responsible for the fines.
6 The need to book in advance.

Language points ◆

How to make comparisons

There are many ways of making comparisons but here we will look at some of the most common ones. You can compare two things by using the structures **más . . . que** 'more . . . than', or **menos . . . que** 'less . . . than', and **tan . . . como** 'as . . . as':

Es mucho más barato alquilar un coche en las Islas Canarias que en la península.
It's much cheaper to rent a car in the Canary Islands than on the mainland.

España está menos poblada que El Reino Unido.
Spain is less populated than the United Kingdom.

Galicia es tan verde como Asturias.
Galicia is as green as Asturias.

When you want to express the idea of 'the most' and 'the least' you need to use the words **más** or **menos** and the article in its masculine or feminine form (**el, la, los, las**). This is called the superlative form.

Los coches en Madrid son los más caros.
Cars in Madrid are the most expensive.

Este es el más barato.
This is the cheapest.

Este es el menos interesante.
This is the least interesting.

Esta es la más ligera.
This is the lightest.

Madrid es la ciudad más grande *de* España.
Madrid is the largest city in Spain.

Note that the preposition **de** has been used in Spanish where English uses 'in':

Mi sobrino Keltxa es el más alto de la familia.
My nephew Keltxa is the tallest in my family.

You can also use another structure: definite article (**el, la, los, las**) plus **más** or **menos** plus **de**:

La más cara de todas es San Sebastián.
San Sebastian is the most expensive (city) one.

Remember that some adjectives have irregular comparative and superlative forms:

adjective	comparative
bueno	**mejor**
malo	**peor**
grande	**mayor**
pequeño	**menor**

Las playas del norte son mejores que las del sur.
The beaches in the north are better than the ones in the south.

Juan es el peor.
Juan is the worst.

Esta maleta es la mayor.
This suitcase is the largest.

Note that **mayor** and **menor** also mean older / oldest and younger / youngest:

Mi hermano Beni es el mayor.
My brother Beni is the oldest.

Mi hermana Sonia es la menor.
My sister Sonia is the youngest.

Yo soy mayor que mis hermanos José y Luisma.
I am older than my brothers José and Luisma.

When the adjective does not refer to anything in particular you need to use the neutral article **lo**:

Lo mejor es ir ahora mismo.
The best thing to do is to go right away.

Lo peor es que no tenemos suficiente dinero.
The worst thing is that we do not have enough money.

Exercise 12

Fill in the gaps with **más que, menos que, peor que, mejor que, el mejor, mayor que, el mayor,** according to your own knowledge about Spain:

1 Creo que hace _____ tiempo en el norte de España _____ en el sur.
2 Creo que la gente gana _____ en España _____ en Inglaterra.

3 Creo que España tiene _____ habitantes _____ Gran Bretaña.

4 Creo que el campo de fútbol del Barça es _____ _____ _____ España.

5 Creo que es _____ barato alquilar un coche en las Islas Canarias _____ en la península.

6 Creo que hace _____ tiempo en España _____ en Inglaterra.

7 Creo que la Reina del Reino Unido es _____ _____ el Rey de España.

8 Creo que se come _____ pescado en España _____ en Inglaterra.

Exercise 13

You would like to rent a car for a week. You are talking to the person working at the local car hire agency. Replace the English prompts with the Spanish equivalent.

JOHN   I'd like to rent a small car for a week, please, unlimited mileage.

SRA. RIVAS Muy bien, ¿un Ford Fiesta está bien?

JOHN   Fine, here is my driving licence.

SRA. RIVAS Bien, ¿me puede dejar su tarjeta de crédito?

JOHN   Here's my credit card. What type of insurance has the car got?

SRA. RIVAS La tarifa incluye el seguro obligatorio del vehículo y el de responsabilidad civil a terceros.

JOHN   How much more do I need to pay to have more protection?

SRA. RIVAS 24 euros al día.

JOHN   Fine. Also, is the tank full?

SRA. RIVAS Sí, llene el depósito antes de devolverlo.

JOHN   OK. Have you got a map of the area?

SRA. RIVAS Sí, aquí tiene uno.

¿Sabía usted? ♦

Spanish people tend to travel during the **puentes**. The number of **puentes** in a year varies since they depend on whether the day of the saint or holiday falls on a weekend. Say, for example, that the 1st of May, which is always a bank holiday in Spain, falls on a Tuesday, then many people will have Monday and Tuesday off. The following dates are always public holidays in Spain regardless of the date they fall on: 1st (**Año Nuevo**) and 6th of January (**El día de Reyes, Epifanía**), Good Friday (**Viernes Santo**), 1st of May (**Día de los trabajadores**), 15th of August (**La Ascensión**), 12th of October (**Día del Pilar**), 1st of November (**Todos los Santos**), 6th of December (**Día de la Constitución**), 8th of November (**La Inmaculada**), and 25th of December (**Navidad**). There are other public holidays in Spain but they vary from one **Comunidad Autónoma** to another. Spanish people tend to **hacer puente** and this means that roads in Spain during that period are very congested and quite dangerous; the number of traffic accidents then is very high. Another busy time is the first and last weekend of July and August, especially August since many Spanish people still take their annual holidays during this month. Do not try to proceed with any official paperwork during the month of August as most public offices shut for the whole month.

3 Carnavales y fiestas

In this unit you can learn about:

- asking for details: **qué** / **cuál** plus **se**
- describing things: adjectives
- introducing a statement you are uncertain about
- using the simple past
- expressing quantity
- common negative words
- Christmas in Spain

Dialogue 1

David has been invited by a Spanish friend to spend some days with his family in **Logroño,** *capital of* **La Rioja,** *during the celebrations on 21 September. He is finding out things about the festival . . .*

Vocabulary ◆

vino (m)	wine
uva (f)	grape
patrón / patrona	patron
mosto (m)	grape juice
corridas (fpl)	bullfights
encierros (mpl)	running / driving of the bulls into the pen before a bullfight

DAVID ¿Qué se celebra el 21 de septiembre?

SANTI Bueno, pues el 21 es San Mateo y toda La Rioja celebra la vendimia, la fiesta es muy popular y hasta ha sido declarada de interés turístico internacional. Pero las fiestas duran casi una semana, ¿eh?, entre el 20 y el 26.

Wine growing areas.

DAVID   ¿Qué es exactamente la vendimia?

SANTI   Es la recogida de la uva.

DAVID   ¿Sabes cuándo empezó la tradición?

SANTI   No estoy muy seguro pero creo que empezó en el siglo XII.

DAVID   ¿Cuáles son los festejos?

SANTI   El pisado de la uva es el acto central de las fiestas y tiene lugar en la céntrica Plaza del Espolón. Después se ofrece el primer mosto a la Virgen de Valvanera, patrona de La Rioja.

DAVID   ¿Mosto, qué es eso?

SANTI   Es el jugo de la uva antes de fermentar.

DAVID   ¡Ah, sí! Me imagino que la comida también tendrá algún papel en las fiestas, ¿no?

SANTI   ¡Claro! En la Plaza del Mercado se puede probar productos típicos riojanos y por supuesto beber nuestros afamados vinos.

DAVID   Supongo que las corridas de toros son también populares en La Rioja, ¿no?

SANTI   Sí, hay bastante afición a los toros. Siempre hay corridas y encierros durante las fiestas. Aunque a mí personalmente no me gustan nada. El año pasado hubo un accidente muy grave durante uno de los encierros. Un chico de 15 años murió unos días después de las fiestas. Un toro lo cogió y le destrozó los pulmones. Y hace unos años ocurrió lo mismo. Deberían prohibirlos.

DAVID Sí, tienes razón. A mí tampoco me gustan.

Exercise 1

Could you now tell a friend about the festival?

1 How long does the festival last and is it popular?
2 As many activities as you can remember.

Language points ♦

How to ask for information

There are obviously many ways to ask for information but one of the most straightforward is by using **qué** and **cuál**. Note that in the following examples the verb is in the impersonal form. To do so you just need to add the pronoun **se** in front of the verb:

¿Qué se celebra el 21 de septiembre?
What is celebrated on the 21st of September?

¿Qué se hace por la noche?
What does one do / would you do at night-time?

¿Qué se come durante las fiestas?
What does one eat / would one eat during the festivals?

Be careful with the different uses of **qué** and **cuál**. **Qué** followed by the verb **ser** is used when you want to find out what something is:

¿Qué es exactamente la vendimia?
What is the 'vendimia'?

¿Qué es el pisado de la uva?
What is the 'pressing of the grape'?

¿Mosto, qué es eso?
'Mosto', what is it?

You only use the verb **ser** after **qué** (**qué es / qué son**) when you need to know what something is (as in the examples above), otherwise, you will normally use **cuál es / cuáles son**:

No sé cuál es el patrón.
I don't know who the saint is.

¿Cuál es el acto principal de las fiestas?
What is the main event in the festival?

Remember the plural of **cuál** is **cuáles**:

¿Cuáles son los festejos?   What are the festivities?

Qué is used with nouns:

¿Qué libro vas a comprar?   Which book are you going to buy?

Qué is also used with verbs:

¿Qué quieres comer?   What do you want to eat?

Cuál is used with verbs when there is a choice to be made:

¿Cuál te gusta más?   Which one do you like more?

Cuál is used in the expression **cuál de**:

¿Cuál de los dos prefieres?   Which of the two do you prefer?

Note that both **cuál** and **qué** can both be translated as 'what'.

Exercise 2

Choose the correct word in the following sentences:

1 ¿Qué / cuál se hace por la mañana?
2 ¿Qué / cuál es el día principal?
3 No sé qué / cuál es pero puede ser un tipo de fruta.
4 ¿Cuáles / cuál es el programa?
5 No sé qué / cuál es el acto principal.
6 ¿Qué / cuál se cocina durante las fiestas?

Adjectives

It's difficult to say where adjectives should go, before or after the noun they qualify. Generally speaking, qualifying adjectives given by the speaker to the object / person go after the noun while those adjectives that are believed to be part of the object / person go before the noun. When you read leaflets, brochures, etc., you will notice that many adjectives go before the noun as they help to create a much more attractive image.

Look at some of the adjectives used in the dialogue:

interés <u>turístico internacional</u>
es el acto <u>central</u> de las fiestas
tiene lugar en la <u>céntrica</u> Plaza del Espolón
después se ofrece el <u>primer</u> mosto
en la Plaza del Mercado todo el mundo puede probar los
productos <u>típicos riojanos</u> y por supuesto saborear los <u>afamados</u>
vinos de La Rioja
las corridas de toros <u>populares</u> en La Rioja

Note the difference between the adjectives, **central** and **céntrica** and their position in the sentence:

es el acto <u>central</u> de las fiestas
it's the main act of the festival

tiene lugar en la <u>céntrica</u> Plaza del Espolón
it takes place in the central Plaza del Espolón

Exercise 3

Fill in the appropriate gap, before or after the noun, with an adjective, **internacional, fundamental, bonito, espectacular, nuevo.** Remember that adjectives agree in number and gender with the noun they describe.

El _____ festival _____ de los patios fue reconocido en 1960 por el entonces Ministerio de Información y Turismo como fiesta de _____ interés _____ aunque no se trata de un _____ concurso _____ pues empezó en 1918. Este _____ festival _____ representa a Córdoba como las Fallas a Valencia y los Sanfermines a Pamplona. Dura todo el mes de mayo. La maceta es uno de los _____ elementos _____ de los patios junto con el pozo.

Preterite tense / *indefinido*

This tense is used to express an action completed at a definite time in the past. Have a look at the Grammar reference on p. 231, if you want to revise the form.

¿Sabes cuándo empezó la tradición?
Do you know when the tradition started?

No estoy muy segura pero creo que empezó en el siglo XII.
I am not sure but I think it started in the twelfth century.

El año pasado hubo un accidente.
There was an accident last year.

Un chico de 15 años murió unos días después de las fiestas.
A 15-year-old boy died a few days after the festival.

Un toro lo cogió y le destrozó los pulmones.
A bull caught him and pierced his lungs.

Remember that you do not use the possessive pronoun (my, your, his) before parts of the body when talking about one's body:

Me rompí *el dedo.*
I broke my finger.

Look out for the spelling of some of the verbs in the preterite form:

La semana pasada empecé a ir al gimnasio.
Last week I started to go to the gym.

¿Cuándo empezaste a estudiar español?
When did you start to study Spanish?

Le destrozó los pulmones.
It pierced his lungs.

Lo destrocé todo.
I destroyed everything.

The verb **morir** (also **dormir**) has a stem change in both the present and the preterite in the third person singular and plural (**él / ella, usted, ellos / ellas, ustedes**):

Un chico murió hace unos días.
A boy died a few days ago.

Yo dormí muy bien ayer.
I slept very well yesterday.

Mi marido no durmió bien.
My husband did not sleep well.

¿Cuántos años tenían tus padres cuando murieron?
How old were your parents when they died?

Exercise 4

Fill in the gaps with the appropriate form of the preterite of the following verbs: **empezar, haber, morir, dormir, hablar,** and **beber:**

1 El otro día _____ a ir a clases de español. (yo)
2 Su hermano _____ en un accidente de tráfico.
3 ¿ _____ con ella ayer? (tú)
4 No _____ muchos problemas el domingo, ¿verdad?
5 El sábado _____ demasiado vino. (nosotros)
6 No _____ nada el fin de semana pasado. (yo)

How to introduce something you believe to be true but you are not certain about

The most common ways of expressing something you believe to be true but would like confirmation about are as follows. Some of them have been used in the dialogue:

<u>Me imagino</u> **que la comida tendrá algún papel en la fiesta, ¿no?**
I imagine food has a role in the festival, hasn't it?

<u>Supongo</u> **que las corridas son también populares en La Rioja, ¿no?**
I suppose bullfights are also popular in La Rioja, aren't they?

Seguro is also used in the same way:

<u>Seguro</u> **que las fiestas duran toda la noche, ¿no?**
I bet the festivals last all night, don't they?

Note the use of the question tag **¿no?** at the end of the sentence.

Que yo sepa is another useful expression used to show knowledge about something you are not one hundred per cent sure about. The difference is that you do not need / expect an answer:

Que yo sepa (from the verb **saber**).
As far as I know, to my knowledge.

Que yo sepa San Isidro es el patrono de Madrid.
As far as I know, San Isidro is Madrid's saint.

Exercise 5

A Bolivian friend is trying to find out about Christmas in Spain. Listen to the recorded information about how one particular family spends Christmas in the Basque Country and answer your friend's questions in Spanish.

1 Me imagino que toda la familia se reúne en casa de sus padres ¿no?
2 Supongo que celebran el 25 y el 26 de diciembre, ¿no?
3 Seguro que su madre prepara una gran cena para Nochebuena, ¿no?
4 Me imagino que reciben los regalos el 25 de diciembre, ¿no?
5 Supongo que salen en Nochevieja, ¿no?
6 Supongo que comen muchos dulces, ¿no?

Text 1

Spanish people really know how to celebrate, not least during **Carnaval.** *A number of towns are well known for their* **Carnaval** *celebrations,* **Santa Cruz de Tenerife** *being the most famous.* **El Carnaval de Cádiz,** *however, is quickly becoming one of the most popular.*

Exercise 6

Read the following information about the **Carnaval de Cádiz** and answer the questions:

1 What is the main motif of the festival?
2 How do the majority of people participate in the celebrations?
3 What do the different groups do?
4 How many people are involved in the different groups?

Vocabulary ♦

Before you read the information look at the following words that appear in the text:

renombre	renown, fame
gaditano	from Cadiz

El Carnaval de Cádiz

Nadie sabe exactamente cuándo empezó a celebrarse esta fiesta pero sí se sabe que se celebró en 1865 y que desde 1885 algunas letras de canciones han adquirido renombre a nivel nacional. El motivo central de todas las celebraciones del carnaval de Cádiz es el humor y la sátira. Todo el pueblo gaditano participa en las populares fiestas y la gran mayoría se une a diferentes tipos de agrupaciones, entre las que se encuentran las comparsas, los coros, los cuartetos y las chirigotas para actuar por la calle desde el domingo de carnaval hasta el domingo de piñata. En total, son más de un centenar de agrupaciones las que participan en el carnaval. Las agrupaciones componen canciones que normalmente hacen referencia a los últimos acontecimientos políticos o a los personajes de actualidad y las cantan durante los desfiles. Los coros, que están compuestos aproximadamente por treinta personas, desfilan en carrozas y cantan tanguillos y cuplés. Los cuartetos, como su mismo nombre indica, los forman cuatro personas y recorren la ciudad a pie cantando coplas. Las comparsas no superan nunca la docena de integrantes y también van a pie como los cuartetos y las chirigotas. Aunque todos los días hay algún festejo, el último domingo es el más importante y es cuando tiene lugar la cabalgata y el carrusel de los coros.

centenar	a hundredth
acontecimiento	event
desfilar	to parade, to march
desfiles (mpl)	parade
recorrer	to cross, to go through a city
superar	to surpass
festejo	celebration, festivity

Language points ◆

How to express quantities

In the text above you have come across a number of useful words /
expressions to describe different quantities:

**algunas letras de canciones han adquirido renombre a nivel
nacional.**
some lyrics have become well known nationally.

Remember that **algunas** in this case is an adjective and therefore takes
the gender of the object:

Algunos hombres creen que la mujer tiene que quedarse en casa.
Some men believe women should stay at home.

Another way of expressing a similar amount other than **algunos /
algunas** is **unos pocos** or **unos cuantos**:

Sólo quedan unos pocos.
There are only a few left.

When you need to express 'more than', remember that in Spanish
you need to use **más de**. **Más de** is used when a number follows the
comparative. Do not use **más que**.

más de un centenar de agrupaciones
more than a hundred groups

Note the difference between **todo el pueblo** and **todos los pueblos**:

Todo el pueblo participa en las celebraciones.
The whole village / town participates in the celebrations.

Todos los pueblos de Cádiz celebran los carnavales.
Every village in Cádiz celebrates carnival.

Other ways of expressing 'the majority' besides **la gran mayoría** are **casi todo el mundo** and **casi todos:**

A casi todo el mundo le gusta el chocolate.
Almost everyone likes chocolate.

Casi todos fueron a la verbena.
Almost everyone went to the open-air dance at night.

La mayoría de los españoles son católicos.
The majority of Spanish people are Catholics.

La gran mayoría de las fiestas se celebran en verano.
The majority of festivals take place in the summer.

Exercise 7

Say whether the following statements are true or false according to your own knowledge:

1 A la mayoría de los españoles les gusta encontrarse con los amigos en el bar.
2 La gran mayoría de las fiestas se celebran en invierno.
3 Todos los pueblos de España celebran su patrón.
4 Hay menos de 35 millones de personas en España.
5 Casi todos los españoles comen en algún restaurante por lo menos una vez al mes.
6 Muy pocos trabajadores comen el menú del día.
7 Algunos pueblos están abandonados.
8 La mayoría de las mujeres españolas de menos de 30 años tienen más de cuatro hijos.

Common negative words

Nada and **nunca:**

Nadie sabe exactamente cuándo empezó a celebrarse esta fiesta.
Nobody knows exactly when the festival was first celebrated.

Las comparsas no superan nunca la docena de integrantes.
The **comparsas** (*group of people in fancy dress*) never include more than twelve members.

Remember that you have to use **no** together with the negative words, **nadie, nada, nunca, ninguno / ninguna, ningún** when these follow the verb:

No hace nada pero siempre tiene dinero.
S/he does not do anything but s/he always has money.

¿Por qué no me esperas nunca?
Why don't you ever wait for me?

No hay nadie en mi casa.
There is no-one in my house / there is not anyone in my house.

No tengo ninguna [enciclopedia].
I don't have any.

However, when the negative word is placed at the beginning (mainly for emphasis), you do not need to use a double negative:

Nadie lo sabe.
No-one knows about it.

Nunca he visto cosa igual.
I have never seen such a thing.

Exercise 8

Rewrite the following sentences in the negative. When you can, give both alternatives according to the position of the negative word:

tener esperanza   to be hopeful

1 Siempre llego a casa antes de las seis.
2 ¿Hay alguien en tu casa?
3 Lo sabe todo el mundo.
4 ¿Tienes algo de beber en tu casa?
5 ¿Por qué hablas con todo el mundo?
6 Manolo siempre va a Italia de vacaciones.
7 ¿Tienes alguna esperanza de aprobar?
8 Mis padres viven con unos amigos.

Text 2 ⁙⟨⟩

Exercise 9

Read the following information about Christmas in Spain and note down the differences between Christmas celebrations in Spain and the United Kingdom or the United States.

Vocabulary ♦

por todo lo alto	in style
cotillón (m)	a special dance party
barra libre	free drinks
turrón (m)	sweet made with almonds and honey
mazapán (m)	marzipan
polvorón (m)	pastry made with lard, flour, sugar and almonds
roscón de Reyes (m)	ring-shaped cake
al compás de	in time to
campanada (f)	sound of a bell

Navidad

Los españoles celebran Navidad y Año Nuevo por todo lo alto y cada persona gasta un promedio de más de trescientos cincuenta euros en lotería, adornos navideños, juguetes y regalos, y como no, en comidas y cenas. La mayoría de los españoles se reúnen para celebrar en familia la Nochebuena, el 24 de diciembre y el día de Navidad mientras que muchos celebran Nochevieja, el 31 de diciembre, en un restaurante o en un hotel. Es bastante popular acudir a uno de los muchos cotillones que se ofrecen para ver el Año Nuevo donde se paga una entrada bastante cara pero con opción a barra libre durante toda la noche. En España también se celebra la Epifanía del Señor, o día de Reyes, el seis de enero. Los platos que se preparan para la cena de Nochebuena varían de un lugar a otro pero el dulce siempre está presente. En todas las casas españolas se puede encontrar turrones para todos los gustos aunque los más populares son aún los tradicionales, el turrón blando de Jijona y el turrón duro de Alicante. Además de los turrones nunca pueden faltar los mazapanes y los polvorones. El día de Reyes también se come el tradicional roscón de Reyes en el que se encuentran pequeñas sorpresas.

Otra actividad común a todos los españoles es la actividad de comer 12 uvas al compás de las 12 campanadas de medianoche, el 31 de diciembre. La mayoría escucha en la televisión las campanadas del reloj que se encuentra en la Puerta del Sol de Madrid.

La lotería es muy popular en España durante todo el año pero es en Navidad cuando la gente compra más números para los dos sorteos especiales, el Sorteo Extraordinario de Navidad y el Sorteo del Niño.

4 Alojamiento

In this unit you can learn about:

- expressing surprise
- some uses of the preterite and the imperfect
- more on **ser / estar / hay**
- using **darse cuenta**
- **turismo rural** in Spain
- time expressions **hace / hacía**
- intensifying the validity of something
- **paradores** in Spain

Dialogue 1

Susan Hawkins arrived at an apartment in Valencia yesterday evening. There are some problems with the apartment and she is now talking to the manager.

Vocabulary ◆

inquilino (m)	tenant
intentar	to try
calentador (m)	boiler (*heater*)
apagar	to switch off
piloto (m)	pilot light
cubiertos (mpl)	cutlery

Exercise 1

Cover up the dialogue and listen to their conversation. After listening to it, give the following information:

1 Problems Mrs Hawkins encountered when she arrived at the apartment.
2 Reason for not getting a reply when she phoned the office.

José	Apartamentos Sol y Sombra, ¿dígame?
Susan	Buenos días. Soy la señora Hawkins y estoy en el apartamento número 4.
José	Sí, dígame. ¿Hay algún problema?
Susan	Sí, llegué anoche y cuando fui a ducharme no había agua caliente y tuve que ducharme con agua fría.
José	¡Qué raro! Los otros inquilinos se fueron ayer por la mañana y no dijeron nada. Pero, ¿por qué no llamó a la oficina cuando notó que no tenía agua caliente?
Susan	Lo intenté, pero creo que la oficina estaba cerrada, es que eran ya las nueve.
José	Sí, cerramos a las 8. ¿Está segura de que el calentador está encendido?
Susan	Me imagino que sí. Yo no he tocado nada.
José	A lo mejor la mujer de la limpieza lo apagó. ¿Puede ver si el piloto está encendido?
Susan	Un momento, voy a mirar, . . . Sí, me parece que sí.
José	Vale. Entonces tenemos que ir a ver cuál es el problema. ¿Y por lo demás? ¿Está todo bien?
Susan	Pues la verdad es que no. El piso está bastante sucio. Cuando fui a hacer un té me di cuenta de que la cocina no estaba limpia y de que además faltaban muchas cosas, sólo hay uno o dos cubiertos, apenas hay tazas . . .
José	¡Qué extraño! Bueno, no se preocupe. Dentro de media hora estoy ahí y arreglamos todo.

Language points ♦

Expressing surprise

There are many ways of expressing surprise but you have just heard in the dialogue some of the most common examples:

¡Qué raro!	How strange!
¡Qué extraño!	How odd!

Another two colloquial ways of expressing surprise or disbelief at what has just been said:

¡No me diga! ¡No me digas!
You don't say! (*don't tell me*)

-¿Sabes que Carmen se casó el otro día?
Do you know that Carmen got married the other day?

-¡No me digas! No sabía nada.
You don't say! (*don't tell me!*), I didn't know.

¿Qué dice?   ¿Qué me dice?
What are you saying? (*formal*)

¿Qué dices?   ¿Qué me dices?
What are you saying? (*informal*)

-¿Sabías que Luis está en el hospital muy enfermo?
Did you know Luis is very ill in hospital?

-¿Qué dices? Si lo vi el lunes y estaba bien.
What are you saying? But I only saw him on Monday and he was fine.

Exercise 2

Match the following questions with their replies:

llevarse bien con alguien   to get on well with somebody
llevarse mal con alguien   to get on badly with somebody

1 ¿Sabías que Santi ya no vive con Concha?

2 ¿Sabías que Manu sale con Laura?

3 ¿Sabías que Andrés ya no vive en Salamanca?

4 ¿Sabes que Antonio está en el hospital?

5 ¿Sabías que María está de vacaciones?

6 ¿Sabías que Pedro se ha ido de la Uni?

a ¡Qué extraño! No me dijo que iba a vivir a otro sitio.

b ¡Qué raro! Pensaba que tenía mucho trabajo.

c ¡No me digas! Pensaba que se llevaban muy bien.

d ¡Qué raro! Sólo le faltaba un año.

e ¿Qué me dices? ¿Está muy mal?

f ¡No me digas! Pensaba que se llevaban mal.

Some comparisons between the simple past (*indefinido*) and the imperfect (*imperfecto*)

These are some of the verbs in the preterite tense you have heard in the dialogue:

Llegué anoche.
I arrived last night.

Fui a ducharme.
I went to have a shower.

Tuve que ducharme con agua fría.
I had to shower with cold water.

Los otros inquilinos se fueron por la mañana y no dijeron nada.
The other tenants left in the morning and they didn't say anything.

¿Por qué no llamó a la oficina cuando notó que ... ?
Why didn't you call the office when you noticed that ... ?

Lo intenté ...
I tried to ...

Remember that the verbs **tener** (**estar, andar**) are irregular in the preterite tense. Have a look at the Grammar reference to remind yourself of the endings:

¿Dónde estuviste ayer?   Where were you yesterday?
Anduvimos mucho.   We walked a lot.

The verbs **ir** and **ser** are irregular in the preterite and are exactly the same.

El día de mi boda <u>fue</u> un día perfecto.
My wedding day was a perfect day.

Ayer <u>se fue</u> de vacaciones.
Yesterday he went on holiday.

Note the spelling of the preterite of **llegar**. Remember that in **ga, gue, gui, go, gu** the letters **g** and **gu** have the same sound (like the 'g' in garden):

Llegué tarde.   I arrived late.
¿A qué hora llegaste?   At what time did you arrive?

You have also heard a number of verbs in the imperfect tense. The imperfect tense has been used because the verbs are used to describe something in the past. One of the main uses of the imperfect tense is for descriptions:

No había agua caliente.	There wasn't any hot water.
No tenía agua caliente.	I didn't have any hot water.
Estaba cerrada.	It was closed.
Eran ya las nueve.	It was already nine o'clock.
No estaba limpia.	It wasn't clean.

In order to understand the difference between the preterite and the imperfect, it helps to think of a scene. Imagine you are describing a scene of a play or a film to a friend. You will use the imperfect tense for the description of the people and for the background of the scene and you will use the preterite for the actions:

La mujer estaba sola, era verano y aunque estaba casi de noche la ventana estaba abierta. La mujer se levantó del sillón, miró por la ventana y la cerró. Volvió al sillón. Se sentó y empezó a ver la tele. No había nada interesante pero estaba aburrida y no sabía qué hacer.

Exercise 3

Complete the following sentences with the appropriate form of the preterite or the imperfect of the verb indicated:

1 Cuando (yo) _____ la puerta _____ abierta (llegar, estar).
2 No _____ toallas en el baño (haber).
3 (yo) _____ a la oficina de objetos perdidos pero _____ cerrada (ir, estar).
4 _____ las once de la noche cuando me _____ Sonia (ser, llamar).
5 ¿Con quién (tú) _____ cuando te _____? (estar, llamar)
6 Susana _____ todo el día en El Corte Inglés pero no _____ nada (estar, comprar).
7 Mi hermana me _____ que su novio _____ muy guapo (decir, ser).
8 Cuando yo _____ de casa _____ muchísimo (salir, llover).
9 Mis padres _____ 22 años cuando _____ (tener, casarse).
10 (nosotros) No _____ porque _____ mucho viento (bañarse, hacer).

Exercise 4

An English friend has asked you to write a note in Spanish to the landlord of the flat where he is staying. These are the things he wants to find out. Write them down in Spanish

toalla   towel

1 When did the other tenants leave?
2 Why is there no hot water?
3 Why are there no towels?
4 Why did the landlord not answer the telephone when he phoned?

Now listen to the reply the landlord has left on your friend's mobile voice mail and translate the information for your friend.

More on *ser, estar* and *hay*

Note that in Spanish when you introduce yourself on the phone, you need to use the first person of the verb **ser** (**soy**), not the third person (**es**):

Soy la señora Hawkins.	It's Mrs Hawkins.
Soy Petra.	It's Petra.

You know that **estar** is used with adjectives when you are describing a temporary state of things. When used in the past tense it normally takes the imperfect tense:

La oficina estaba cerrada.	The office was closed.
La cocina no estaba limpia.	The kitchen was not clean.

When talking about the time in the past tense, the verb **ser** normally takes the imperfect tense:

Eran ya las nueve.
It was already nine o'clock.

Era la una cuando llegó a casa.
It was one o'clock when s/he arrived home.

Likewise when you want to describe what was / wasn't in a place, you need to use the verb **haber** (**hay**) in the imperfect tense:

No había agua caliente.	There was not any hot water.
No había toallas.	There were not any towels.

Exercise 5

Ana has booked a house in the south of Spain. She expected to find a basket of food in the house but it wasn't there when she arrived. The following is the conversation between her and the person in charge of the house. Fill in the gaps with the appropriate form of **estar, ser,** and **haber**.

MANUEL ¿Cómo _____ la casa cuando llegaste?

ANA La verdad es que _____ bastante limpia pero no _____ nada.

MANUEL ¿No _____ la cesta con la comida y la botella de vino en la mesa de la cocina?

ANA No, sólo _____ una caja de leche en la nevera pero _____ pasada.

MANUEL ¡Qué extraño! ¿Qué hora _____ cuando llegaste?

ANA _____ las once de la mañana.

MANUEL ¡Ah! Creo que _____ demasiado temprano, la mujer lleva las cosas al mediodía. ¿No fue más tarde?

ANA No sé, me fui a dormir porque _____ muy cansada.

MANUEL ¿Y no _____ nada cuando te levantaste?

ANA No, nada.

Darse cuenta de

This verb means 'to realise'. It consists of the verb **dar** in the reflexive form and the noun **cuenta**:

Me di cuenta de que la cocina no estaba limpia.
I realised the kitchen was not clean.

Dar is irregular in the preterite: **di, diste, dio, dimos, disteis, dieron**:

¿Te diste cuenta de lo sucio que estaba?
Did you notice how dirty it was?

Darse is a reflexive verb therefore you need to use the respective reflexive pronoun (**me, te, se, nos, os, se**):

¿Te diste cuenta de que no había vino?
Did you realise there was no wine?

Pete se dio cuenta de que no tenía suficiente dinero.
Pete realised he did not have enough money.

Note that the Spanish verb **realizar** does not mean to realise in the sense of understanding. **Realizar** means to carry out something, similar to the verb **hacer:**

¿Ya has realizado todo lo que tenías que hacer?
Have you already done everything you had to do?

In the dialogue you have seen another verb that means something very similar to **darse cuenta,** that is **notar:**

¿Cuándo notó que no tenía agua caliente?
When did you notice that you did not have any hot water?

You could also have used the verb **ver:**

¿Cuándo vio que no tenía agua caliente?
When did you notice you didn't have any hot water?

Exercise 6

Match the following questions with their respective answers

1 ¿Notaste que Lola empezó a llorar de repente?

2 ¿Te diste cuenta de que John vino con una amiga nueva?

3 ¿Notaste que todo el mundo estaba muy serio?

4 ¿Te diste cuenta de que el novio de Antonia no estaba allí?

5 ¿Notaste que la puerta del dormitorio estaba cerrada?

a Por supuesto, ¿no sabías que tenía otra novia?

b ¿No sabías que ya no salen juntos?

c Sí, claro, creo que Lola está un poco deprimida.

d No, no me di cuenta.

e No, no lo noté. Yo me lo pasé muy bien.

Text 1

People are discovering that Spain is not only a country of beaches and **sangría**, *they are discovering its beautiful interior in* **turismo rural**. *One of the best ways to get to know the real Spain is to make use of the growing number of agro-tourism sites. These are farms or old houses that have been restored and converted into small hotels.*

Exercise 7

Read the following extract on *La Ramallosa*, a place in *Cáceres* in the province of *Extremadura*, in the west of Spain, and answer the questions after the text. The text describes how the owners started the project.

Vocabulary ♦

caserío (m)	country house and its outbuildings
siglo (m)	century
paraje (m)	area, region
contar con	to have (*in this context*), to count on (*someone*)
lamentable	deplorable, pitiful
sin embargo	however
reto (m)	challenge
infernal	infernal
esfuerzo (m)	effort
puntero	outstanding,
pozo (m)	well
recurrir a	to turn to (*someone*), to resort to
encajar	to fit together

In your own words, summarise the following points as gleaned from the text on the opposite page:

1 Reason for bad state of the buildings
2 Positive aspects of the project
3 Type of materials used
4 Financial help received

Language points ♦

Hace / hacía

Remember that the time expression **hace** is used with the present tense. The present perfect is used in English:

Hace mucho tiempo que no fumo.
I **haven't smoked** for a long time.

La Ramallosa

Cuando en 1994 decidimos reconstruir el viejo caserío del siglo XIX que teníamos en el paraje de La Ramallosa, sólo contábamos con las ruinas de un antiguo núcleo rural que hacía más de 40 años que se encontraba deshabitado y abandonado . . .

El estado del caserío era lamentable . . . Sin embargo, el reto merecía la pena pues el conjunto, su ubicación, la arquitectura de la zona y el modelo de alojamiento que teníamos en mente, contrarrestaban con ilusión el esfuerzo titánico que supondría convertir aquellas ruinas en un alojamiento rural puntero. El acceso era infernal; más de once km. de un camino que entonces, era prácticamente intransitable; sin más agua que en un típico pozo, a un nivel inferior al de las casas, y con una zona a rehabilitar de más de 2.500 metros cuadrados de calles y edificaciones.

A medida que la obra avanzaba todo iba encajando porque, no sólo era más barato recurrir a los materiales y soluciones tradicionales sino que, además, era lo más adecuado . . . y la imaginación es gratis.

Lo poco que había, lo conservamos y potenciamos y, el resto, lo reconstruimos, pero nunca contra corriente . . .

No podemos olvidar tampoco las ayudas económicas que nos facilitó la Comunidad Europea a través del *Programa Leader* que, aunque con mucho retraso, posibilitaron en gran medida la rehabilitación de nuestro Caserío.

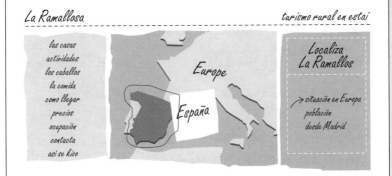

La Ramallosa   turismo rural en estai

las casas
actividades
los caballos
la comida
como llegar
precios
ocupación
contacta
así se hizo

Europe

España

Localiza
La Ramallos

→ situación en Europa
población
desde Madrid

Hace una semana que no voy a clase.
I haven't been to class for a week.

¿Hace mucho tiempo que estudias español?
Have you studied Spanish for a long time?

When you use the time expression hacía you need to use the imperfect tense. Note that in English the pluperfect is used:

Hacía más de 40 años que se encontraba abandonado.
It had been empty for more than 40 years.

Hacía más de un mes que no comía pescado.
I had not eaten fish for more than a month.

Hacía un año que no venía a España.
S/he had not visited Spain for a year.

Hacía mucho tiempo que no te veía.
I had not seen you for a long time.

¿Cuánto tiempo hacía que no la veías?
How long has it been since you last saw her?
(*Literally,* How long is it since you had last seen her?)

Exercise 8

Complete the following sentences with the appropriate form of the indicated verb:

1 Hace un mes que no _____ al cine (ir).
2 Hacía más de un año que no _____ a tu madre (ver).
3 Hacía mucho tiempo que _____ viajar por México (querer).
4 ¿Cuánto tiempo hace que lo _____ ellos? (saber)
5 Hacía más de una semana que nosotros lo _____ (saber).
6 ¿Hace mucho que _____ (tú) aquí? (estar)
7 Hacía sólo un mes que Luisa _____ con él cuando le dejó (salir).
8 ¿Hacía mucho tiempo que (tú) lo _____? (conocer)

More uses of *ser* in the imperfect tense

El estado del caserío era lamentable.
The state of the house was pitiful.

El acceso era infernal.
The access was a nightmare.

un camino que entonces era prácticamente intransitable
a path that was then almost impassable

The verb **ser** has been used in the imperfect tense in all the examples above because the verb describes the state of the house, the access and the path. The writer of the text has used the verb **ser** instead of **estar** presumably because he felt all the problems were kind of inherent rather than temporary. In a different situation, for example, after a heavy snow fall, you could have used the verb **estar**.

El camino estaba prácticamente intransitable.
The path was almost impassable.

Exercise 9

Fill in the gaps with **ser** or **estar** in the imperfect tense:

patinar   to skid, to skate

1 ¿Por qué no viniste ayer?
   Es que el camino _____ imposible. Había muchas hojas en la carretera y el coche patinaba.
2 ¿Cómo _____ la gente?
   _____ muy simpática.
3 ¿Por qué la carretera _____ cerrada?
   Porque había habido un accidente.
4 ¿Cómo _____ la comida en la India?
   La comida _____ buena pero picaba mucho.

No sólo ... sino (que)

The expression **no sólo ... sino** 'not only ... but also' is used when you want to intensify the validity of something. Note that the conjunction **sino** is used instead of **pero**:

No sólo era más barato recurrir a los materiales y soluciones tradicionales sino que, además, era lo más adecuado.
Not only was it cheaper to resort to traditional materials and solutions but, also, it was the most appropriate.

Note that when you are using two different verbs you need to use the word **que** after **sino**:

No sólo estudia español sino que también estudia alemán.
Not only does s/he study Spanish but s/he also studies German.

When there is only one verb you do not need to use **que**:

No sólo existe aquí sino en todas en las ciudades de España.
Not only does it exist here but in all the Spanish cities.

Exercise 10

Complete the following sentences with **no sólo … sino (que)** according to the model:

Example: **Tiene un brazo roto y el coche está destrozado.**
   No sólo tiene un brazo roto sino que además /
   también el coche está destrozado.

1 Es guapo y tiene mucho dinero también.
2 Viene tarde y trae una botella de vino malísima también.
3 Ocurre aquí y en el sur también.
4 Ha muerto su mujer y ha perdido la casa también.
5 Escribe libros y pinta cuadros también.
6 Me ha mandado una carta y dinero también.

¿Sabía usted? ♦

La Red Paradores de Turismo de España is a chain of government-run hotels located in beautiful settings.

Hay en España más de 86 paradores repartidos por su geografía. El primer parador inaugurado en 1928 fue el Parador de Gredos en plena Sierra de Gredos en la provincia de Ávila. Desde entonces se ha restaurado un gran número de edificios del Patrimonio Nacional desde castillos medievales hasta antiguos conventos y palacios. Estos se encuentran en magníficos parajes naturales (como el Parador de Fuente Dé en los Picos de Europa) o en edificios históricos (como el Parador de Santo Domingo de la Calzada en La Rioja). No sólo ofrecen instalaciones cómodas y una variada oferta gastronómica de la cocina española sino que, entre todo el esplendor del pasado, también se encuentran instalaciones modernas como piscinas, pistas de tenis, salas de reuniones, etc. De entre todos destacan el Parador de Granada y el Parador de los Reyes Católicos en Santiago de Compostela. Este último se encuentra en el Hospital Real, albergue de peregrinos de finales del siglo XV. El Parador de Granada está ubicado en los jardines de la Alhambra y tiene vistas sobre el Generalife, los jardines de Secano y el Albaicín.

Parador, Granada. Photo: Tepa

5 Trabajando en España

In this unit you can learn about:

- ▶ how to express agreement / conformity
- ▶ the pluperfect tense
- ▶ more differences between the preterite and the imperfect
- ▶ how to introduce an idea having said something to the contrary: **sin embargo, no obstante**
- ▶ how to write a CV and a letter of presentation
- ▶ using adjectives to describe people

Dialogue 1

Julia Pedman arrived in Spain a few weeks ago. She would like to stay in Spain so she has sent her CV to some Spanish companies. One of the companies has invited her to an interview ...

Exercise 1

Cover the dialogue, listen to the first part of the interview and answer the questions:

1 What did she do after leaving her job?
2 Why did she leave the job?
3 Has she got any Spanish language certificates?

Vocabulary ♦

marcharse / irse	to leave, to go away
aclarar	to clarify
si no me equivoco	if I am not wrong

ahorrar	to save (*money*)
ponerse enfermo	to become ill
aprovechar	to take advantage / to use
mejorar	to improve
no obstante	nevertheless
matricularse	to enrol
Diploma Superior de Español	official title together with Diploma Básico de Español awarded by the Ministerio de Educación y Ciencia of Spain
convocatoria (f)	examination session

SR. LÓPEZ   Buenos días señorita Pedman, siéntese por favor.

JULIA   Muchas gracias.

SR. LÓPEZ   ¿Cómo está? ¿Ha encontrado la oficina fácilmente?

JULIA   Sí, gracias. Las indicaciones estaban muy claras.

SR. LÓPEZ   Me alegro. Bueno, recibimos su currículum hace unos días y quisiera hacerle algunas preguntas y aclarar algunos de los puntos que usted mencionó en él. En primer lugar me gustaría saber por qué dejó la compañía Goldhawk donde, si no me equivoco, estuvo casi 5 años.

JULIA   Sí, ¡cómo no! Cuando empecé a trabajar allí sólo pensaba quedarme un año como máximo. Quería trabajar y ahorrar dinero para viajar por el mundo. Pero cuando llegó la hora no pude irme, mi madre se puso muy enferma y me quedé a cuidarla. Hace dos años conocí a una chilena que vivía en Inglaterra desde hacía mucho tiempo pero que quería volver a su país. Un día volvió a Chile y después de un tiempo allí me invitó a su casa. Así que aproveché la ocasión y me fui.

SR. LÓPEZ   Esto fue hace un año más o menos, y ¿qué ha estado haciendo hasta ahora?

JULIA   Estuve viajando por Latinoamérica y después estuve unos 6 meses en Santiago de Chile para mejorar mi español. Ya había estado anteriormente en México y Guatemala pero sólo unas semanas. Fue durante este viaje cuando decidí venirme a España. Quería vivir en un país de habla hispana sin vivir demasiado lejos de Inglaterra.

SR. LÓPEZ   Hablando del español, no menciona en el currículo ningún título.

JULIA   Ya lo sé. La verdad es que no he hecho ningún examen todavía pero tenía pensado hacer el Diploma Superior de Español.

SR. LÓPEZ   Está bien, ya veo que usted habla español muy bien así que no hay ningún problema. No obstante, sería una buena idea hacerlo lo antes posible.

JULIA   Sí claro. Ya me he matriculado para la convocatoria de mayo.

Language points ♦

Expressing agreement / conformity

You saw in the dialogue a few ways of expressing agreement. Some of the most common expressions have the word **claro**:

Sí claro
Claro que sí
¡Pues claro (que sí)!
¿Vienes a la fiesta?   Are you coming to the party?
¡Pues claro (que sí)!   Of course I am.

Another polite way is **¿cómo no?** It is used more in Latin America:

¿Me pasas el agua?   Would you pass me the water?
¡Cómo no!   Of course.

You can also use **por supuesto (que sí)**:

¿Has estado ya en casa?   Have you already been home?
Por supuesto.   Of course.

Or both together, **claro, por supuesto:**

¿Te despediste de Juan?   Did you say goodbye to John?
Claro, por supuesto.   Well, of course.

Another common expression is **desde luego (que sí):**

¿Vas a ir a la fiesta de Sonia?   Are you going to Sonia's party?
Desde luego.   Of course.

You can also use them in the negative to express disagreement:

¿Has hablado con él?   Have you spoken with him?
Por supuesto que no.   Of course not.

Exercise 2

Match the questions with the correct answers:

1 ¿Te apetece ir al cine?

2 ¿Hiciste todo lo que te mandé?

3 ¿Le dijiste que habíamos cambiado la hora?

4 ¿Has ido ya al médico?

5 ¿Vienes conmigo al hospital?

6 ¿Quieres venir a cenar a casa esta noche?

a Sí, claro. No sé por qué no está aquí.

b Sí, claro. ¿Cuándo tienes hora?

c Por supuesto, ¿a qué hora quieres que vaya?

d Desde luego. Te lo prometí, ¿no?

e Claro, por supuesto. Me ha recetado unas pastillas.

f Pues claro. Ya sabes que siempre me apunto para ir al cine.

Pluperfect tense (*pretérito pluscuamperfecto*)

This tense is used in the same way in Spanish as in English. It is used to express a past action completed prior to another past action. You need to use the imperfect tense of **haber** (**había**) plus the past participle that you have learnt with the present perfect:

Ya lo había hecho para cuando yo llegué.
S/he had already done it when I arrived.

¿Cuándo la habías visto?
When had you seen her?

Pepe ya lo había hecho.
Pepe had already done it.

Nosotros ya habíamos ido antes.
We had already gone earlier.

¿Por qué se lo habíais dicho?
Why had you said it to him / her?

Ellos ya lo habían oído antes.
They had already heard it before.

Note that it is commonly used with **ya** ('already'):

Ya lo había pensado.
I had already thought about it.

Exercise 3

Write the following sentences according to the model:

Example:

Pedro salió y María llegó.
Pedro ya había salido cuando María llegó.

1 Nosotros hablamos con él y su madre llegó.
2 ¿Te levantaste y te llamé?
3 Yo comí y Lola apareció.
4 Nerea cocinó y le expliqué que éramos cinco.
5 Limpié y mi padre llamó a la puerta.
6 Antonio terminó el informe y llegó su jefe.

Preterite and imperfect tense

Most verbs which express some kind of mental activity are used in the imperfect tense: **saber, querer, poder, pensar, creer, conocer.** When you say 'I knew that' probably you have known about it for a while, it involves duration and that is why in Spanish you use the imperfect tense **lo sabía**:

Sólo pensaba quedarme un año.
I only thought about staying for a year.

Quería trabajar y ahorrar dinero.
I wanted to work and save money.

José podía hacerlo con los ojos cerrados.
José could do it blind-folded (*Literally*, with his eyes closed).

Creía que estabas en Londres.
I thought you were in London.

No conocía a mucha gente en Madrid.
I did not know many people in Madrid.

The English translation of these verbs changes according to whether they are used in the imperfect or in the preterite. As you know, the preterite is used for actions completed at a specific time in the past. When these verbs are used in the preterite, they refer to the precise moment of the action and their meaning is quite particular.

You need to use the preterite of **conocer** when you are talking about the moment of meeting a person. When you want to talk about knowing a person well, you need to use the imperfect tense of **conocer**:

Hace dos años conocí a una chilena.
Two years ago I met a Chilean woman.

¿Cuándo conociste a tu novio?
When did you meet your boyfriend?

Yo pensaba que la conocía bien pero . . .
I thought I knew her well but . . .

Poder in the preterite refers to the precise time of trying to do it but being/not being able to do it:

Cuando llegó la hora no pude irme.
When the time arrived I could not go (*you wanted to but couldn't*).

Jesús no pudo hacerlo.
Jesús could not do it (*but he tried*).

Jesús no podía usar el ordenador.
Jesús could not use the computer (*it is a fact because he didn't know how to*).

Pensar / creer in the preterite refers to the moment of thinking about it for the first time:

Lo pensé ayer.	I thought about it yesterday.
¿Se lo creíste?	Did you believe it?

Pensaba que estabas en Londres.
I thought you were in London.
(*You thought this was the case for a while*)

Creía que estabas en el hospital.
I thought you were in hospital.

Saber in the preterite refers to the the moment of hearing about it:

Lo supe el domingo.
I found it out / heard about it on Sunday.

No sabía que estabas mal.
I did not know you were ill.

Querer in the preterite refers to the fact that the action has / has not happened:

No quise ir a la reunión.
I did not want to go to the meeting.
(*I refused to go*)

Sebas no quería ir al cine.
Sebas did not want to go to the cinema.
(*It is difficult to know whether he went or not*)

No quería ir al cine pero fui.
I did not want to go to the cinema but I went.

Exercise 4

Rewrite the following sentences in the past:

Example: **Lo conozco desde hace tres años.**
          Lo conocí hace tres años.

1   La conozco bien.
2   Lo sé desde ayer.
3   Andrés no quiere ir al teatro (no fue).
4   Laura no puede hacerlo (lo intentó).
5   ¿Qué piensas de ella?

6 La conozco desde ayer.
7 No sé qué hace en España.
8 No quiere hacerlo (no sabes si lo hizo o no).

How to introduce an idea despite having made a comment to the contrary

no obstante   nevertheless

> **No obstante, sería una buena idea hacerlo lo antes posible.**
> Nevertheless it would be a good idea to do it as soon as possible.

sin embargo   however

> **Podía haberle mentido, sin embargo, no lo hice.**
> I could have lied to her/him, however, I did not do it.

a pesar de eso   in spite of that
así y todo   even so

> **Hará todo lo que pueda por llegar lo antes posible, así y todo no estará aquí a tiempo.**
> S/he will do her/his best to arrive as soon as possible, even so, s/he will not be here on time.

de todas maneras   anyway, at any rate

> **No me dieron el trabajo. De todas maneras, no estoy segura si lo quería o no.**
> I wasn't offered the job. Anyway, I am not sure I wanted it.

Exercise 5

Match the following sentences:

1 No tengo mucho tiempo	a no obstante, está todavía enferma
2 Estudió mucho	b así y todo fue a la fiesta
3 Estaba destrozada por la muerte de su padre	c sin embargo, no era feliz
4 Ha ido tres veces al médico	d de todas maneras, llámale por si acaso
5 Ganaba mucho	e sin embargo, no aprobó
6 Creo que no te ayudará	f no obstante, lo intentaré hacer

Curriculum vitae

Datos personales

Nombre y apellidos _____

Lugar y fecha de nacimiento: _____

Dirección: _____

Teléfono de contacto: _____

E-mail: _____

Estado civil: _____

Formación académica

Estudios realizados y títulos obtenidos _____

Centros y fechas correspondientes _____

Formación complementaria

Estudios realizados diferentes a la formación académica

_____

Experiencia profesional

Información de las empresas en las cuales has trabajado, los cargos ocupados, las funciones, los logros y las fechas en forma cronológica inversa

Idiomas

Precisa el nivel oral y escrito con títulos reconocidos si se poseen.

Informática

Conocimiento de programas y aplicaciones, Internet

Datos de interés

Información sobre otras actividades, aficiones, intereses, disponibilidad para viajar, etc.

Exercise 6

Read the following text about Sonia Rodríguez Martín and write as much as you can of her curriculum vitae.

Me llamo Sonia Rodríguez Martín. Nací en Burgos el 4 de diciembre de 1969. Empecé mis estudios de E.G.B. en la escuela Santa María en Burgos en el 76. En 1984 entré en el Instituto San Vicente donde realicé mis estudios de BUP y COU. Después en 1988 fui a la Universidad de Deusto en Bilbao para estudiar filología inglesa. Cuando terminé la carrera en el año 93 me fui un año a Inglaterra a practicar inglés. Allí trabajé como profesora de español en varias empresas en la City. Cuando volví a España estuve sin trabajar casi un año durante el cual estudié francés en la Escuela Oficial de Idiomas de Madrid. Llegué al nivel intermedio. Por suerte encontré trabajo en una escuela privada 'Lucas Rey' en la que di clases de inglés durante 4 años. Dejé ese trabajo en el año 99. Como quería trabajar en la universidad, me presenté a las Oposiciones y afortunadamente las pasé. Me puse a dar clases de inglés y de literatura inglesa en la Universidad de Granada en el año 2000 donde todavía estoy. Durante mi trabajo en la escuela privada realicé unos cursillos de informática donde aprendí a utilizar el ordenador, hojas de cálculo, bases de datos, etc. Uso Internet todos los días. Me gusta mucho leer y escribir. Estoy en estos momentos escribiendo una obra de teatro.

Exercise 7

The following are some jobs advertised in a national newspaper and the type of person they are looking for. Write down as many examples as you can find in the texts above of 'good communication skills', and 'Management / personnel skills'.

Responsable del Centro de Reparaciones de Telefonía Móvil de Madrid

Buscamos una persona muy dinámica, orientada al cliente, con instinto comercial y con capacidad para motivar y dirigir a un equipo joven.

Director financiero
Buen manejo de recursos humanos, capacidad de organización y de relaciones interpersonales.

Técnico / a comercial

Capacidad para la comunicación y negociación.

Gestores comerciales

Buscamos personas, con vocación y espíritu claramente comercial. Dinámicas y con iniciativa, que posean altas dotes de comunicación, fluidez verbal, capacidad de aprendizaje y de desarrollo personal.

Jefe de Ventas

Buscamos una persona con excelentes aptitudes comerciales, gran capacidad de trabajo y dotes para la supervisión de personal. Es imprescindible poseer total disponibilidad para viajar.

GESTOR DE COMPRAS DE FRUTAS Y HORTALIZAS

El puesto requiere una persona dinámica, organizada, con dotes de mando, buen negociador y acostumbrado a trabajar por objetivos.

ABOGADOS CON EXPERIENCIA EN ASESORAMIENTO TRIBUTARIO

Capacidad para trabajar en equipo, excelentes dotes de comunicación, dinamismo e iniciativa.

Adjectives to describe people

Exercise 8

Here is a list of adjectives that could be used to describe a person. Many of them are very close to their equivalents in English. Remember that those adjectives that end in e and ta do not change gender. Match them with their English equivalent:

dinámico/a	trustworthy
adaptable	willing
ambicioso/a	responsible
analítico/a	enthusiastic
creativo/a	independent
fiable	objective
responsable	efficient
dispuesto/a	optimistic
eficiente	hard-working
trabajador/a	independent
entusiasta	adaptable
estable	ambitious
independiente	willing / helpful
objetivo/a	creative
optimista	analytical
voluntarioso/a	balanced / stable

Many professions require a certain type of person. Which three qualities do you think a musician (**músico**), a doctor (**médico**) and an accountant (**contable**) should have?

Cómo elaborar una carta de presentación adecuada

Nombre de la empresa

Sr.

Dirección completa de la empresa   lugar y fecha

Según su anuncio publicado en _____ el día _____ me es
grato adjuntarles mi currículum vitae, para que tengan buen
conocimiento, tanto de mis aptitudes como de mi experiencia
profesional. Mi experiencia profesional demuestra mi capacidad
para la gestión y dirección de equipo y una elevada iniciativa. Me
considero una persona dinámica, trabajadora y emprendedora, por
eso creo que podría encajar satisfactoriamente en el equipo de la
empresa que Ud. dirige. Esperando recibir noticias suyas, a fin de
concertar una entrevista personal, reciba un cordial saludo.

Exercise 9

You have seen the following job advertisement in a local newspaper.
Write a letter to go with your CV.

Responsable de tienda

Ref: 7.134

Funciones: animar y dirigir un equipo de entre 5 y 9 dependientas
implantar la colección de la tienda de la manera más
adecuada

Requisitos: tener entre 25 y 35 años
un buen nivel cultural
conocimientos de informática a nivel de usuario
capacidad y experiencia en la conducción de equipos
agudo sentido del comercio

Se valorarán conocimientos de inglés

Perfil: persona entusiasta
gran sentido de la responsabilidad
espíritu de grupo
disponibilidad para viajar. Vehículo propio
disponibilidad inmediata

Se ofrece renumeración a convenir en función de la experiencia
aportada así como una interesante proyección profesional

Text 1

El empleo en España

Salario mínimo

Existe en España un salario mínimo interprofesional fijado en la Ley
de Presupuestos Generales del Estado.

Pagas extras

El empresario tiene la obligación de abonar al trabajador dos gratificaciones extraordinarias al año, una en el mes de diciembre (en
las fiestas de Navidad) y la otra en el mes que esté fijado en el
contrato (normalmente en el mes de agosto que suele ser el mes
de las vacaciones).

Contratos

Hay muchos tipos de contratos pero quizás el más común sea el contrato indefinido que puede ser a tiempo completo o a tiempo parcial. El contrato temporal o eventual tiene una duración máxima de 6 meses, prorrogables hasta 2 o 3 años. Puede pasar a contrato indefinido en cualquier momento. Mucha gente llega a tener este tipo de contrato a través de una ETT (empresa de trabajo temporal).

Seguridad Social

Cuando empiezas a trabajar para una empresa tienes que darte de alta en la Seguridad Social. Esto quiere decir que tienes que cotizar al Sistema de Seguridad Social.

Note: When you start to work you need to tell Social Security that you are now employed (**darse de alta**) which means you will start to pay a certain percentage of your wages to **Seguridad Social**. This amount of money will be deducted at source. This payment will give you a right to the National Health Service (**Insalud**) and to unemployment benefits. It also gives your dependants the right to the National Health Service.

Exercise 10

Looking at the text above, can you find the Spanish for the following expressions?

> part-time   full-time   minimum wage
> that can be extended   Social Security   to pay
> bonus (added to the main salary)

6 El fútbol

In this unit you can learn about:

- ▶ progressive tenses: present and past tenses
- ▶ how to introduce a true statement
- ▶ using direct and indirect speech (i)
- ▶ the first Spanish football team

Many Spanish people, men and women, are very passionate about football so it will be quite useful to learn some of the vocabulary you will need in order to talk to them about their favourite sport.

21 de diciembre de 2002

Liga-Clasificación general

Posición	Equipo	Ptos	J	Ganó	E	P	GF	GC	Diff
1	Real Sociedad	**32**	14	9	5	0	26	15	+11
2	Valencia CF	**28**	14	8	4	2	24	7	+17
3	Real Madrid	**27**	14	7	6	1	29	15	+14
4	Celta Vigo	**27**	14	8	3	4	20	13	+7
5	Real Betis	**23**	14	6	5	3	24	15	+9
6	Deportivo La Coruña	**23**	14	6	5	3	19	17	+2
7	RCD Mallorca	**23**	15	7	2	6	21	26	−5
8	Atlético Madrid	**21**	15	5	6	4	20	17	+3
9	Racing Santander	**20**	15	6	2	7	17	16	+1
10	Barcelona	**19**	15	5	4	6	22	19	+3
11	Málaga CF	**18**	15	4	6	5	20	22	−2
12	Osasuna	**18**	14	5	3	6	16	19	+3
13	Athletic Bilbao	**18**	15	5	3	7	21	28	−8
14	Sevilla FC	**17**	14	4	5	5	12	11	+1
15	Valladolid	**17**	14	5	3	7	13	17	−4
16	Alavés	**16**	15	4	4	7	17	25	−8
17	Villarreal	**15**	15	3	6	6	14	18	−4
18	Rayo Vallecano	**15**	15	4	3	8	16	23	−7
19	RCD Espanyol	**10**	14	3	1	10	14	26	−12
20	Recreativo Huelva	**9**	14	2	3	9	12	28	−16

Exercise 1

Here is a list of words related to football. There are many words in Spanish which have the same meaning. For example, a football ground is **el estadio** and **el campo**. In the two columns, there are words which have the same meaning. Can you match them?

el árbitro	el guardameta
el técnico	el campo
el hincha	el entrenador
la tarjeta	el aficionado
el portero	la cartulina
el estadio	el colegial

Exercise 2

The following are also words related to football. Classify them according to the headings, completing the table below.

People	Stadium	Actions

> la portería   empatar   el defensa   las gradas   el hincha
> el banquillo   el delantero   marcar goles   estadio / campo
> cometer una falta   perder   el árbitro   el centrocampista
> la plantilla   suplentes   titulares   el entrenador   el césped
> el lateral izquierdo / derecho   ganar   el portero

Dialogue 1

A football manager is being interviewed by a journalist. The manager has recently joined the club and is talking about the future of his team.

Vocabulary ♦

mostrar ganas de destacar	to show a desire to stand out
lograr	to achieve
implantar	to implement
mostrar	to demonstrate
tirar la toalla	to throw in the towel
contar con	to count on (*someone*)

Exercise 3

Cover up the dialogue and listen to their conversation. After listening to it answer the following questions:

1 How does the manager feel about his players?
2 Why have the players not yet taken on board the new system the manager wants to introduce?
3 How is managing his new team different from other teams he has recently managed?
4 Does the manager have any problems with Carlos, one of his players?

LUIS ¿Cómo está viendo a su equipo?

EDU Pues la verdad es que estoy satisfecho con la actitud de los jugadores, quienes cada día están mostrando unas ganas dignas de destacar. El problema es que nos faltan buenos resultados y tenemos prisa por lograrlos.

LUIS ¿Están asimilando sus futbolistas el sistema de juego que usted desea implantar?

EDU Los jugadores van asimilando poco a poco lo que se pretende de cada uno, pero en tres semanas no se pueden hacer milagros.

LUIS ¿Está teniendo que cambiar algunos conceptos de su filosofía tras observar el nivel y la situación del equipo?

EDU En los tres últimos años trabajé con dos equipos que jugaban para ser campeón y ahora es distinto. Un equipo que está abajo no juega igual que los que ocupan las primeras posiciones, porque los futbolistas no son capaces de mostrar todo lo que tienen. Ahora, tenemos que ganar partidos para subir puestos y luego ya veremos qué somos capaces de hacer. Si seguimos fallando, dentro de poco no habrá nada que hacer para salvarnos. Pero no vamos a tirar la toalla todavía.

LUIS ¿Sigue teniendo problemas con Carlos? Parece que anda diciendo por ahí que no está contento con su sistema de juego.

EDU No, en absoluto. Puedo contar con él. Bien es verdad que no hizo un gran partido la semana pasada.

LUIS No, la verdad es que no. La prensa fue muy dura con usted. A pesar de ir perdiendo no hizo ningún cambio.

EDU Si le he de decir la verdad, hay problemas internos de los que no voy a hablar en estos momentos.

Language points ♦

Progressive tenses (i)

The progressive tenses in Spanish are used to express that an action is taking place. Although one of the most common auxiliaries used in the progressive tenses is the verb **estar**, you can use other verbs as auxiliaries: **ir, seguir, andar, salir**. This depends on the context.

To form the progressive tense you need to use the appropriate tense of the auxiliary verb plus the present participle.

The present participle of -**ar** verbs consists of the verb root plus -**ando** and of -**er** and -**ir** verbs the verb root plus -**iendo**.

¿Estás hablando con tu hermano?
Are you talking to your brother? (*informal*)

¿Qué está comiendo?
What are you eating? (*formal*)

Estoy viendo una película.
I am watching a film.

¿Cómo está viendo a su equipo?
How do you think your team is doing? (*Literally*, how are you seeing your team?)

Cada día están mostrando unas ganas dignas de destacar.
Day by day they are showing a clear wish to shine.

¿Están asimilando sus futbolistas el sistema de juego?
Are your players assimilating the game's system?

Los jugadores van asimilando poco a poco.
The players are assimilating little by little.

¿Está teniendo que cambiar algunos conceptos?
Are you having to change some concepts?

Si seguimos fallando
If we continue to make mistakes (*missing the target*)

¿Sigue teniendo problemas con Carlos?
Are you still having problems with Carlos?

A pesar de ir perdiendo
Despite losing

Remember that many verbs have a stem change in the present participle:

dormir	durmiendo
decir	diciendo
pedir	pidiendo
sentir	sintiendo

construir, leer, oir, ir have the **y** in the present participle:

construir	construyendo
leer	leyendo
oir	oyendo
ir	yendo

Note: this tense is never used with the verbs **ir** and **venir**:

Estoy yendo is incorrect	**voy ahora mismo** is correct
	I am going right now
Estoy viniendo is incorrect	**vengo ahora mismo** is correct
	I am coming right now

Remember that if you are using a reflexive verb, you can attach the reflexive pronoun (**me, te, se, nos, os, se**) to the present participle (**limpiando, poniendo,** etc.). The reflexive pronoun can also go just before the auxiliary (**estar, seguir, ir,** etc.):

Estoy quitándome la camiseta.	I am taking off my t-shirt.
Me estoy quitando la camiseta.	I am taking off my t-shirt.

Note that a written accent has been added to **quitando** when the pronoun is added to the end.

Estoy peinándole.	I am combing his / her hair.

Ir plus the present participle is used instead of **estar** as an auxiliary of the present participle adding a sense of happening slowly and progressively:

¿Cómo vas?   How are you getting on?
Voy mejorando.   I am getting better (slowly).

Andar plus the present participle is normally translated as 'to be', but it gives the sentence a pejorative sense:

Anda contando mentiras por ahí.
S/he is going around telling lies.

Anda diciendo por ahí que no está contento.
He is going around saying that he is not happy.

Seguir plus the present participle means 'to keep on, to go on, to continue':

Sigue trabajando en la fábrica.
S/he is still working in the factory.

Salir plus a present participle is normally used with the verbs **ganar** and **perder**:

Pedro siempre sale ganando.
Pedro always ends up being the winner.

Luis siempre sale perdiendo.
Luis always ends up being the loser.

Exercise 4

Rewrite the following sentences using the present progressive with **estar**:

1 Sale con un futbolista de Manchester.
2 Luis juega en un equipo japonés.
3 Nosotros entrenamos para los Juegos Olímpicos.
4 Preparo la cena para un grupo de hinchas del Arsenal que acaba de llegar de Londres.
5 Leo el periódico porque busco un artículo del portero Cabanillas.
6 ¿Quiénes juegan?

Exercise 5

Match the following:

1	¿Qué anda diciendo por ahí?	a	Salió perdiendo como siempre.
2	¿Por qué sigues estudiando?	b	¡Qué va! No se están molestando ni en intentarlo.
3	¿Cómo va María después del accidente?	c	Que no tienes ni para pagar el alquiler.
4	¿Cómo le salió a Juan el negocio?	d	Va mejorando pero aún se encuentra en el hospital.
5	¿Por qué andas haciendo eso?	e	Pues, porque me gusta y porque quiero tener un trabajo fijo.
6	¿Están haciendo todo lo posible por terminarlo?	f	Pues, porque lo necesita Laura para mañana.

How to introduce a true statement

To introduce a true statement, use:

la verdad es que
si he de decir la verdad

Both expressions are used to introduce a statement that is true. They convey a feeling of confession:

Pues la verdad es que estoy satisfecho con la actitud de los jugadores.
Well, the truth is that I am satisfied with the players' attitude.

Si le he de decir la verdad, hay problemas internos.
If I must tell you the truth, there are internal problems.

Other expressions are:

bien es verdad que
si bien es verdad que

These expressions are used to introduce an idea that in some way removes the certainty of what had being said previously:

Bien es verdad que no hizo un gran partido la semana pasada.
It is true he did not have a good match last week.

Si bien es verdad que no nos queda mucho tiempo, todavía podemos rescatar algo.
Although it is true we do not have much time left, we can still rescue something.

Para decirte la verdad and **a decir verdad** are also used to convey a feeling of confession:

Para decirte la verdad estoy cansada de todo.
To tell you the truth, I am tired of everything.

A decir verdad, ya no me apetece ir de vacaciones contigo.
To tell you the truth, I don't feel like going on holiday with you.

Exercise 6

A English coach who has not been in Spain for long has asked you to help him with the translation into Spanish of a number of facts he needs to tell the chairman of the team. Translate the following statements for him:

1 The truth is that I am not happy with the goalkeeper.
2 Although it is true we have good players in the team, we still need to buy a left wing.
3 If I must tell you the truth, I think Jaime is not fit.
4 Although it is true the referee did not help us, we lost because we did not play well.
5 To tell you the truth, we need another goalkeeper.

Dialogue 2

Exercise 7

Listen to the following dialogue between two friends. Carlos wants to know whether Andrés has spoken to Luis. He also wants to know what Luis has said because he has not phoned him and feels bad about it.

CARLOS   ¿Fuiste a ver a Luis?
ANDRÉS   Sí, fui ayer por la tarde como te dije, estuve hablando con él toda la tarde.

CARLOS	¿Qué le dijiste que estaba haciendo?
ANDRÉS	Le dije que estabas entrenándote y que ibas a ver al médico después.
CARLOS	Y, ¿qué te respondió?
ANDRÉS	Pues que había estado toda la tarde intentando hablar contigo y que le habías prometido llamarle.
CARLOS	¿Estaba deprimido?
ANDRÉS	Bastante, me contó que el lunes había estado hablando con el técnico y que le había dicho que quería irse del equipo, que no estaba contento aquí y que estaba dispuesto a hablar con la prensa.
CARLOS	¿Te dijo si había hablado con Ricardo?
ANDRÉS	Me explicó que fue a verlo a su casa pero que no estaba, que se había ido de vacaciones unos días a Málaga. Después me preguntó si no querías hablar con él.

Progressive tenses (ii)

When you are talking about a past action, the auxiliary verb must take the appropriate tense.

Preterite

Estuve hablando con él toda la tarde.
I was talking to him all afternoon.

El lunes **estuvo hablando** con el técnico.
On Monday he was talking to the coach.

Siguió jugando hasta los 38.
S/he continued to play until s/he was 38.

Imperfect

¿Qué le dijiste que **estaba haciendo**?
What did you tell her/him I was doing?

Le dije que **estabas entrenándote**.
I told her/him you were training.

¿Qué **andabas haciendo** por ahí?
What were you doing around there?

Perfect

¿Qué <u>has estado haciendo</u> todo el día?
What have you been doing all day?

Ellos <u>han estado esperándote</u> toda la mañana.
They have been waiting for you all morning.

Pluperfect

<u>Había estado</u> toda la tarde <u>intentando</u> hablar contigo.
S/he had been trying to talk to you all afternoon.

<u>Había estado siguiéndole</u> todo el día.
S/he had been following him all day.

Exercise 8

Fill in the gaps with the appropriate tense of the verb **estar**: imperfect or preterite:

1 _____ (yo) jugando al tenis cuando me rompí el brazo.
2 ¿_____ (tú) hablando con él todo el día?
3 Cuando llegué los jugadores _____ entrenándose.
4 El árbitro _____ hablando con un jugador cuando tiraron una botella al campo.
5 Los suplentes _____ discutiendo el sistema de juego con el entrenador toda la mañana.
6 El defensa _____ atándose las botas cuando marcaron el gol.
7 Los hinchas _____ cantando durante todo el partido.

Direct and indirect speech (i)

Direct speech is when you reproduce a message word for word:

El entrenador dijo 'Raúl <u>está</u> en forma.'
The coach said, 'Raúl is fit.'

Indirect speech is, on the other hand, when you reproduce the message with some changes:

El entrenador dijo que Raúl <u>estaba</u> en forma.
The coach said that Raúl was fit.

When reproducing a message in indirect speech you must remember to change all the necessary tenses and words (time, space, etc.). You do not need, however, to change the tenses when the main clause (**dice que**) is in the present:

'**Vine hace una hora.**'
'I came an hour ago.'

Dice que vino hace una hora.
S/he says he came an hour ago.

'**He jugado con los mejores futbolistas del mundo.**'
'I have played with the best football players in the world.'

Dice que ha jugado con los mejores futbolistas del mundo.
He says he has played with the best football players in the world.

Tense changes are needed when referring to something said in the past (you will see other changes in future units).

The following statements could have been the actual words used by Luis when talking to Andrés in the dialogue you have just heard:

Andrés: **Pues que había estado intentando hablar contigo**
Indirect speech: Pluperfect

Luis' words: '<u>He estado</u> toda la tarde intentando hablar con él.'
Direct speech: Present perfect

'I have been trying to talk to him all afternoon.'

Andrés: . . . <u>había estado hablando</u> **con el técnico**
Indirect speech: Pluperfect continuous

Luis' words: '**He estado hablando con el técnico.**'
Direct speech: Present perfect continuous

'I was talking to the coach.'

Andrés: . . . **le había dicho que** <u>quería</u> **irse del equipo**
Indirect speech: imperfect

Luis' words: '**Quiero irme del equipo.**'
Direct speech: present

'I want to leave the team.'

Andrés: . . . **que no** <u>estaba</u> **contento**
Indirect speech: imperfect

Luis' words: '**No** <u>estoy</u> **contento.**'
Direct speech: present

'I am not happy.'

Andrés: ... **que estaba dispuesto a hablar con la prensa**
Indirect speech: imperfect

Luis' words: '**Estoy dispuesto a hablar con la prensa.**'
Direct speech: present

'I am prepared to go to the press.'

Andrés: **Me preguntó si no querías hablar con él.**
Indirect speech: imperfect

Luis' words: '**¿No quiere hablar conmigo?**'
Direct speech: present

'Doesn't he want to talk to me?

Andrés: **Me dijo que quería ir.**
Indirect speech: imperfect

Luis' words: '**Quería ir.**'
Direct speech: imperfect

'I want to go.'

Direct speech	Indirect speech
Present	Imperfect
Imperfect	Imperfect
Preterite	Pluperfect
Present perfect	Pluperfect

Exercise 9

Change the following direct speech statements into the appropriate indirect speech:

Example: '**Me llamo Lorena.**'
Me dijo que se llamaba Lorena.

1 'Quiero marcar tres goles.'   Me dijo que ...
2 'Necesito hablar con el técnico.'
3 'Raúl se fue a otro equipo.'
4 'El césped está muy mal.'
5 'Toda la plantilla estaba de mal humor.'

6 'Hemos perdido porque hemos jugado muy mal.'
7 'Ganaron porque Sánchez jugó muy bien.'
8 'Ángel está lesionado.'

Remember that when changing direct to indirect speech, you may also have to change other words:

Direct speech	Indirect speech
Hoy	Ese día, aquel día
Ayer	El día anterior
Mañana	Al día siguiente

'Ayer la vi en el campo.'
'I saw her in the stadium yesterday.'

Lola me dijo que la había visto el día anterior.
Lola told me she had seen her in the stadium the day before.

But

'Hoy tengo lecciones con Laura.'
'I have lessons with Laura today.'

Me dijo que ayer tenía lecciones con Laura. (*talking the following day*)
S/he told me s/he was having lessons with Laura yesterday.

'Mañana voy a jugar con José.'
'I am going to play with José tomorrow.'

Me dijo que hoy iba a jugar con José. (*talking the following day*)
S/he told me s/he was going to play with José today.

Other changes:

Direct speech	Indirect speech
Aquí	Allí
Este, esta, esto	Ese, esa, eso, aquel, aquella, aquello

'**Vivo aquí desde hace muchos años.**'
'I've lived here for many years'

Me dijo que vivía allí desde hacía muchos años.
S/he told me s/he had lived there for many years.

You also have to take into consideration any changes in personal and possessive pronouns:

'**Este coche es <u>mío</u>.**'
'This car is mine.'

Me dijo que ese coche era <u>suyo</u>.
S/he told me that that car was his/hers.

'**No quiero hablar <u>contigo</u>.**'
'I don't want to talk to you.'

Me dijo que no quería hablar <u>conmigo</u>.
S/he told me s/he didn't want to talk to me.

Exercise 10

Fill the gaps with the appropriate word:

1 'No quiero hablar contigo de esto otra vez.'
Me dijo _____ no _____ hablar _____ de _____ otra vez.

2 'Te llamo mañana.'
Me dijo que _____ _____ al día _____.

3 'No pudo jugar ayer.'
Me dijo que no _____ _____ jugar el día _____ _____.

4 'No quiero hablar con ella de esto otra vez.'
Me contó que no _____ hablar con ella de _____ otra vez.

5 'Fui al teatro la semana pasada.'
Me contó que _____ _____ al teatro la semana pasada / la semana anterior.

6 'He estado aquí todo el día.'
Me dijo que _____ _____ _____ todo el día.

As you have seen, you need to use **que** to join both statements:

'**Tengo un dolor de cabeza terrible.**'
'I have a really bad headache.'

Me dijo que tenía un dolor de cabeza terrible.
S/he told me s/he had a really bad headache.

Interrogative pronouns (**cuándo**, **dónde**, **cómo**, etc.) used in direct speech are kept in indirect speech either with **que** or without it:

'**¿Cómo te apellidas?**'
'What is your surname?'

Me preguntó cómo me apellidaba.
S/he asked me what my surname was.

Me preguntó que cómo me apellidaba.

When you are transforming a question which does not have an interrogative pronoun (**cuándo**, **dónde**, **cómo**, etc.) into indirect speech, you need to use the conjunction **si**:

'**¿Quieres venir conmigo al cine?**'
'Do you want to come with me to the cinema?'

Me preguntó si quería ir al cine con ella.
She asked whether I wanted to come with her to the cinema.

Exercise 11

Fill in the following gaps:

1 ¿Quieres quedarte en mi casa?   Me preguntó _____ quería dormir en su casa.

2 ¿Dónde viven tus padres?   Me preguntó _____ _____ vivían mis padres.

3 ¿Vas a ir a ver la última película de Almodóvar?   Me preguntó _____ iba a ver la última película de Almodóvar.

4 ¿Por qué no hablas con ella?   Me preguntó _____ _____ no hablaba con ella.

5 ¿Te gusta este vestido?   Me preguntó _____ me gustaba ese vestido.

Exercise 12

You have just come back from Aurora's house. She is letting a flat to Enrique, a friend you have in common. Aurora has asked you to tell Enrique her concerns about the state of the flat and the payment of the rent. How would you tell her the following?

Example: '<u>Le dejé</u> un recado en el contestador pero no <u>me ha contestado</u>.' Me dijo que te había dejado un recado en el contestador pero que no le habías contestado.

1 '*Estoy* cansada de esperar *sus* llamadas.'
2 '*Llevo* mucho tiempo esperando un emilio con detalles del estado del piso.'
3 '*Hace* mucho tiempo que no *recibo* el alquiler.'
4 'Esperaba recibir un cheque *la semana pasada*.'
5 '*Quiero* saber si *puede* pagar o no.'

Text 1

Read the following text on the birth of the first Spanish football team.

Vocabulary ♦

pujante	booming
cargados	loaded
hulla (f)	coal
técnico	coach (*football*) or technician
repletos	packed
naciente	growing
extraño	strange, peculiar
acordar	to agree
unirse	to join together
cantera (f)	a club's own training school
sinfín (m)	a large number

El primer equipo de fútbol en España: Athletic Club

El club nació cuando florecían las relaciones comerciales y culturales ente Vizcaya y la pujante Inglaterra. Los barcos británicos llegaban a las costas de Vizcaya cargados con hulla y repletos de técnicos ingleses especializados que se incorporaban a las nacientes industrias vizcaínas. Muchos jóvenes de la burguesía vasca acudían a los prestigiosos colegios británicos a estudiar, principalmente carreras técnicas industriales. De este intercambio cultural nació el interés por el nuevo deporte inglés, el fútbol. Como por arte de magia los jóvenes deportistas empezaron a practicar el extraño juego.

Así surgió el primer equipo de fútbol de Bilbao. Se llamó Bilbao Foot-ball Club. En 1898 se creó el primer club de fútbol vasco: el Athletic Club. Los dos equipos fueron rivales al principio pero después acordaron unirse y formaron una selección llamada Vizcaya.

El Athletic celebró su centenario en 1998. Junto con el Real Madrid y el Barcelona son los únicos equipos que nunca han bajado a Segunda. En el Athletic sólo juegan jugadores de origen vasco. La cantera del Club ha producido un sinfín de futbolistas de prestigio internacional.

Exercise 13

1 Why did British ships go to Vizcaya?
2 Why did young Basque people go to the United Kingdom?
3 What has Athletic Club got in common with Barcelona and Real Madrid?
4 What is different about Athletic Club?

7 La salud

In this unit you can learn about:

▶ using the future tense (i)
▶ how to express probability / uncertainty / guesswork
▶ how to interrupt and introduce a new topic
▶ using the conditional (i)
▶ using indirect speech (ii)
▶ how to give advice (i)
▶ papers needed to use the **INSALUD** (the Spanish Health Service)
▶ acronyms used in the Health Service

Exercise 1

Arrange the following symptoms into the four headings. Some of the symptoms could go under more than one heading:

malestar general fiebre alta estornudos tos	

malestar general   fiebre alta   estornudos   tos
dolor de cabeza   molestias musculares   dolor de garganta
mareos   vómitos   dolor de estómago
escalofríos   ronquera

resaca (hangover)	**gripe** (flu)	**resfriado** (cold)	**migraña** (migraine)

Dialogue 1 🔊

Lucía bumps into an acquaintance. After a while Lucía enquires about a friend they have in common that she has not seen for a while.

Vocabulary ◆

tiene para rato	it will be a long time before he is well (*in this context*)
análisis (m)	(*medical*) test / tests
dar el alta	to discharge from hospital / the certificate your doctor gives you to start work again
llevarse bien	to get on well

Exercise 2

Cover up the dialogue and listen to their conversation. After listening to it, answer the following:

1 Where is Andrés and why?
2 Why does Lucía want to know whether he is at 'El Clínico'?
3 Why does Lucía not want to see Andrés' parents?

LUCÍA   Oye, por cierto ¿No sabrás por dónde anda Andrés? Hace un montón de tiempo que no lo veo. ¿No estará ya en Tailandia?

SONIA   ¡No irás a decirme que no lo sabes! Pensaba que todos sus amigos lo sabían.

LUCÍA   Pero, ¿de qué me hablas?

SONIA   Pues que ya lleva tres semanas en el hospital. Le operaron de un tumor en la cabeza hace dos semanas.

LUCÍA   ¡Oh, no! Y, ¿cómo está ahora?

SONIA   Tranquila, mujer, salió bien de la operación, y se está recuperando pero tiene para rato. Me imagino que no le darán el alta por mucho tiempo . . .

LUCÍA   Perdona que te interrumpa pero ¿cómo se lo encontraron? Yo lo vi hace cosa de dos meses y estaba bien. Estaba pensando en hacer un viaje por Asia . . .

SONIA   Empezó a tener dolores de cabeza, a marearse, así que fue
          al médico y después al hospital a hacerse unos análisis . . .
LUCÍA   Oye, ¿no estará en el Clínico?
SONIA   Sí, ¿pues?
LUCIA   No, es que uno de mis hermanos que es médico trabaja allí
          y podría hablar con los médicos que le tratan.
SONIA   Sería fantástico, ya sabes como es lo de los hospitales. Por
          cierto, yo iba a visitarle ahora, ¿por qué no vienes conmigo?
LUCÍA   ¿No estarán con él sus padres? Es que no nos llevamos muy
          bien.
SONIA   No creo. Normalmente van por la mañana para llevarle algo
          de comer. Es que no le gusta nada la comida de los hospi-
          tales. Seguro que ya no están ahí.
LUCÍA   Vale, entonces voy a hacerle una visitilla pero sólo podré
          quedarme un rato. Tengo que estar en casa antes de las seis.

Language points ◆

Future tenses (i)

The future tense is used in Spanish the same way as it is in English
to refer to an action that will happen. It is more commonly used
in the written language. The form **ir a** plus an infinitive is used in
everyday conversation.

Mañana voy a visitar a Lola.
Tomorrow I am going to visit Lola.

¿Cuándo vas a hacerte el análisis de sangre?
When are you going to have the blood test done?

Remember that the future tense of regular verbs is formed by adding
the following personal endings to the inifitive: -é, -ás, -á, -emos, -éis,
-án:

No iré aunque me lo pida.
I will not go even if s / he asks me to.

¿Volverás pronto?
Will you come back soon?

¿Trabajará Luis mañana?
Will Luis work tomorrow?

Also remember that some verbs are irregular in the future tense. Have
a look at them in the Grammar reference at the back of the book.

Note that the present tense is also used to refer to the future:

El tren sale a las 4.
The train leaves at 4.

¿Vienes conmigo el domingo?
Are you coming with me on Sunday?

Exercise 3

Match the following questions with their answers:

1	¿Hará buen tiempo mañana?	a	Creo que será en agosto.
2	¿Cuándo lo sabrás?	b	Creo que lo tendrá todo terminado esta tarde.
3	¿Vendrá tu hermano a la boda?	c	No sé si podré venir o no.
4	¿Irás con tu madre?	d	Sí, creo que hará calor.
5	¿Cuándo tendrá todo hecho?	e	No sé si lo sabré antes del domingo.
6	¿Cuándo podrás venir?	f	Creo que vendrá pero no estoy segura.
7	¿A qué hora saldréis de la oficina?	g	No, iré con mi hermana.
8	¿Cuándo será la boda?	h	Saldremos a las seis.

Exercise 4

Answer the following questions according to the model:

> Example: ¿Has hecho ya la carta?
> No, pero la haré luego.

1 ¿Has ido ya al banco?
2 ¿Ha venido ya Juan?
3 ¿Sabes ya cuándo viene tu madre?
4 ¿Tenéis ya los billetes?
5 ¿Ha salido ya con el perro?
6 ¿Le has dicho todo?
7 ¿Le has mandado ya el emilio?
8 ¿Habéis comido ya?

How to express probability / uncertainty / guesswork

The future tense is also used in Spanish for expressing other ideas:

to express probability / uncertainty / guesswork:

¿No sabrás por dónde anda Andrés?
Do you know by any chance where Andrés is?

¿No estará en el Clínico?
Is he by any chance in the Clínico? Could he be at the Clínico?

¿Qué hora será?
I wonder what time it is.

Serán como las cuatro.
It's probably about 4 o'clock.

¿Quién llamará a estas horas? ¿Será Luis?
I wonder who is calling at this time, I wonder whether it is Luis. / Could it be Luis?

To express surprise or doubt:

¿No estará ya en Tailandia?
He's not in Thailand, is he?

¡No irás a decirme que no lo sabes!
Don't tell me you don't know!

¡No me dirás que has sacado el carné de conducir!
Don't tell me you have got your driving licence!

to express indignation:

| ¡Tendrás cara! | You have got a cheek! |
| ¡Será idiota! | S/he is such an idiot! |

to express orders:

| ¡No matarás! | Don't kill! |

Harás ahora mismo lo que te digo ...
You will do straightaway what I tell you ...

Exercise 5

Fill in the gaps with the future tense of the appropriate verb: **ser** (3 times), **estar** (twice), **ir**, **vivir**, and **decir**:

1 ¿En qué _____ pensando? (él)
2 ¿Quiénes _____ esos hombres?
3 ¿ _____ posible que todavía esté aquí?
4 Tú _____ lo que quieras pero yo no me voy de aquí.
5 ¡Si _____ de acuerdo con ella! (tú)
6 ¿De qué _____ la vecina? No trabaja en ningún sitio.
7 ¿ _____ tu hermano el que llama?
8 Tú _____ allí ahora mismo.

How to interrupt a conversation and introduce a new topic

por cierto by the way

Oye, por cierto, ¿no sabrás por dónde anda Andrés?
By the way, do you by any chance know where Andrés is?

Por cierto, yo iba a visitarle ahora.
By the way, I was going to visit him now.

Perdona que te interrumpa. Sorry to interrupt.

Perdona que te interrumpa pero ¿cómo se lo encontraron?
Sorry to interrupt you (*informal*), but, how did they find it?

Perdone que le interrumpa pero creo que eso no es verdad.
Sorry to interrupt you (*formal*) but I don't think that's true.

Antes de que se me olvide. Before I forget.

Antes de que se me olvide, ¿a qué hora es la película?
Before I forget, what time does the film start?

Antes de que se me olvide, ¿cuáles son las horas de visita?
Before I forget, what are the visiting hours?

Eso me recuerda. That reminds me.

Eso me recuerda, ¿en qué habitación está?
That reminds me, which room is s / he in?

Eso me recuerda, ¿fuiste ya al médico?
That reminds me, have you already been to the doctor?

Exercise 6

Translate the following sentences:

1 Before I forget, do you know whether Juan is better?
2 That reminds me, have you got an appointment with the doctor?
3 By the way, how is your stomach now?
4 Sorry to interrupt but have you visited Andrés?
5 Before I forget, do you know whether these pills are any good?
6 By the way, have you received the results of the blood test?

The conditional (i)

The conditional is formed by adding the personal endings, -ía, -ías, -ía, -íamos, -íais, -ían to the infinitive:

Tomaría otra copa pero he venido en coche.
I would have another drink but I have come by car.

Viviría en Granada pero mi trabajo está aquí.
I would live in Granada but my work is here.

Trabajaría en ese hospital pero está muy lejos.
I would work in that hospital but it is a long way away.

¿Irías con ella?
Would you go with her?

¿Se quedaría con ella?
Would s/he stay with her?

The same verbs that are irregular in the future tense are irregular in the conditional. Look at the Grammar reference for more information:

¿Lo harías tú?   Would you do it?
Podría hablar con él.   I could speak to him.
Pilar dijo que vendría hoy.   Pilar said she would come today.

The conditional is used in Spanish in the same way as in English:

Iría mañana pero no puedo.
I would go tomorrow but I can't.

¿Beberías el agua en la India?
Would you drink the water in India?

Dijeron que vendrían hoy.
They said they would come today.

Dijo que lo haría un día de estos.
S/he said s/he would do it one of these days.

It is also used, as the future tense, to express probability, uncertainty, and guesswork. The only difference being that the conditional is related to an action that has already passed:

¿Qué hora sería cuando llegamos a casa?
What time could it have been when we arrived at home?

Serían las tres de la madrugada.
It was probably 3 a.m.

¿Vendrían en avión?
Could they have come by plane?

¿Quién llamaría a esas horas?
Who could have phoned at that time?

¿Serían los vecinos?
Could it have been the neighbours?

Exercise 7

Match the following questions with the correct answers:

1 ¿Qué hora sería cuando vino Luis?
2 ¿Quién llamaría cuando estábamos cenando?
3 ¿Vendría en avión?
4 ¿Tendría dolor de cabeza?
5 No estaría solo, ¿no?
6 ¿Estarían en casa cuando llamamos?

a Creo que vendría en tren.
b No creo, estaría con su hermana.
c Creo que serían las tres.
d No creo, estarían fuera.
e Creo que sería la vecina.
f No creo, me imagino que estaría cansado.

Exercise 8

Fill in the gaps with the appropriate form of the conditional of the following verbs: **comer, hacer, irse, visitar, quedarse, venir, escribir,** and **ser**:

1 _____ más pero estoy llena (yo).
2 Estoy segura de que lo _____ si se lo pides (ella).
3 Me _____ contigo ahora mismo pero no puedo (yo).
4 La _____ pero no me gustan los hospitales (yo).
5 ¿Te _____ mañana con ella? (tú).
6 Mis padres _____ pero cuestan mucho los billetes.
7 ¿Le _____ si te doy la dirección electrónica? (tú)
8 Cuando él llegó, _____ las cinco.

The conditional is also used to express courtesy when you are asking for something:

¿Podría decirme dónde hay una farmacia por aquí?
Could you tell me where there is a chemist nearby?

¿Me dejarías tu coche?
Would you lend me your car?

¿Vendrías conmigo al hospital?
Would you come with me to the hospital?

¿Me prestarías tus libros para el examen?
Would you lend me your books for the exam?

¿Te importaría ir ahora mismo?
Would you mind going right now?

Exercise 9

An English friend whose Spanish is not very good has to send an email to a friend asking her to help him. He has asked you to write down the correct conditional tenses of the verbs **poder, importar, venir, gustar**. In some instances two of them could be suitable.

Querida Susana

El mes que viene iré a Madrid a pasar dos semanas. Llegaré al aeropuerto de Barajas a las 11 de la noche, ¿ _____ venir a recogerme? Si no puedes, ¿ _____ Juan venir a recogerme? No sé si alquilaré un coche, pero si no tengo suficiente dinero, ¿ _____ dejarme tu coche unos días? No sé tampoco dónde quedarme, ya sabes que no ando bien de dinero, ¿ _____ quedarme las dos semanas en tu casa? Cuando esté en Madrid, tengo que ir a ver a un amigo que está muy enfermo en el hospital pero no quiero ir solo, ¿ _____ conmigo? También me _____ pasar unos días en la Sierra, ¿ _____ coger unos días de vacaciones? Por último, necesito encontrar información del último libro de Rosa Montero, ¿ _____ ir a alguna librería y preguntar por él?

Perdona por pedirte tantos favores pero es que tengo muchos problemas.

Indirect speech (ii)

The future tense in direct speech changes to the conditional tense when the message is reproduced in indirect speech:

'Iré al hospital si tengo tiempo.'
'I will go to hospital if I have the time.'

Me dijo que iría al hospital si tenía tiempo.
S/he told me s/he would go to hospital if s/he had the time.

'Tomaré los antibióticos.'
'I will take the antibiotics.'

Me dijo que tomaría los antibióticos.
S/he told me s/he would take the antibiotics.

'¿Irás a Barcelona con Lola?'
'Will you go to Barcelona with Lola?'

Me preguntó si iría a Barcelona con Lola.
S/he asked me whether I would go to Barcelona with Lola.

'¿Cuándo llamarás a Luisma?'
'When will you call Luisma?'

Me preguntó que cuándo llamaría a Luisma.
S/he asked when I would call Luisma.

Direct speech	Indirect speech
Future	Conditional

Remember that the future is used in indirect speech when the main clause (**dice que**) is in the present:

'Veré al médico más tarde.'
'I will see the doctor later.'

<u>Ella dice</u> que verá al médico más tarde.
<u>She says</u> she will see the doctor later.

But

<u>Ella dijo</u> que vería al médico más tardé.
<u>She said</u> she would see the doctor later.

'Seguiré tomando las pastillas.'
'I will keep on taking the pills.'

<u>Ella dice</u> que seguirá tomando las pastillas.
<u>She says</u> she will keep on taking the pills.

But

<u>Ella dijo</u> que seguiría tomando las pastillas.
<u>She said</u> she would keep on taking the pills.

Exercise 10

Change the following direct speech statements into the appropriate indirect speech:

Example: **'¿Estarás en casa mañana?'**
Me preguntó si estaría en casa al día siguiente.

1 'Vendré el lunes sin falta.'   Me dijo que _____
2 'Iré sola si no quieres venir.' Me dijo que _____
3 '¿Cuándo llegarás?   Me preguntó que _____
4 ¿Pintarás la casa?   Me preguntó si _____
5 ¿Me ayudarás luego?   Me preguntó si _____
6 'Saldré más tarde.'   Me dijo que _____

How to give advice (i)

When you want to tell someone what you would do if you were them,
you need to use one of the following expressions plus the conditional:

Yo que tú / él / ella / usted / vosotros/as / ellos / ellas / ustedes

Yo que tú iría a Urgencias.
If I were you, I would go to Casualty.

Yo que él iría ahora mismo.
If I were him, I would go straight away.

Yo en tu / su / vuestro lugar

Yo en tu lugar me haría un análisis de sangre.
If I were you, I would have a blood test.

Yo en su lugar hablaría con un especialista.
If I were him / her, I would talk to a specialist or
If I were you (*formal*), I would talk to a specialist.

Yo en vuestro lugar no tomaría esas pastillas.
If I were you (*plural*), I wouldn't take those pills.

Si yo fuera tú / usted / él / ella / vosotros/as / ustedes / ellos / ellas

Si yo fuera tú iría a un médico privado.
If I were you, I would go to a private doctor.

Si yo fuera usted no lo firmaría.
If I were you (*formal*), I wouldn't sign it.

Si yo fuera vosotros no iría en coche.
If I were you (*plural*), I wouldn't go by car.

Exercise 11

Answer the following questions according to the model. Just choose one of the three different options:

¿Adónde irías de vacaciones?   (la India)

Example: **Yo que tú iría a la India /**
Yo en tu lugar iría a la India /
Si yo fuera tú iría a la India

1	¿Dónde te quedarías tú?	(hoteles)
2	¿Cuándo irías a la India?	(en Navidad)
3	¿Comerías ensaladas?	(no, sólo cosas calientes)
4	¿Qué vacunas te pondrías?	(polio, hepatitis)
5	¿Tomarías las pastillas contra la malaria?	(sí)
6	¿Te pondrías la vacuna contra el cólera?	(no)
7	¿Viajarías en autocar?	(no)
8	¿Beberías agua del grifo?	(no, sólo agua mineral)

Text 1

Exercise 12

An English friend who is spending some time with you in Spain thinks he may be suffering from hay fever. He is not sure because he has not suffered from it before. You have found the following information on the worst areas in Spain for hay fever sufferers and it also contains some advice. Read it and make notes for your friend on areas of Spain to avoid.

Vocabulary ♦

fiebre del heno (m)	hay fever
maleza (f)	scrub
empeorar	to worsen
mejorar	to improve
premisas (pl)	premises

Alergia al polen

La presencia en la atmósfera de pólenes de plantas no cultivadas es la causa más importante de fiebre del heno en España; en segundo lugar se encuentra el polen del olivo en las zonas sur, centro y este de la península. El polen de la Parietaria judaica, que es un tipo de maleza, también presenta una gran importancia pero sólo en la zona costera mediterránea. Para los alérgicos a las plantas no cultivadas, los meses más severos corresponden a mayo y junio aunque pacientes muy sensibilizados pueden presentar ya síntomas los días soleados a partir del mes de febrero. En este periodo los pacientes empeoran con las salidas al campo y mejoran en los días lluviosos.

El paciente alérgico debe respetar unas premisas básicas durante la estación de exposición a pólenes alergénicos:

- Mantener las ventanas cerradas por la noche.
- Utilizar aire acondicionado con filtros.
- Disminuir las actividades al aire libre durante las 5–10 de la mañana y de 6–10 de la tarde.
- Mantener cerradas las ventanillas cuando viaje en coche.
- Poner filtros al aire acondicionado del automóvil.
- Permanecer el mayor tiempo posible dentro de casa durante los días de mayores concentraciones de pólenes.
- Evitar salir los días de viento.
- Tomarse las vacaciones en zonas libres de pólenes, por ejemplo, la playa.
- No cortar el césped.
- No tumbarse sobre el césped.
- No secar la ropa en el exterior durante los días de recuentos altos. El polen puede quedar atrapado en ella.
- Ponerse gafas de sol al salir a la calle.

Exercise 13

Match the following expressions (all of them can be used to wish people well) with their English equivalents:

1 Que te mejores.
2 Que te pongas bien pronto.
3 Que te recuperes pronto.

4 Que te manden pronto para casa.
5 Que te den el alta pronto.
6 Que no sea nada grave.

7 Que sea leve.

a I hope it is nothing serious.
b I hope you recover soon.
c I hope you are released from hospital soon.
d I hope you get better.

e I hope you get better soon.
f I hope you are sent home soon.

g I hope it is not serious.

How to use the Spanish National Health Service (INSALUD)

Insalud, Instituto nacional de Salud

Exercise 14

A friend who suffers from a number of ailments is planning to come and live in Spain for a while. She has asked you to send her information on what she needs to do so she can use the Spanish Health Service. You have come across the following information about the subject on the Internet. Read it and fill in the table below to send to your friend.

Vocabulary ♦

disponer de	to have, to have available
INSS	Instituto Nacional de la Seguridad Social
convenios (mpl)	agreements
solicitar	to apply for, to request
organismo	organisation
asignar	to assign, to allocate
desplazamiento	travelling

Los usuarios de países de la UE deberán disponer del formulario E.111. Si no dispone de él, el INSS a través de su Departamento de Convenios Internacionales los solicitará al organismo extranjero correspondiente. En el Centro de Salud más próximo a su domicilio presentará el formulario E.111, original y copia, junto con el pasaporte o DNI para que le asignen médico.

Si un usuario miembro de la UE precisa Tratamiento con Diálisis Renal en sus desplazamientos por España, este debe ser solicitado al INSALUD por el organismo correspondiente del país de origen, con suficiente antelación según formulario E.111–D1.

En caso de venir a España para recibir un tratamiento específico, este será previamente solicitado por la Seguridad Social de su país de origen, que hará la reserva en el Centro Hospitalario español correspondiente y le entregará el formulario E.112.

	Doctor	**Dialysis**	**Specific treatments**
Documents / forms needed			
Organisation / people responsible for obtaining the documents			

¿Sabía usted? ♦

Generally speaking, **siglas** (abbreviations) and **acrónimos** (acronyms) are synonymous. When the abbreviation results in a word that can be read, we do not need to pronounce the abbreviation letter by letter: **el SIDA, los PACs**, etc. Sometimes we add a letter in order to make it easier to read it as a word (this is, strictly speaking, an acronym) e.g. in **la RENFE** (**Red Nacional de los Ferrocarriles Españoles**) the vowel **E** has been added. Until recently we used to put a full stop between each individual letter but this tendency is disappearing.

UE	Unión Europea	European Union
INSALUD	Instituto Nacional de la Salud (el INSALUD)	NHSS
INSS	Instituto Nacional de la Seguridad Social	Social Security
D.N.I. / DNI	Documento Nacional de Identidad	Identity Card
PAC	Punto de Atención Continuada (los PACs)	
UVI	Unidad de Vigilancia Intensiva (la UVI)	Intensive Care Unit
TSI	Tarjeta Sanitaria Individual	NHSS Card
SIDA	Síndrome de Inmunodeficiencia Adquirida (el SIDA)	AIDS
NIF	Número de Identificación Fiscal (el NIF)	National Insurance Number

8 La educación

In this unit you can learn about:

▶ education
▶ using the future and conditional perfect
▶ using indirect speech (iii)
▶ how to deny a statement
▶ some verbs with prepositions: **optar** and **contar**
▶ the passive voice with **se** (i)
▶ how to express impersonality
▶ the Spanish educational system

Dialogue 1

Sara is doing a translation course and Asun wants to know how the exam went.

Exercise 1

Match the following words you will hear in the dialogue with their respective description:

1 las notas	devolver el dinero que ya has pagado
2 la matrícula	la cancelación
3 reembolsar	los resultados de los exámenes
4 la anulación	con anticipación, con cierto espacio de tiempo
5 antelación (f)	la inscripción
6 convocatoria (f)	cita o llamada a un examen / concurso

Exercise 2

Cover the dialogue, listen to their conversation and tick where appropriate.

	True	False
Sara has just done her exams.	____	____
Sara had the flu.	____	____
Sara has been given her enrolment fee back.	____	____
Sara is sure she is going to continue her studies.	____	____
Sara wants to stay in Madrid.	____	____
Sara has not talked to her tutor.	____	____

ASUN   Habrás hecho ya el examen de traducción, ¿no?

SARA   ¡Qué va! Lo iba a hacer pero no pude porque justo antes del examen cogí una gripe terrible. Para ahora ya habría recibido las notas y todo . . .

ASUN   Pero, te habrán devuelto el dinero de la matrícula, ¿no?

SARA   ¡Qué más quisiera yo! Sólo reembolsan el dinero si haces la anulación con más de 15 días de antelación y yo les llamé sólo 2 días antes del examen.

ASUN   Pues te dejarán hacer el examen en la siguiente convocatoria . . .

SARA   Espero que sí, no estoy muy segura . . .

ASUN   De todas formas, seguirás estudiando para el examen, ¿no?

SARA   No lo sé. Para septiembre ya habré terminado las horas que me pagaron mis padres y el examen es en diciembre. No sé si tendré dinero para pagar más clases.

ASUN   Podrías trabajar, ¿no?

SARA   Sí, pero no estoy segura si quiero quedarme en Madrid hasta diciembre.

ASUN   Pero habrás hablado con tu tutor, ¿no?

SARA   ¡Qué va! Ya lo habría solucionado todo pero mi tutor está de vacaciones y no vuelve hasta septiembre. Así que no sé qué voy a hacer.

ASUN   Yo que tú no decidiría nada de momento. Habla con tus padres a ver lo que te dicen.

Language points ♦

Future perfect

The future perfect tense is formed by using the future of the auxiliary verb **haber** (**habré, habrás, habrá, habremos, habréis, habrán**) and the past participle. Look at the Grammar reference at the back of the book for more information.

Habrás hecho ya el examen de traducción, ¿no?
You must have already done your translation exam, haven't you?

Pero, te habrán devuelto el dinero de la matrícula, ¿no?
They have returned the enrolment fee, haven't they?

Ya habrán terminado los exámenes.
I presume they will have finished the exams by now.

This tense is used to express a future action that will be completed prior to another future action:

Para septiembre ya habré terminado las horas.
By September I will have completed the hours.

Para el verano ya habré hecho todos los exámenes.
I will have finished all the exams by the summer.

Para cuando ella llegue yo ya me habré ido.
By the time she arrives I will have left.

The future perfect tense is also used to express probability / uncertainty / guesswork about a past event:

¿Habrá llegado ya?
I wonder whether s/he has already arrived.

¿No te habrás matriculado?
I wonder whether you have enrolled.
(*You haven't enrolled, have you?*)

Supongo que lo habrá hecho.
I imagine s/he has done it by now.

¿Habrá aprobado el examen?
I wonder whether s/he has passed his/her exam.

Exercise 3

Change the following questions according to the model.

Example: **¿Irá a matricularse?**
            ¿Habrá ido a matricularse?

1   ¿Irá a matricularse?
2   ¿Aprobará todas las asignaturas?
3   ¿Repetirán el curso?
4   ¿Se pondrá nerviosa en el examen?
5   ¿Sabrán todas las preguntas?
6   ¿Le darán la licenciatura?
7   ¿Vendrá a tiempo?
8   ¿Reconocerá las tres novelas?

Conditional perfect

The conditional perfect is formed by using the conditional of the auxiliary **haber** (**habría, habrías, habría, habríamos, habríais, habrían**) and the past participle:

Lo habría hecho pero no pude.
I would have done it but I couldn't.

Habría ido a verlo pero no tuve tiempo.
I would have gone to see him but I did not have the time.

This tense is used to express what would have taken place had something else not intervened:

Ya lo habría solucionado todo para ahora pero mi tutor está de vacaciones.
I would have resolved everything by now but my tutor is on holiday.

Lo habría hecho pero no pude.
I would have done it but I couldn't.

Ellos habrían venido pero se les averió el coche.
They would have come but their car broke down.

Exercise 4

Form sentences according to the model:

Example: Yo / hablar / con el jefe / no estar.
Yo habría hablado con el jefe pero no estaba.

1 Nosotros / terminar / no haber luz.
2 Ellos / irse de vacaciones / no tener dinero.
3 Yo / estudiar inglés / no haber profesores.
4 Yo / matricularse / no tener los papeles.
5 Ella / aprobar / no encontrarse bien.
6 Ellos / estudiar más / su madre estar enferma.

Exercise 5

Match the following statements:

1 ¿Estarían en casa cuando llamamos?

2 ¿Tendrían algún problema con el coche?

3 ¿Saldrían juntos?

4 Vendría solo, ¿no?

5 ¿Sería fácil el examen?

6 Dijo que vendría antes de las cinco.

a Lo dudo, se habría sentido demasiado solo.

b ¡Qué extraño! ya habría llegado si dijo eso.

c No creo, nos lo habrían dicho.

d No creo, nos habrían llamado por teléfono.

e Lo dudo, Laura no habría suspendido.

f Lo dudo, habrían abierto la puerta.

Indirect speech (iii)

The future perfect tense in direct speech changes to the conditional perfect tense when the message is reproduced in indirect speech:

'Ya habrá hecho todos los exámenes.'
'S/he has probably already finished all the exams.'

Me dijo que ya habría hecho todos los exámenes.
S/he told me that s/he would have already done all the exams.

'Ya se habrá matriculado.'
'S/he has probably enrolled.'

Me dijo que se habría matriculado.
S/he told me s/he would have probably enrolled.

'Ya lo habré hecho para el lunes.'
'I will have it done by Monday.'

Me dijo que ya lo habría hecho para el lunes.
S/he told me s/he would have done it by Monday.

'¿Lo habrás hecho para el lunes?'
'Will you have done it by Monday?'

Me preguntó que si lo habría hecho para el lunes.
S/he asked me if I would have done it by Monday.

Direct speech	Indirect speech
Future perfect	Conditional perfect

Remember that the future perfect is used in indirect speech when the main clause (dice que) is in the present:

'José habrá suspendido porque el profesor no ha dicho nada.'
'José has probably failed because the teacher has not said anything.'

<u>Dice que</u> José habrá suspendido porque el profesor no ha dicho nada.
S/he says José has probably failed because the teacher has not said anything.

But

Dijo que José habría suspendido porque el profesor no había dicho nada.
S/he said José would probably have failed because the teacher had not said anything.

Exercise 6

Change the following direct speech statements into the appropriate indirect speech:

Example: **'Supongo que lo habrá hecho.'**
Ella dijo que suponía que lo habría hecho.
Ella dice que supone que lo habrá hecho.

1 'Supongo que habrá llegado.' Ella dijo que _____
    Ella dice que _____
2 '¿No habrás visto a Luis?' Él me preguntó si _____
3 '¿Lo habrás terminado para Me preguntó si _____
  el verano?'
4 'Creo que ya habrá llamado.' Dijo que _____
    Dice que _____
5 'Supongo que ya habrá Dijo que _____
  terminado la licenciatura.' Dice que _____
6 'Supongo que habrá suspendido.' Dijo que _____

How to deny a statement

¡Qué va!   Not at all

This expression is quite informal:

Habrás hecho ya el examen de traducción, ¿no?
You have done the translation exam, haven't you?

¡Qué va!
Not at all!

¿Tendrás suficiente dinero para el curso, ¿no?
You have enough money for the course, haven't you?

¡Qué va! No tengo ni para comer.
Not at all, I don't even have enough to eat.

¡Qué más quisiera yo!   I wish!

Pero, te habrán devuelto el dinero de la matrícula, ¿no?
They have given you the money back for the enrolment fee,
haven't they?

¡Qué más quisiera yo!
I wish!

¿Habrás aprobado todos los exámenes, ¿no?
You have passed all the exams, haven't you?

¡Qué más quisiera yo! Suspendí uno.
I wish! I failed one.

Exercise 7

Listen to the answers given to the following questions. Tick those
questions that have not taken place:

1   Habrás visto a tu madre, ¿no?
2   Habrás pagado ya todo, ¿no?

3   Habrás aprobado Historia, ¿no?

4   Te habrás matriculado, ¿no?
5   Habrás ido a la universidad, ¿no?

6   Saldrás con nosotros luego, ¿no?

Exercise 8

Read the following information on some changes that will take place
in the Spanish educational system in 2004 and decide the most appropriate heading for each part:

1. Repeticiones   2. Grupos de refuerzo   3. Itinerarios desde los
14 años   4. Idioma extranjero   5. Reválida

Educación, cómo les va a afectar el cambio

Las novedades comenzarán en el curso 2004–2005. Los estudiantes empezarán a encauzar su futuro desde los 14 años.

_____. A partir de 3° de Educación Secundaria Obligatoria (ESO) los alumnos optarán entre dos itinerarios: Orientación Técnico-Profesional o Científico-Humanística. Para poder elegir, recibirán un Informe de Orientación Escolar que les sirva de guía. Tendrán que orientar su futuro hacia la Universidad o hacia la Formación Profesional dos años antes que actualmente. En el curso siguiente, en 4°, volverán a tres opciones: Orientación Tecnológica, Científica o Humanística. Por cualquiera de estas vías se consigue obtener el título de graduado de Educación Secundaria.

_____. En los cuatro cursos de la ESO se repetirá si se suspenden tres o más asignaturas (sólo se repite una vez por año). Sin embargo, como hasta ahora, en el primer ciclo de Primaria (de 6 a 8 años) no se podrá repetir curso. Los alumnos que suspenden alguna asignatura en junio podrán realizar una prueba extraordinaria: es una nueva versión de la convocatoria de septiembre, que ahora se adelanta 3 meses.

_____. Con el título de bachiller se podrá acceder a la Prueba General de Bachillerato (PGB), que sustituye a la Selectividad y es necesaria para acceder a Formación Profesional de Grado Superior y a los estudios universitarios. Habrá hasta cuatro oportunidades para superar esta prueba, que será escrita y contará con una parte común y otra específica. La nota del título de bachiller se obtendrá de la media entre la reválida y el expediente de Bachillerato.

_____. En 1° y 2° de ESO todos los alumnos estudiarán las mismas asignaturas, pero se crearán grupos de refuerzo para aquellos estudiantes que tengan dificultades en el aprendizaje o para inmigrantes con problemas de comprensión lingüística.

_____. Una de las asignaturas que más pretende potenciar la nueva ley es la lengua extranjera (sobre todo, inglés), cuyo estudio se adelanta de los 8 a los 6 años. Se facilitará la preparación del profesor. En la prueba de reválida se incluye un examen escrito y otro oral de esta asignatura.

Source: Article from magazine _Mía_, 15–21 April 2002

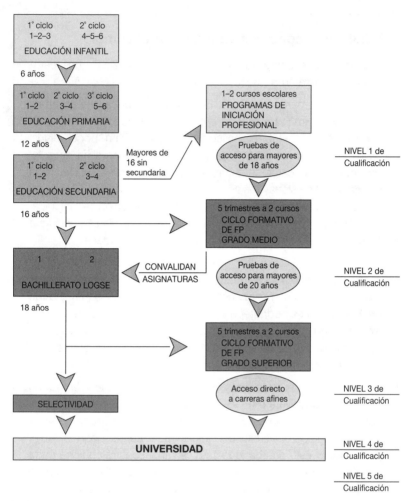

The new educational system.

Exercise 9

Find the equivalents in the Spanish text:

1 Para 1   currently
2 Para 2   to fail
            test
            examination session
            to move forward

3 Para 3   to overcome
             grade
             academic record
4 Para 4   learning
5 Para 5   to increase its importance

Exercise 10

Read the article again and say whether the following statements are true or false:

1 Para 1 Students will have to start choosing whether they want to go to university or do Vocational Qualifications two years earlier.
2 Para 2 Students who fail some subjects in June can re-take them in September.
3 Para 3 To be able to have access to university you need to pass the 'Prueba General de Bachillerato'.
4 Para 4 All the students will study the same subjects.
5 Para 5 Learning a foreign language will start at the age of 8.

Some verbs with prepositions

Optar entre   to choose between

Los alumnos optarán entre dos itinerarios.
The pupils will choose between two routes.

Optar por   to opt for, to choose

Optaron por el coche más barato.
They opted for the cheapest car.

Opté por callarme.
I chose not to say anything.

Contar con   to have, to have at one's disposal, to consist of

Contará con una parte común.
It will consist of a general examination. (*all students have to do this part*)

El director contará con más poder.
The director will have more power.

Contar con   to rely on, to count on

¡Cuenta conmigo!
You can rely on me.

¿Puedo contar con él?
Can I rely on him?

Contar con   to think, to expect

No contaba con encontrarte aquí.
I didn't think I was going to find you here.

Contaba con ir hoy pero . . .
I thought I was going to go today but . . .

Exercise 11

Fill in the gaps with the corresponding verb and preposition:

1 Tienes que _____ _____ las seis asignaturas, no puedes estudiar todas.
2 No sabía qué estudiar pero al final él _____ _____ humanidades. (in the preterite)
3 No _____ _____ la nieve y llegaron tarde. (in the imperfect tense)
4 Ellos _____ _____ hacer el examen en septiembre. (in the preterite)
5 La reválida _____ _____ dos pruebas.
6 No puedes _____ _____ él, ya sabes que está muy enfermo.
7 _____ _____ terminar hoy. (in the imperfect)

The pronoun *se*

The pronoun **se** has many different uses. The first two below you have seen in other chapters.

Reflexive

Se is the third person, singular and plural, reflexive pronoun:

Se levanta todos los días a las 6 de la mañana para estudiar.
S/he gets up every day at 6 a.m. to study.

Se quejaron del examen.
They complained about the exam.

Indirect object

The indirect object **le** changes to **se** when it is followed by a direct object: **lo, la, los, las:**

Se lo di ayer.	I gave it to her/him.
Se lo diré mañana.	I will tell her/him tomorrow.
Se los daré el domingo.	I will give them to her/him on Sunday.

Passive voice

A passive sentence turns the object of an active sentence into the subject. In the English language the verb *to be* plus a past participle is used in the passive voice:

Active: Alejandro Amenábar directed the film. (*the film is the object*)

Passive: The film was directed by Alejandro Amenábar. (*the film is the subject*)

Active: George Orwell wrote *Animal Farm*. (*Animal Farm is the object*)

Passive: *Animal Farm* was written by George Orwell. (*Animal Farm is the subject*)

We will be looking at how the pronoun **se** is used in the passive voice. In the next chapters you will study other ways of forming passive sentences.

Se plus a verb in the third person (singular or plural)

Have a look at the following sentences taken from the article on education:

Pero se crearán grupos de refuerzo para aquellos estudiantes . . .
But support groups will be created for those students . . .

En la prueba de reválida se incluye un examen escrito y otro oral de esta asignatura.
In the final exam a written and an oral exam of this subject is included.

La nota del títuto de bachiller se obtendrá de la media entre la reválida y el expediente de Bachillerato.
The grade of the certificate of 'bachiller' will be obtained from the average between the final exam and the academic record of 'Bachillerato'.

Note that the verb has to agree (singular or plural) with the subject.

Pero se crearán grupos de refuerzo.
Support groups will be created.

Pero se creará un grupo de refuerzo.
A support group will be created.

Se solucionó el problema.
The problem was resolved.

Se solucionaron los problemas.
All the problems were resolved.

¿Se han hecho todos los exámenes?
Have all the exams been done?

¿Se ha hecho ya el examen de inglés?
Has the English exam been done?

This construction is often used on signs:

Se venden fincas	Farms sold
Se alquilan sombrillas	Sunshades for rent
Se vende piso	Flat for sale

Exercise 12

Change the following sentences into the passive voice using the pronoun **se**:

Example: **Construyeron la iglesia el año pasado.**
           Se construyó el año pasado.

1 Construyeron la universidad en 1968.
2 Encontraron los exámenes en su habitación.
3 Descubrieron muchos errores en el examen.
4 Resolvieron el error.
5 Lo hicieron el año pasado.
6 Firmaron la carta la semana pasada.
7 Anularon la reunión.
8 Crearon un nuevo curso.

How to make impersonal sentences

There are a number of ways of making impersonal sentences (when the subject is not important). One common way is by using the pronoun **se**.

Se plus the verb in the third person singular

Have a look at some of the sentences taken from the text you have read about the Spanish educational system:

En los cuatro cursos de la ESO <u>se repetirá</u> si se suspenden tres o más asignaturas.
During the four years of ESO people (one) will repeat (a year) if three or more subjects are failed.

Con el título de bachiller <u>se podrá</u> acceder a la Prueba General de Bachillerato (PGB).
With the title of 'bachiller' people will (one will) have access to the PGB.

Other common impersonal sentences:

¿Se vive bien en Madrid?
Does one live well in Madrid? (*Do people live well in Madrid?*)

Se bebe mucho vino tinto en España.
In Spain people drink lots of red wine.

No se puede entrar.
Entrance forbidden (*people cannot enter*).

No se puede fumar.
Smoking forbidden (*people cannot smoke*).

No se puede decir eso aquí.
One cannot say that here.

Exercise 13

Translate the following sentences into Spanish using the pronoun **se**:

Example: People can send the essay by post.
Se puede mandar el trabajo por correo.

1 One can pass the exam without studying.
2 Drinking is forbidden.
3 Eating beef is forbidden in India.
4 People live well in Barcelona.

9 La inmigración en España

In this unit you can learn about:

- ▶ immigration in Spain
- ▶ using the passive voice (ii)
- ▶ **ser** and **estar** plus a past participle
- ▶ plural of nouns / adjectives ending in a stressed vowel
- ▶ how to add more information: **asimismo**, **además**
- ▶ expressions with **gota**, **punto**, **altura**
- ▶ how to ask for information
- ▶ papers needed for obtaining work and a residence permit

Text 1 [⫶))👂]

The number of people from Africa trying to enter Europe illegally through Spain has been increasing steadily. During the summer period a large number of people lose their lives when they try to cross the Straits of Gibraltar (Estrecho de Gibraltar) in very flimsy boats or rafts called pateras. Many of the people end up on the beaches around Algeciras and Tarifa in the south of Spain, west of Málaga, in the Comunidad Autónoma of Andalucía. Read the following article published in El País about the arrest of illegal immigrants in the south of Spain.

Vocabulary ◆

goteo (m)	dripping (verb: **gotear** to drip; **gota** drip)
punto (m)	place, spot, point
a la altura	in the region of
indocumentados	without documents
varones (m)	male (*plural of* **varón**)
mayor de edad	of age

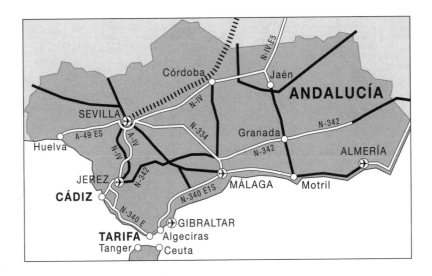

término municipal (m)	municipal district
matriculado	registered (*car, boat*)
	enrolled (*in school, at university*)
natural de	native of
junto a	together with
delito (m)	crime (**crimen** is a very serious crime, normally murder)
turismo (m)	vehicle, private car
asimismo	also, too
deambular	to stroll
menor de edad	under age
tutelado por	under the auspices of

Detenidos en el Campo de Gibraltar otros 23 indocumentados

La llegada de inmigrantes irregulares a las costas de Cádiz continúa como un goteo. Agentes de la Guardia Civil interceptaron ayer a otras 23 personas en distintas operaciones en varios puntos del Campo de Gibraltar. A la altura del kilómetro 86,5 de la carretera Jerez–Los Barrios fueron interceptados tres marroquíes que estaban indocumentados. Poco después fueron localizados en Tarifa otros tres marroquíes, varones y mayores de edad.

En el mismo término municipal, en el puerto de Facinas, fue interceptado un vehículo matriculado en A Coruña cuyo conductor era A.H., natural de Marruecos y vecino de Milán (Italia), que fue detenido junto a su acompañante H.O.A., también marroquí y vecino de Algeciras. Ambos están acusados de cometer un delito contra los derechos de los ciudadanos extranjeros al transportar en el interior del turismo a tres indocumentados de origen marroquí.

Asimismo, en Facinas, la Guardia Civil también interceptó, mientras deambulaban por la zona conocida como Paraje Cumbre Tarifa, a otros dos marroquíes.

En el puerto de Algeciras fueron localizadas otras dos personas, una de ellas menor de edad, que fue trasladada al colegio de Nuestra Señora del Cobre, tutelado por la Junta de Andalucía.

Todos los detenidos, a excepción del menor, serán devueltos a Marruecos en las próximas horas, después de ser conducidos hasta la comisaría de policía de Algeciras, donde se iniciaron los trámites para su repatriación.

Exercise 1

Read the article again and say which are true or false:

1 These are the first immigrants to be arrested.
2 They were all arrested in the same place.
3 All the people arrested were Moroccan nationals.
4 The people arrested did not carry identity papers.
5 All the people arrested will be sent to Morocco.

Exercise 2

Answer the following questions in English:

1 ¿Dónde viven las personas interceptadas en el coche?
2 ¿De qué están acusados A.H. y H.O.A?
3 ¿Cuántas personas son menores de edad?
4 ¿Quiénes serán devueltos a Marruecos?

Language points ◆

The passive voice (ii)

Have a look at the following examples taken from the text:

fueron interceptados tres marroquíes

fueron localizados en Tarifa otros 13 marroquíes

fue interceptado un vehículo matriculado en A Coruña

fue detenido junto a su acompañante

fueron localizadas otras dos personas, una de ellas menor de edad, que fue trasladada al colegio de Nuestra Señora del Cobre

Todos los detenidos . . . , serán devueltos a Marruecos . . . después de ser conducidos, hasta la comisaría de policía de Algeciras

You will probably have noticed that the participles, interceptados, localizados, interceptado, detenido, localizadas, trasladada, devueltos, conducidos, agree both in number and gender with the subject:

interceptados	marroquíes (masculine, plural)	Verbs: interceptar
localizados	marroquíes (masculine, plural)	localizar
interceptado	vehículo (masculine, singular)	
detenido	acompañante (masculine, singular)	detener
localizadas	personas (feminine, plural)	
trasladada	una de ellas (feminine, singular)	trasladar
devueltos	los detenidos (masculine, plural)	devolver
conducidos	los detenidos (masculine, plural)	conducir

Note that if the subject consists of both a masculine and a feminine, you need to use the masculine form:

El joven y la mujer fueron conducidos hasta la comisaría.
The youngster and the woman were driven to the police station.

You have already learned how to make the passive with the pronoun **se**. This one, constructed with the verb **ser**, is very similar to the English passive; you need to use the verb **ser** ('to be') in the appropriate tense plus the past participle of the verb that agrees in gender and number with the subject as we have just seen. Although the passive with **ser** is not commonly used in spoken language, it is very common in written Spanish, especially in the media:

Fueron interceptados tres marroquíes.
Three Moroccan nationals were intercepted.

Fueron localizados en Tarifa otros 13 marroquíes.
Another thirteen Moroccan nationals were found in Tarifa.

Fue interceptado un vehículo matriculado en A Coruña.
A car with an A Coruña number plate was intercepted.

En el puerto de Algeciras fueron localizadas otras dos personas.
Another two people were found in the port of Algeciras.

Todos los detenidos serán devueltos a Marruecos.
All those arrested will be sent back to Marroco.

después de ser conducidos hasta la comisaría de policía de Algeciras
after being driven to the police station in Algeciras

As you can see, the verb **ser** has been used in the past tense (**fueron / fue**), the future (**serán**) and the infinitive (**ser**) according to what was needed. Do not forget that after a preposition you need to use the infinitive form of the verb:

después de ser conducidos   after being driven
antes de ser detenidos   before being arrested

If you want to mention the person who carried out the action, you need to use the preposition **por** followed by the subject:

Don Quijote **fue escrito por Cervantes.**
Don Quixote was written by Cervantes.

Exercise 3

Match the following sentences:

jornalero   day labourer

1 El cuadro fue expuesto en el museo.

2 Los cuadros serán expuestos en el museo.

3 Los inmigrantes fueron trasladados ayer.

a Los contrataron como pintores.

b Los trasladaron ayer.

c Lo expusieron en el museo.

4 Los rumanos han sido
   contratados como pintores.
5 Los polacos fueron
   contratados como pintores.

d Los expondrán en el museo.

e Los han contratado como
  pintores.

Exercise 4

Fill in the gaps with the appropriate past participle of the following verbs: **devolver, trasladar, interrogar, localizar, detener,** and **rescatar** ('to rescue'). Remember that they have to agree in number and gender with the subject.

superviviente   survivor

1 Los 19 supervivientes han sido _____ a un centro de salud en Tarifa para recibir asistencia médica, a excepción de tres magrebíes que han sido _____ por la Guardia Civil.
2 Los otros tres inmigrantes indocumentados fueron _____ en el interior de un turismo.
3 Los mayores de edad han sido _____ a su país.
4 Una de las jóvenes que viajaba en una patera fue _____.
5 Juan fue _____ en la Comisaría.

Exercise 5

Translate the following sentences into Spanish using the verb **ser** plus a past participle:

1 The tourists were taken to the hotel (trasladar).
2 The hotel was built a long time ago (construir).
3 The swimming pool will be cleaned tomorrow (limpiar).
4 The motorway will be closed next week (cerrar).
5 The group was arrested (detener) yesterday.

Ser and *estar* plus a past participle

You will probably have noticed one example in the article in which the past participle is accompanied by the verb **estar** rather than **ser**:

Ambos están acusados de cometer un delito.
Both are accused of having committed a crime.

The best way to explain the difference between the use of **ser** and **estar** with a past participle is by describing **ser** plus a past participle as an action and **estar** plus a past participle as a state / a description:

Los asesinos fueron detenidos ayer.
The assassins were detained yesterday.

Los asesinos están detenidos desde anoche.
The assassins have been detained since last night.

La puerta estaba abierta cuando llegué.
The door was open when I arrived. (*Someone had opened the door before my arrival.*)

La puerta fue abierta cuando llegué.
The door was opened when I arrived. (*Someone opened the door as I arrived.*)

Exercise 6

Fill in the gaps with either **ser** or **estar**; use as many tenses as you can:

Example: **Los documentos _____ destruidos por los ladrones.**
Los documentos fueron destruidos por los ladrones.
Los documentos han sido destruidos por los ladrones.
Los documentos serán destruidos por los ladrones.

1 Las cartas _____ abiertas por la policía.
2 El documento _____ terminado hace unos días.
3 El documento _____ hecho desde hace una semana.
4 El artículo _____ escrito por Vargas Llosa.
5 Ya _____ todo hecho cuando llegué.

Plural of nouns / adjectives that end in a stressed vowel

Note that you need to add **-es** to nouns and adjectives ending in the stressed vowels **í, ú,** to form the plural (as you do to words ending in a consonant):

un marroquí	tres marroquíes
un iraní	algunos iraníes
un hindú	algunos hindúes
irregular	irregulares
operación	operaciones

However, there are some common words that nowadays simply take an -s in the plural form:

champú	champús
esquí	esquís
menú	menús

Other irregular plurals are:

film	films
comic	comics
poster	posters

Exercise 7

Make the plural sentences singular and the singular sentences plural:

Example: **El marroquí se quedó en el hospital.**
Ese menú es fantástico.

Los marroquíes se quedaron en el hospital.
Esos menús son fantásticos.

1 Los marroquíes se quedaron en el sur de España.
2 El menú es muy barato.
3 Estos posters son fantásticos.
4 El joven israelí se fue a Estados Unidos.
5 Este rubí es muy caro.
6 Los iraquíes están muy sorprendidos.
7 Ese esquí es de tu hermano.
8 Me gusta este film.

How to add more information

Asimismo (also)

You will also see this adverb spelled **así mismo**; both are correct. This adverb is not used very much in the spoken language. Other ways of expressing the same idea are:

También

También estuvo en India / Estuvo también en India.
S/he was also in India.

Además

Además nos trajo una botella de Reserva / Nos trajo además una botella de Reserva.
S/he also brought us a bottle of Reserva.

De la misma manera (de igual manera)

De la misma manera, la Guardia Civil interceptó a un marroquí.
The Guardia Civil also intercepted a Moroccan national.

When **de la misma manera** is used to mean **asimismo,** it must go at the beginning of the sentence. Otherwise it means something different:

Lo hizo de la misma manera.
S/he did it the same way.

Text 2

Exercise 8

A friend of yours has asked you to find information on work permits in Spain. You have come across the following article in the Spanish magazine Mía. *Read it and fill in the worksheet so you can send it to him / her.*

La abogada responde

'Soy extranjero, ¿qué tipo de permiso de trabajo necesito?

'He venido de vacaciones y quisiera quedarme más tiempo, pero con un empleo.'

Existen varios tipos de permisos de trabajo según sean tus circunstancias personales y tus planes de permanencia en España. El tipo A se concede para trabajos de temporada de duración limitada, y no puede exceder de nueve meses. El B, para trabajar en una profesión, actividad y ámbito geográfico concretos. Su límite de vigencia es de un año. El permiso C permite trabajar en cualquier actividad dentro de cualquier lugar del territorio nacional y tiene una vigencia de tres años. Y, por último, el permiso de trabajo de tipo D se otorga para ejercer una actividad por cuenta propia y tiene una vigencia de un año. Los tipos B y D pueden ser renovados.

	Time limitations	Geographical limitations	Activity limitations	Renewal
Type A				
Type B				
Type C				
Type D				

Vocabulary ◆

Here are some expressions with words you have learnt in this unit:

gota:	**gota a gota**	drop by drop
	no veo ni gota	I am as blind as a bat
	una gota de vino	a drop of wine
punto:	**llegar a punto**	to arrive on time
	con puntos y comas	in minute detail
	dar en el punto	to hit the nail on the head
	llegar en punto	sharp, on the dot
	estar en su punto	done to a turn, just right
	estar a punto de	to be about to
	hasta cierto punto	up to a point
	poner a punto	to tune up (*car, machine*)
altura:	**a estas alturas**	at this stage
	estar a la altura de las circunstancias	to rise to the occasion

Exercise 9

Fill in the gaps with the appropriate expression from the ones with **punto**, **gota** and **altura**:

1 Se lo dije todo _____.
2 La carne está _____.

3 Tu hermano estuvo _____ como siempre.
4 Él nunca llega _____.
5 Tengo que ir al oculista porque _____.
6 Estaba _____ de salir cuando me llamaron por teléfono.

Now it is your turn, translate the following sentences using some of the expressions with **punto**:

a You must arrive on the dot.
b You have hit the nail on the head.
c You are right but up to a point.
d I was about to tell him the truth when you came in.

Dialogue 1

Listen to the conversation between an immigration officer and Lucía.

Exercise 10

Fill in the following in English:

Reason for journey:

Money:

Friends in Spain:

Problem with her clothes:

ADUANERO	¿Le importaría decirme cuál es la razón de su visita?
LUCÍA	¡Cómo no! Quisiera viajar por España.
ADUANERO	¿Y cuánto tiempo piensa quedarse?
LUCÍA	Tengo un vuelo abierto pero me gustaría quedarme un mes.
ADUANERO	¿Podría decirme cuánto dinero trae?
LUCÍA	Bueno, la verdad es que no traigo mucho pero mi familia me va a mandar más si lo necesito.

ADUANERO   Pero dígame exactamente cuánto tiene.

LUCÍA   Creo que unos 500 euros.

ADUANERO   Me imagino que ya sabrá que con ese dinero no tiene ni para dos semanas. ¿Conoce a alguien en España?

LUCÍA   Tengo una amiga que vive en Sevilla. Es profesora de baile.

ADUANERO   Y, ¿usted piensa quedarse a trabajar aquí?

LUCÍA   No, no. Tengo que regresar a mi país después de mis vacaciones.

ADUANERO   Bueno, ¿tiene algún inconveniente en abrir las maletas por favor?

LUCÍA   No, en absoluto.

ADUANERO   La ropa que tiene en las maletas es un poco extraña, ¿no? Parece que tiene ropa de invierno cuando estamos en julio.

LUCÍA   Es que pienso ir a las montañas y me habían dicho que podía hacer frío.

ADUANERO   Es verdad que hace más fresco en la sierra pero no como para llevar este tipo de ropa.

How to ask for information

There are many ways you could ask for information and you have just heard in the dialogue some common ones:

Le / te importaría decirme

¿Le importaría decirme cuál es la razón de su visita?
Would you mind telling me the reason for your visit?

¿Le importaría decirme si tiene intención de trabajar aquí?
Would you mind telling me if you intend to work here?

Podría/s decirme

¿Podría decirme cuánto dinero trae?
Could you tell how much money you have brought?

¿Podría decirme la edad que tiene?
Could you tell me your age?

Dígame / dime

Pero dígame exactamente cuánto tiene.
But tell me how much exactly you have.

Dígame si quiere quedarse aquí.
Tell me if you want to stay here.

Tienes / tendrías algún inconveniente en . . .

¿Tiene algún inconveniente en abrir las maletas por favor?
Do you mind opening the suitcases, please?

¿Tendría algún inconveniente en abrir ese bolso por favor?
Would you mind opening that bag, please?

Exercise 11

Match the following parts of the sentence:

1	Les importaría decirme	a	cúal es vuestro número de teléfono
2	Tendría algún inconveniente en	b	a qué hora van a venir
3	Podrías decirme	c	por qué está aquí
4	Dígame	d	qué es lo que quieres comer el domingo
5	Os importaría decirme	e	volver mañana por la mañana

Exercise 12

Listen to the following extract from a news programme about a group of immigrants who have been offered a job in Lleida (Cataluña):

jornalero	day laborour
patronal	association
sector agrícola	agriculture sector
vendimia	grape harvest
burlar	to sneak across
frontera	border

Listen to the recording again and answer the following questions:

1 How many immigrants have gone to Lleida?
2 Which kind of work are they going to do?
3 Where are the workers from?

Translate into Spanish: 'They have been contracted as day labourers.' Now listen to the recording again and listen to how the presenter says it.

¿Sabía usted? ✦

Every citizen of the European Union who intends to reside for more than three months in another Member State is required to have a residence permit (**permiso de residencia**). This document, which serves only to confirm the right of residence enjoyed by all Union citizens, is issued on presentation of certain documents, which vary according to the circumstances of the person making the request.

If you intend to stay in Spain for more than three months, you must apply for a residence permit within thirty days of arriving in the country. Your application (**solicitud**) should be addressed to the Foreign Residents Office (**Oficina de Extranjeros**) or, failing that, to the police in the province where you intend to establish your residence or carry on an economic activity. To find out the competent authority in your case, contact the mayor's office in the municipality where you are resident, a police station, the **Delegación del Gobierno** (a government delegate's office) or the **Subdelegación del Gobierno** (government subdelegate's office) in your province.

Documents required:

Together with your application for a residence permit, you must submit the original plus photocopies of your current identity card or passport, three passport photos, and, if expressly asked for, a medical certificate, which can be requested only on the grounds of public health. Depending on your status during your stay in Spain (employee, job-seeker, self-employed, retired, not working, student), you may be required to produce other documents.

US citizens with ordinary passports, valid for a minimum of six months, who wish to stay in Spain for business or as tourists for up to ninety days do not need a visa.

10 El trabajo y la banca

In this unit you can learn about:

- ▶ employment and banking
- ▶ active and passive sentences
- ▶ how to express the fact that an action is finished
- ▶ benefits for the unemployed in Spain
- ▶ some uses of **por** and **para**
- ▶ how to present a list of ideas / reasons in an argument

Dialogue 1

Liz, an Australian woman travelling in Spain, has been offered a job in Madrid and would really like to stay. She is now at an **oficina de extranjeros** *finding out more about how to obtain a work permit. Cover the dialogue and listen to the conversation. Before you listen to it, have a look at some words you will hear in the dialogue.*

Vocabulary ♦

temporada (f)	a period of time, a spell
temporada alta	high season
temporada baja	low season
solicitud (f)	application form
aportar	to provide
antecedentes penales (mpl)	criminal record
sacar	to get, to withdraw *(money from a bank)*
tamaño (m)	size
titulación homologada (f)	confirmed degree *(qualification)*
apartado (m)	section

LIZ   Buenos días, mire, soy australiana y me gustaría quedarme
           en España una temporada.

SRA. PUJOL   Bien, ¿va a estudiar, trabajar o tiene algún otro motivo?

LIZ   A trabajar, me han ofrecido un trabajo en una compañía de
           Internet pero necesito el permiso.

SRA. PUJOL   Bueno, entonces sus empleadores tienen que rellenar en
           esta solicitud todos sus datos – nombre, apellidos, domi-
           cilio, nacionalidad, fecha de nacimiento, etcétera – y en este
           otro apartado tienen que rellenar los datos del empresario o
           persona que desea contratarla.

LIZ   Vale, de acuerdo.

SRA. PUJOL   Además usted tiene que aportar la fotocopia del pasaporte
           o documento de viaje con validez para entrar en España, el
           certificado de antecedentes penales del país de origen, un
           certificado médico oficial . . .

LIZ   Perdone que le interrumpa, pero por teléfono me dijeron que
           no necesitaba tantos papeles. Mire, es que el otro día me
           robaron el bolso donde llevaba mis documentos y todavía
           no he podido sacar todos de nuevo.

SRA. PUJOL   Lo siento mucho pero le informaron mal o quizás usted les
           entendió mal porque no es posible hacer nada sin estos do-
           cumentos. También necesita seis fotografías tamaño carnet
           y la titulación homologada.

LIZ   Entonces, ¿no puedo hacer nada hasta que recupere todos
           mis papeles?

SRA. PUJOL   Ya lo siento, pero no.

Exercise 1

Listen to the dialogue again and answer the following questions:

1 Why would she like to stay in Spain?
2 Why did she think she did not need so many papers?
3 Why can she not show all the papers needed?
4 Can she obtain her work permit?

Language points ♦

Active and passive sentences

As you learned in the previous chapter, the passive with **ser** is used in English much more than in Spanish. In the spoken language you should use other forms. You already know how to express the passive with the pronoun **se**. Now you will learn another way. Have a look at the following sentences from the dialogue:

Me dijeron por teléfono que no necesitaba tantos papeles.
I was told on the phone that I didn't need so many papers.

Me robaron el bolso donde llevaba mis documentos.
My bag in which I was carrying all my documents was taken.

Lo siento mucho pero le informaron mal.
I'm sorry but you (*formal*) were informed wrongly / were given the wrong information.

If you do not want to say who has carried out the action, you need to use the third person plural of the verb in the tense appropriate to the situation:

Me dieron toda la información.
I was given all the information. *or* They gave me all the information.

Me lo han dicho esta mañana.
I was told (have been told) this morning. *or* They told me this morning.

Me lo dirán el domingo.
I will be told on Sunday. *or* They will tell me on Sunday.

When using verbs (**decir, robar, dar**) which normally need an indirect object (**me, te, le, nos, os, les**) never use the passive; make the sentence active by using the third person plural of the verb with the appropriate indirect object:

Me dijeron que estabas enfermo.
(*Literally,* they told me) I was told you were ill.
Do not try to use the passive: *****fui dicho que estabas enfermo**

Le han robado.
(*Literally,* they have robbed her/him) S/he has been robbed.
Do not say: *****ha sido robado / a**

Me dieron las llaves del piso.
(*Literally,* they gave me the keys of the flat) I was given the keys of the flat.

Le dijeron que no estabas en Madrid.
S/he was told you were not in Madrid.

Localizaron a otros 13 marroquíes.
Another 13 Moroccan nationals were found.

Construyeron el puente en ocho meses.
The bridge was built in eight months.

Les llevaron al hotel.
They were taken to the hotel.

Exercise 2

Change the following passive sentences into active statements using the third person plural:

1 La exposición fue suspendida.
2 Los cuadros fueron destrozados.
3 Las personas fueron trasladadas a comisaría.
4 Dos estudiantes fueron detenidos y trasladados también a la comisaría.
5 Los dos estudiantes fueron interrogados.
6 Uno de los estudiantes fue golpeado.

Exercise 3

Translate the following statements into Spanish:

1 I was robbed in El Rastro.
2 I was told about it yesterday morning.
3 He will be offered a contract.
4 I was only given half the money.
5 He was told a lie.
6 I wasn't told anything.
7 I was offered a job yesterday.
8 He will be told the truth.

Exercise 4

Have a look at the following banking terms and match them with the appropriate definition or information related to them:

1 Saldo mínimo necesario   a   Las hay de todas clases: de mantenimiento, por transferencias, por no mantener el saldo, por enviar los extractos, etc.

2 Tramo no renumerado   b   Es la cantidad mínima de dinero que hay que tener en la cuenta para que nos den los intereses pactados.

3 Comisiones   c   Son los números rojos. Pueden cobrarte hasta un 25% si tu cuenta corriente está 'en rojo'.

4 Descubiertos   d   A veces los bancos te cobran si ingresas un cheque de otra entidad.

5 Tarjetas de crédito y débito   e   En algunas cuentas corrientes existe una cantidad de dinero que no cuenta a la hora de recibir los intereses.

6 Ingresos de cheques de otras entidades   f   Algunas entidades cobran una cantidad anual por conceder una tarjeta de crédito.

7 Extractos de cuentas   g   Es la información de tu cuenta con los últimos movimientos.

Dialogue 2 ⟨))⌣⟩

Tom wants to open an account at the bank and is enquiring about the different accounts available. Before listening to the dialogue, have a look at some of the words you are going to hear. The words on the right are synonyms or definitions of the words, on the left.

Vocabulary ♦

la nómina	el sueldo
domiciliar	pagar el sueldo (nómina) directamente al banco
cobrar	recibir dinero
trámite (m)	formalidad, paso
recibos domiciliados (mpl)	pagar los recibos (la luz, el teléfono, etc.) directamente desde el banco
la cuota	cantidad de dinero que tienes que pagar
los desfavorecidos	personas que necesitan la ayuda de otros
el importe	el valor en dinero de una cosa
el folleto	libro de pocas páginas

Exercise 5

Listen to the dialogue. Listen out for the following questions and then put them in the order they occur in the dialogue:

• Have you got many cash machines?
• Have you thought of paying your bills by direct debit?
• How much do you charge for the Cuenta 2000?
• Which cards could I have?
• How much is the fee for the credit card?
• Could you give me the brochures related to the account?
• How much credit would I have?

TOM   Quisiera abrir una cuenta corriente en su banco pero no estoy seguro de cuál sería la cuenta que más me podría interesar.

EMPLEADO	Bueno, pues tenemos varias cuentas. ¿Trabaja en España?
TOM	Sí, acabo de empezar a dar clases de inglés en una escuela, aquí en Madrid.
EMPLEADO	Y ¿tiene pensado domiciliar su nómina con nosotros?
TOM	Sí. Me gustaría disponer de mi nómina unos días antes de cobrarla, ¿es posible?
EMPLEADO	Con la Cuenta 2000 podrá disponer de su nómina unos días antes de recibir el cobro.
TOM	Y ¿cuánto cobran por ese servicio?
EMPLEADO	No hay ningún tipo de interés ni trámite especial. Además pagaremos sus recibos domiciliados en caso de descubierto, hasta el importe de su nómina.
TOM	¿Hay alguna cuota de administración?
EMPLEADO	No hay ningún tipo de comisión.
TOM	¿Qué tipos de tarjetas podría tener? Me han dicho que hay una tarjeta visa de la Cruz Roja, ¿es cierto?
EMPLEADO	Sí, le han informado bien. Con la tarjeta Visa Cruz Roja podrá ayudar a los más desfavorecidos. Cruz Roja se beneficia con el 0,7% del importe de las compras que haga.
TOM	¿Cuál sería mi crédito?
EMPLEADO	Bueno, eso depende de su salario, el límite de crédito es de 3.000 euros.
TOM	¿Cúanto es la cuota?
EMPLEADO	El primer año es gratuita aunque si usted lo desea puede pagarla y nosotros daremos el dinero íntegramente a Cruz Roja. Después del primer año, la cuota es de 10 euros anuales.
TOM	También me han dicho que el banco lleva abierto muchos años en España, ¿tiene muchos cajeros automáticos aquí?
EMPLEADO	Somos uno de los bancos más grandes de España y tenemos más de 350.000 cajeros.
TOM	Bien, creo que eso es todo de momento. ¿Podría darme todos los folletos relacionados con la cuenta para poder leerlos con más tiempo?
EMPLEADO	Sí, claro. Aquí los tiene.

TITULAR DE LA TARJETA			
NIF	Nombre	Primer apellido	Segundo apellido / /
Límite solicitado		Profesión	Fecha de nacimiento
Nacionalidad	☐ Varón ☐ Mujer ☐ Soltero/a ☐ Casado/a ☐ Viudo/a ☐ Divorciado/a ☐ Separado/a		Teléfono
Domicilio	Código Postal	Población	Provincia

DOMICILIACIÓN BANCARIA	
Banco o Caja y Sucursal	┌── CÓDIGO CUENTA CLIENTE (C.C.C) ──┐
Domicilio .... C.P.	ENTIDAD SUCURSAL D.C. NÚMERO DE CUENTA DE CARGO
Población .... Provincia	☐☐☐☐ ☐☐☐☐ ☐☐ ☐☐☐☐☐☐☐☐☐☐
Nombre del Solicitante y Titular de la Cuenta de Cargo	N.I.F. ....
(Cuando no coincida con el Titular de la Tarjeta)	

Exercise 6

Listen to the conversation again and choose the correct answer:

1 Does Tom work in Spain?
   a He teaches English in a university.
   b He teaches English in a school.
   c He teaches Spanish in a school.
2 What are the benefits of Cuenta 2000?
   a You can withdraw money before your wages are paid in without any extra charges.
   b You can withdraw money before your wages are paid in with a very small charge.
   c You cannot withdraw money before your wages are paid in.
3 What is the Cruz Roja credit card?
   a Cruz Roja receives 0.6 percent of the amount you spend on the credit card.
   b Cruz Roja receives 0.7 percent of the amount you spend on the credit card.
   c Cruz Roja receives 0.5 percent of the amount you spend on the credit card.
4 What is the amount of credit you can get?
   a It depends on the salary, but the maximum is 2,000 Euros.
   b It depends on the salary, but the maximum is 2,500 Euros.
   c It depends on the salary, but the maximum is 3,000 Euros.
5 How many cash machines does the bank have in Spain?
   a 300,000
   b 350,000
   c 35,000

Language points ♦

How to express the fact that an action is finished

Some times the auxiliary **haber** cannot be used to express some actions and another verb is used as an auxiliary. This auxiliary (**tener, deber, estar, andar,** etc.) is then followed by an infinitive (**pensar**), a gerund (**pensando**) or a participle (**pensado**). You already know a number of these auxiliaries.

Auxiliaries plus an infinitive:

Tener que

> **Tengo que volver al banco.**
> I have to go back to the bank.

Deber

> **Debo ir inmediatamente.**
> I must go inmediately.

Deber de

> **Deben de ser como las cuatro.**
> It must be around 4 o'clock.

Ir a

> **Voy a sacar dinero del cajero.**
> I'm going to get some money from the cash machine.

Acabar de

> **Acabo de hablar con la secretaria.**
> I have just talked to the secretary.

Auxiliaries plus a gerund:

Estar

> **Luis está leyendo su extracto de cuenta.**
> Luis is reading his bank statement.

Andar

> **Anda diciendo que no tiene dinero.**
> S/he is going around saying s/he has no money.

Seguir

> **Sigo intentando abrir una cuenta.**
> I am still trying to open an account.

Continuar

¿Sigues metiendo todo tu sueldo en la cuenta?
Are you still paying all of your wages into the account?

Auxiliaries plus a participle:

In the dialogue you heard the verb **tener** and the verb **llevar** plus a participle. Both **tener** and **llevar** plus a participle are used to convey the fact that an action is finished.

¿Tiene pensado domiciliar su nómina con nosotros?
Have you thought about paying in your salary to us?

¿Tienes pensado ir de vacaciones este verano?
Have you thought about going on holiday this summer?

¿Tienes estudiados todos los temas?
Have you studied all the topics?

El banco lleva abierto muchos años en España.
The bank has been open for many years in Spain.

Esta tienda lleva cerrada más de un año.
This shop has been closed for more than a year.

¿Cuántos libros llevas leídos?
How many books have you (already) read?

Note that the participle agrees in gender and in number with the object:

¿Cuántos <u>periódicos</u> lleva <u>leídos</u>?
How many newspapers has s/he (already) read?

¿Cuántas <u>revistas</u> llevas <u>leídas</u>?
How many magazines have you (already) read?

Sometimes **tener** and **llevar** can replace one another:

Llevo estudiada toda la gramática.
I have studied all the grammar.

Tengo estudiada toda la gramática.
I have studied all the grammar.

Exercise 7

Fill in the gaps with the appropriate participle:

> Example: **¿Cuántas veces llevas _____ ese libro? (leer)**
> **¿Cuántas veces llevas leído ese libro?**

1 ¿Cuántas hojas tienes _____ ? (leer)
2 ¿A dónde tienes _____ ir? (pensar)
3 ¿Cuántos días lleva _____ la tienda? (cerrar)
4 ¿Desde cuándo tenías _____ volver a Inglaterra? (pensar)
5 ¿Desde cuándo lo tienes _____? (preparar)
6 Creo que lleva _____ la película tres veces (ver).
7 Ellos tienen _____ dos habitaciones en el mejor hotel de Madrid (reservar).

Text 1

You have come across the following article on the unemployed in the European Union. Before you read it, have a look at the following expressions (e.g. phrases such as 'to apply sanctions').

Exercise 8

Match the Spanish phrases with their English equivalents:

1 aplicar sanciones
2 las diferencias radican cuando / en
3 incentivar la búsqueda de empleo
4 la cobertura a los parados
5 contar con prestaciones
6 forma involuntaria
7 por despido

8 fin de contrato

9 abonar prestaciones
10 reincorporarse al mercado de trabajo

a end of contract
b to have benefits
c to apply sanctions
d to rejoin the job market
e the differences lie in
f to pay benefits
g to encourage the search for employment
h the cover for the unemployed
i due to dismissal
j involuntary way

Note: Two large Spanish trade unions are **Comisiones Obreras (CC OO)** and **Unión General de Trabajadores (UGT).**

Different types of unemployment benefits are: **el nivel contributivo:** for those who have been employed and have made the necessary contributions; **el nivel asistencial:** for those who have not made the necessary contributions; **el sistema eventual agrario:** for those people who are employed in the agriculture sector on a temporary basis.

Las desigualdades entre los parados europeos

Prácticamente todos los países comunitarios aplican sanciones cuando el parado rechaza un 'empleo razonable', y las exigencias son mayores a medida que la permanencia en la situación de desempleo se prolonga. Las diferencias radican cuando se concreta el concepto de 'oferta adecuada'. Ahí es cuando cada país tiene su propio modelo y sus normas para incentivar la búsqueda de empleo por parte del parado, según varios informes comparativos elaborados por el Ministerio de Trabajo y por los sindicatos CC OO UGT . . .

En la cobertura a los parados no existen estadísticas comparativas del conjunto de países de la Unión Europea. En España un 40% de los desempleados no cuenta con ninguna prestación ni ayuda del Estado. Los datos de febrero de trabajo indican que en ese mes había 570.000 parados que estaban protegidos en el nivel contributivo, 385.000 en el asistencial y 218.000 en el sistema eventual agrario. Del total de 1.666.049 desempleados, 437.000 no tenían ninguna cobertura.

El modelo de España exige para acceder a las prestaciones haber perdido el empleo de forma involuntaria (por despido o fin de contrato) y haber cotizado más de doce meses. En otros ordenamientos también pueden tener cobertura los demandantes de un primer empleo y los trabajadores que se reincorporen al mercado de trabajo después de largos periodos de inactividad por estudios o cuidado de familiares. Esto no es posible en España, como tampoco el acceso a la protección cuando el pase a la situación de desempleo es voluntario por parte del trabajador, y que en la mayoría de los países cuenta con alguna prestación aunque sea más limitada. La legislación de Grecia es otra excepción y los parados solamente tienen derecho a ayudas por seis meses y siempre que hayan perdido el empleo por un despido.

La doble vía de protección (contributiva y asistencial) es una característica común con otros modelos europeos. En Alemania existe además la prestación de desempleo parcial por causas atmosféricas, destinada a los trabajadores del sector de la construcción para los periodos de inactividad obligada que se pueden dar entre el 1 de noviembre y el 31 de marzo de cada año.

Otros países de la UE abonan prestaciones contributivas por un periodo máximo más largo que el español de 24 meses, que en Alemania llega hasta los 32 meses, en Francia a 60 meses, en Países Bajos a cuatro años y en el caso de Bélgica es ilimitado.

Source: Extract from an article published by El País, of 12 May 2002

Exercise 9

Tick the statements that are false:

☐ Every country applies sanctions to the unemployed who reject a 'reasonable employment'.

☐ The differences lie in the description of the concept 'adequate offer'.

☐ Each country has its own system and norms to encourage the search for employment.

☐ In Spain 40 per cent of the unemployed do not receive any benefits.

☐ In Spain, in order to receive benefits, it does not matter how the unemployed has lost his / her job.

☐ In Spain it is not possible to receive unemployment benefit if you are looking for your first job.

☐ In Germany workers from the construction sector receive unemployment benefit during the winter.

☐ The unemployed in many countries of the European Union receive unemployment benefit for a longer period than in Spain.

Language points ♦

Some uses of *por* and *para*

Para

To express the idea of 'in order to', 'for the purpose of':

> **normas para incentivar**
> norms to (in order to) encourage

> **El modelo de España exige para acceder a las prestaciones ...**
> The Spanish model demands ... to (in order to) have access to benefits.

> **para los periodos de inactividad obligada**
> for the purpose / for periods of forced inactivity

To express a deadline:

> **Lo necesito para el lunes.**
> I need it for / by Monday.

To express a specific period of time:

> **El contrato es para seis meses.**
> The contract is for six months.

To express direction:

> **Este tren va para Santiago.**
> This train goes to Santiago.

To express the idea of 'to be about to':

> **Estaba para salir cuando llamaste.**
> I was about to leave when you called.

Por

To express the cause of or reason for something:

> **por despido**
> due to dismissal

> **por estudios o cuidados de familiares**
> due to studies or looking after family members

> **por causas atmosféricas**
> due to the weather

To express a period of time:

por un periodo máximo más largo que el español
for a maximum period longer than the Spanish one

To express who has carried out the action in a passive sentence:

(fueron) elaborados por el Ministerio de Trabajo y por los sindicatos
carried out by the Ministry of Employment and by the trade unions

To express the idea of 'on the part of':

por parte del trabajador
on the part of the worker

por parte del parado
on the part of the unemployed person

To express apology and gratitude:

Perdona por no haberte llamado antes.
I'm sorry I haven't called before.

Gracias por todo lo que has hecho por mí.
Thanks for everything you have done for me.

To express the idea that there are still things to do:

Las camas están por hacer.
The beds are yet to be made.

Note the difference between the following two sentences:

Lo hizo por ti.
S/he did it for because of you. (*for example, she talked to somebody to defend you*)

Lo hizo para ti.
S/he did (made) it for you. (*for example, she made a cake for you*)

As you can see both have the same English translation. In the first sentence she did it because she likes you or because you could not do it. In the second instance she did something concrete for you. You are getting a cake.

Exercise 10

Fill in the gaps with the appropriate preposition **por** or **para**:

1 Lo necesito _____ conseguir prestaciones.
2 Le despidieron _____ mandar demasiados correos electrónicos privados.
3 El comunicado fue escrito _____ el Presidente.
4 He comprado esta camisa _____ ti.
5 Recibió las prestaciones _____ ocho meses.
6 _____ reincorporarte al mercado de trabajo debes hacer este cursillo.
7 Me subieron el sueldo _____ haber trabajado en Navidad.
8 Me han dicho que _____ trabajar en España necesito estos documentos.
9 No puede ir _____ la nieve.
10 Lo tienes que terminar _____ junio.
11 Quiere pedirte perdón _____ lo que te hizo.
12 Está _____ llover, ¿quieres salir?

How to present a number of reasons in an argument (in opposition or in agreement)

por una parte	por un lado	on the one hand
por otra parte	por otro lado / de otro lado	on the other hand
por otra	por otro	on the other

Por una parte el problema de la inmigración es un problema internacional.
On the one hand the problem of immigration is an international problem.

De otro lado, cada país debe tomar las medidas necesarias para ayudar a los inmigrantes ilegales.
On the other hand, each country must take the necessary measures to help the illegal immigrants.

When both **por una parte** and **por otra parte** come within the same sentence you do not need to repeat **parte**:

Por una parte el pueblo no quiere demasiada gente de fuera, por otra hay falta de mano de obra.
On the one hand, the people do not want too many people from outside, on the other, there is a lack of workers.

en primer lugar	in the first place
en segundo lugar	in the second place, secondly
por último / en último lugar	lastly, finally

En primer lugar me gustaría destacar la importancia de su riqueza biológica, en segundo el papel del Ministerio de Medio Ambiente y por último el papel de los ciudadanos.
In the first place I would like to highlight the importance of the biological wealth, secondly, the role of the Ministry of Environment and, finally, the role of citizens.

Exercise 11

Present the following ideas as a summary at the beginning of a presentation using the expressions **en primer lugar**, etc.

Example: **En primer lugar voy a hablar sobre . . . ,**
en segundo sobre . . . y por último . . .

1 La nueva ley del paro
   Los objetivos del gobierno
   Las medidas que se van a tomar
2 El problema actual del paro
   Las causas
   Las posibles soluciones
3 El problema del SIDA en África
   La ayuda de la Unión Europea
   La ayuda internacional

11 El medio ambiente

In this unit you can learn about:

- ▶ the environment
- ▶ using the subjunctive
- ▶ agreement of tenses
- ▶ how to give advice / an order
- ▶ the subjunctive with subordinators of time: **cuando, en cuanto, una vez que**
- ▶ how to make a complaint
- ▶ a campaign in Andalucia to save the forests

Dialogue 1

Liz is thinking of going on holiday to **Cádiz** *and wants to know more about the area, especially about the* **Parque de Doñana**. *She is talking about it to a Spanish friend who is in a hurry because she has to teach shortly. Before you listen to the dialogue, have a look at the following words that will appear in the conversation.*

Vocabulary ♦

aves migratorias (fpl)	migratory birds
Patrimonio de la Humanidad (m)	World Heritage
dunas (fpl)	dunes
marismas (fpl)	marsh regions
pinares (mpl)	pine forests
balsa de lodos (m)	dam of sludge (*mud*)
minas (fpl)	mines
vertido (m)	spillage
tortillas de camarones (mpl)	shrimp fritters (**camarones** is the name given in the South of Spain to shrimps)

LIZ   Quiero visitar la provincia de Cádiz y he oído hablar del Parque de Doñana pero no estoy segura por qué es famoso. Antes de que vayas a dar la clase, ¿por qué no me cuentas algo del parque?

ROSA   Sí, claro, pero no sé tanto, ¿eh? He estado en Cádiz muchas veces pero sólo he visitado el parque una vez, hace muchos años. El Parque de Doñana es un parque enorme, famoso por los millares de aves migratorias que pasan por él. Es un parque único en Europa y creo que en los 90 fue declarado Patrimonio de la Humanidad.

LIZ   ¿Dónde está exactamente?

ROSA   Se encuentra entre las ciudades de Cádiz, Huelva y Sevilla.

LIZ   Y, ¿cómo es el paisaje?

ROSA   Pues, hay mar, playas, dunas, marismas, pinares. No sé qué más contarte.

LIZ   Me gustaría saber un poco sobre el estado medioambiental.

ROSA   Pues teniendo en cuenta que hubo un desastre ecológico hace unos años no está tan mal, podría ser peor.

LIZ   ¡Anda! ¿Qué pasó?

ROSA   Pues verás, en 1998 una balsa de lodos de unas minas en Aznalcóllar se rompió y el vertido afectó gravemente al río Guadiamar. En cuanto se supo lo que había pasado, la gente se movilizó y se hizo todo lo posible por evitar la contaminación de las aguas del Parque pero murieron muchísimas aves y peces.

LIZ   Parece mentira que haya minas tan cerca de un parque tan especial, ¿no?

ROSA   Nadie se lo creía tampoco cuando pasó pero ya sabes cómo son las cosas. Mira, de todas maneras cuando vayas a Cádiz no te olvides de pasar por Sanlúcar de Barrameda que ya verás cómo te va a gustar. Una vez que estés allí pide unas tortillas de camarones en uno de los bares de la plaza y bebe una botellita de manzanilla.

LIZ   Pero, ¿manzanilla no es una infusión?

ROSA   ¡Ah, claro! Cuando estés en Sanlúcar ten cuidado con lo que pides. La manzanilla es una bebida típica de Sanlúcar, algo parecido al jerez y está muy buena. Cuando quieras tomarte una manzanilla para el estómago no pidas simplemente una manzanilla, pide una infusión si no, a lo mejor te sacan una manzanilla fresquita. Pero mira, tan pronto como termine la clase, te pasas por mi casa y te doy unos folletos.

Exercise 1

Listen again to the dialogue and tick the statements that are false:

☐ Liz has not heard about the Parque Doñana.
☐ Rosa has been in the park many times.
☐ In 1994 there was an ecological disaster.
☐ The situation is not as bad as it could have been.
☐ Many birds and fish died.
☐ Rosa advises Liz to have shrimp fritters and camomile tea.

Language points ♦

The subjunctive

Up to now you have learnt a number of tenses (present, preterite, imperfect, perfect, pluperfect, future, etc.) in what is called the 'indicative mood'. In Spanish there is another 'mood' called the subjunctive mood. The word subjunctive means subjectivity. Therefore, whenever there is a possibility that the action you are referring to may not take place, you use the subjunctive. This does not mean, however, that the subjunctive mood is always used in expressions of doubt or uncertainty. This mood in the respective tenses (present, imperfect, perfect and pluperfect) is used a great deal in Spanish, in both the spoken and written language. There are still some subjunctives used in the English language: 'If I were a rich woman' instead of 'If I was a rich woman', but its use is dying out.

The present subjunctive for **-ar** verbs is formed by adding the following endings to the verb: **-e, -es, -e, -emos, -éis, -en**:

Espero que trabajes más.	I hope you work more.
Espero que trabajéis más.	I hope you (*plural*) work more.

When you are using an irregular verb or stem-changing verbs (**cerrar, empezar**, etc.), you need to use the beginning of the first person singular of the present tense indicative and add the appropriate ending above.

Present indicative:

Todos los días <u>cierro</u> la tienda a las seis.
I close the shop every day at six o'clock.

Present subjunctive:

Espero que <u>cierren</u> pronto.
I hope they close early / soon.

Present indicative:

Las clases <u>empiezan</u> a las nueve.
The classes start at nine o'clock.

Present subjunctive:

Espero que las clases <u>empiecen</u> a las diez.
I hope the classes start at ten o'clock.

The present subjunctive for -er and -ir verbs is formed by adding the following endings to the verb: **-a, -as, -a, -amos, -áis, -an:**

Espero que <u>bebas</u> poco.
I hope you drink little.

Espero que <u>recibas</u> muchas postales.
I hope you receive many cards.

When you are using irregular verbs (**tener, venir**, etc.), the same rule applies. You need to use the root of the first person singular of the present indicative and then add the appropriate ending.

Present indicative:

No <u>tengo</u> mucha suerte, ¿verdad?
I am not very lucky, am I?

Present subjunctive:

Espero que <u>tengas</u> mucha suerte.
I hope you are very lucky.

Present indicative:

Mañana <u>vengo</u> a las ocho.
Tomorrow I am coming at eight.

Present subjunctive:

Espero que <u>vengas</u> a las ocho.
I hope you come at eight.

The verbs **saber, ir, estar, dar, venir, tener** and **haber** are some common irregular verbs:

Espero que <u>sepa</u> dónde está el restaurante.
I hope s/he knows where the restaurant is.

Espero que <u>vayamos</u> juntos.
I hope we go together.

Espero que <u>estés</u> en casa a las ocho.
I hope you are at home at eight o'clock.

Espero que le <u>den</u> lo que le deben.
I hope they give her/him what they owe her/him.

Espero que no <u>haya</u> problemas.
I hope there aren't any problems.

Espero que Sonia <u>venga</u> pronto.
I hope Sonia comes soon.

Espero que no <u>tengas</u> muchos problemas.
I hope you don't have many problems.

Agreement of tenses

In this unit and units 12 and 13 we will be looking only at structures in which the main clause is in the present indicative. When the main clause (**espero que, quiero que, es posible que,** etc.) is in the present indicative, the subordinate clause takes the present or the perfect subjunctive. It depends on whether the action has happened or is yet to happen:

Espero que venga pronto.
I hope s/he comes early.

Espero que haya venido pronto.
I hope s/he has come early.

Main clause	Subordinate clause
Present indicative	Present subjunctive Perfect subjunctive
Espero que (I hope that . . .)	**lo haga bien** (he does it well) **lo haya hecho bien** (he has done it well)

Exercise 2

The verb **esperar** always takes the subjunctive when the subject in the main clause and the subject in the subordinate clause are not the same person:

Espero que vengas mañana. *I* hope *you* come tomorrow.
Espero que vengan el domingo. *I* hope *they* come on Sunday.

But

Espero ir al parque. I hope to go to the park.
Javier espera volver pronto. Javier hopes to come back soon.

Choose the correct form of the verb:

1 Espero que (tú) no vengas / vienes tarde.
2 Espero que (tú) salgas / sales pronto.
3 Espero que (yo) voy / ir mañana.
4 Espero que (tú) comes / comas toda la tortilla.
5 Espero que no (la casa) vale / valga mucho.
6 Espero que (él) está / esté bien.
7 Espero que (yo) tengo / tener suerte.
8 Espero que lo pasas / pases bien en Barcelona.
9 Espero que apruebes / apruebas los exámenes.
10 Espero que no lo sepa / sabe.

Exercise 3

Fill in the gaps with the present subjunctive:

Example: **Espero que no _____ toda la botella (tú, beber).**
Espero que no bebas toda la botella.

1 Espero que no _____ (tú, fumar).
2 Espero que _____ mañana (tú, venir).
3 Espero que _____ la verdad (él, saber).
4 Espero que _____ todos en la fiesta (ellos, estar).
5 Espero que _____ a la hora (ella, llegar).
6 Espero que _____ el domingo (tú, trabajar).
7 Espero que no _____ problemas (tú, tener).
8 Espero que todavía _____ entradas (haber).
9 Espero que _____ de vacaciones a Cáceres (nosotros, ir).

How to give advice / an order

There are a number of ways in Spanish to advise or to give an order:

Put the verb in the second person present tense:

Te pasas por mi casa y te doy unos folletos.
Come to my house and I'll give you some brochures.

Vienes pronto y comemos algo.
Come early and we'll eat something.

Use a question:

¿Por qué no me cuentas algo del parque?
Why don't you tell me something about the park?

¿Por qué no vamos al parque?
Why don't we go to the park?

Use the imperative: **tú** (informal), affirmative:

Pide unas tortillas de camarones en uno de los bares de la plaza y bebe una botellita de manzanilla.
Ask for some shrimp fritters in one of the bars in the square and drink a small bottle of manzanilla.

Recicla las botellas.
Recycle the bottles.

Note this imperative takes the third person singular of the present indicative:

Recarga las pilas.   Recharge the batteries.
Corta la hierba.   Cut the grass.

There are some useful verbs that have an irregular imperative:

Ten cuidado con lo que pides.
Be careful what you ask for.

Pon las botellas en el contenedor verde.
Put the bottles in the green container.

Ven pronto y comemos juntas.
Come early and we'll eat together.

Dime la verdad.
Tell me the truth.

Vete de aquí, es peligroso.
Get out of here, it's dangerous.

Sal temprano.
Leave early.

Note that when you need to use a pronoun (**me, te, se, le, lo, la, nos, os, les, los, las**), it joins on to the verb:

Dame el folleto.	Give me the brochure.
Pásame la sal.	Pass me the salt.

You need to add the accent to the imperative form of verbs of more than one syllable (**pasar, escribir,** etc.) when you add a pronoun:

Escríbeme pronto.	Write to me soon.
Regálale un libro.	Give her/him a book (*as a present*).

But

Dile que no tengo tiempo.	Tell him I haven't got the time.

Imperative: **tú** (informal), negative:

No pidas simplemente una manzanilla, pide una infusión.
Don't ask simply for a manzanilla, ask for an infusion.

Cuando vayas a Cádiz, no te olvides de pasar por Sanlúcar de Barrameda.
When you go to Cadiz, don't forget to go to Sanlucar de Barrameda.

No vayas a la central nuclear.
Don't go to the nuclear power station.

No hagas fuego en el pinar.
Don't light a fire in the pine forest.

To form the imperative in the negative form you need to use the second person singular of the present subjunctive of the verb:

No tires las pilas a la basura.	Don't put the batteries in the bin.
No compres cosas de marfil.	Don't buy ivory items.

Note that when you are using a pronoun with the imperative in the negative form, you place the pronoun before the verb:

No me digas.	Don't tell me.
No le compres nada a Pepe.	Don't buy Pepe anything.

Imperative: **usted** (formal), affirmative:

Use bien los recursos naturales.
Use the natural resources carefully.

Respete el medio ambiente.
Respect the environment.

To form this imperative you need to use the third person singular of the present subjunctive:

Use el transporte público.	Use public transport.
Ande en bicicleta.	Ride a bike.

Imperative: **usted**, negative:

No olvide llevar las pilas a un lugar seguro.
Don't forget to take the batteries to a safe place.

No malgaste los recursos naturales.
Don't waste the natural resources.

To form this imperative you need to use the third person singular of the present subjunctive:

No deje las luces encendidas.
Don't leave the lights on.

No lave el coche todos los días.
Don't wash the car every day.

Summary of the imperative

Third person of the present tense:

Lleva las botellas al contenedor.

No plus second person singular of the present subjunctive:

No tires los periódicos.

Third person singular of the present subjunctive:

Deje las toallas en el suelo si quiere toallas limpias.

No plus third person singular of the present subjunctive:

No deje las toallas en el suelo si no necesita toallas limpias.

Exercise 4

Read the following advice on how to be a good 'green citizen'. Unfortunately, some of the do's and don'ts have been mixed up. Tick the sentences that give the wrong advice and change them so that they are good advice:

1 Lleva tus propias bolsas cuando vayas a comprar.
2 No compres cosas de marfil o coral.
3 No utilices pilas recargables.
4 Tira las pilas en cualquier sitio.
5 Compra animales de especies protegidas.
6 Utiliza los transportes públicos.
7 Cambia el agua de la piscina todos los días.
8 Ahorra papel escribiendo por los dos lados.
9 No recicles los periódicos.
10 Apaga la luz cuando no estés en la habitación.

Exercise 5

A Spanish friend of yours is thinking of going to India and has asked you for some advice. You haven't been to India but your brother has, so you have asked him to give you a list of do's and don'ts. Here is the list. Translate it for your friend.

- Book the hotel for the first night in India.
- Don't take any taxi at the airport, take an official taxi.

- Don't drink tap water, always buy mineral water.
- Eat with your right hand; don't eat with your left hand.
- Travel by train, it is very comfortable.
- Don't stay in very cheap hotels; they can be dangerous.
- Be careful at the stations.
- Remove your shoes before entering the temples.
- Don't drive at night time; it is dangerous.
- If you are invited for dinner, eat something before going as they normally have dinner very late.

Text 1

Exercise 6

Read the following information about a campaign launched by **El Ministerio de Medio Ambiente** of **Andalucía** to protect their forests. Before you start reading, complete the following exercise. It will help you to understand the article better. Match the words in the left column that appear in the article with their definitions or synonyms. Make sure you understand them before you start reading.

convivir	parar
heredar	asistir a, ir a
prueba (f)	es la acción de talar, cortar los árboles
albergar	es el tubo en el coche por donde sale humo
frenar	vivir con otra persona o cosa
talas (fpl)	el cuidado del ganado (animales como las vacas)
pastoreo (m)	recibir dinero / posesiones después de la muerte de alguien
implicar	la demostración
compromiso (m)	alojar, dar protección
acudir a	cuando estás dispuesto a hacer algo
tubo de escape (m)	envolver

National Parks.

Campaña 'Mira por tus bosques'

La naturaleza y el hombre pueden y deben convivir en armonía y equilibrio. Los bosques que hemos heredado de las generaciones anteriores constituyen una prueba de que esta posibilidad es una realidad. Por una parte albergan una extraordinaria riqueza biológica, fruto de muchos millones de años de evolución, purifican el aire y frenan el avance de la erosión y de los desiertos. De otro lado, proporcionan una serie de recursos indispensables para la vida y el desarrollo humanos, cuya disponibilidad y permanencia en el tiempo dependen del uso racional que de ellos hagamos.

Sin embargo, en los últimos decenios, la situación de nuestros bosques ha empeorado considerablemente, de forma que la deforestación se ha convertido en uno de los problemas medioambientales más graves de Andalucía. Las talas abusivas, el exceso de pastoreo, las malas prácticas agrícolas, la contaminación, el crecimiento de las urbanizaciones, y muy especialmente los incendios forestales, son algunas de las causas del deterioro del patrimonio forestal andaluz.

El programa 'Mira por tus bosques', promovido por la Junta de Andalucía, pretende implicar a todos los andaluces en las tareas de defensa, conservación y restauración de los bosques, con el convencimiento de que sólo con el compromiso y la participación directa, activa y decidida de los ciudadanos, podremos recuperar nuestro medio natural.

¿Cómo podemos ayudar a prevenir los incendios forestales?

Muchos incendios forestales ocurren porque nos comportamos en el bosque como si estuviéramos en la ciudad. Cuando acudimos al campo es necesario adaptar nuestro comportamiento a las condiciones del medio natural.

- **No enciendas fuego en el monte.**
  Una comida campestre no merece el más pequeño incendio. Es mejor llevar comidas preparadas o acudir a bares y restaurantes de la zona.

- **No abandones residuos y basuras.**
  Especialmente vidrios y papeles, ya que pueden contribuir al inicio y mantenimiento de un incendio. La naturaleza no debe ser el vertedero de nuestros residuos.

- **Visita el bosque caminando o en bicicleta.**
  Así podemos tener un contacto más directo con la naturaleza. En el bosque no deben usarse vehículos a motor, sobre todo en verano. Un tubo de escape demasiado caliente puede iniciar un fuego.

- **Acampa en lugares adecuados.**
  Al usar campings y áreas de acampada, además de obtener mayor comodidad y seguridad, se evitan riesgos innecesarios.

Exercise 7

Read the following statements and tick those ones that convey the ideas found in the text:

☐ Nature and mankind can live together in harmony.
☐ We do not have proof of this reality but it is a possibility.
☐ Forests purify the air and stop the development of erosion and deserts.
☐ Forests also offer many resources.
☐ The situation regarding the forests has improved in the past decades.
☐ The most important cause of the deforestation is the growth in housing.
☐ The programme 'Look after your forests' tries to involve everybody in Andalucia.
☐ It is only possible to recover the natural resources through the commitment and participation of the citizens.

Exercise 8

Translate the advice (just the headings) given to prevent forest fires.

Subjunctives with subordinators of time

The following subordinators of time take the subjunctive when they refer to actions that will take place in the future:

Antes de que / después de que plus subjunctive:

Antes de que vayas a dar la clase, ¿te importaría contarme algo del parque?
Before you go to teach, would you mind telling me something about the park?

Antes de que salgas, ¿te importaría arreglarme esto?
Before you leave, would you mind fixing this for me?

Después de que termines, podemos salir.
After you finish we can leave.

When the action has already happened, the verb takes the indicative:

Decidimos ir al museo después de que llegaron.
We decided to go to the museum after they arrived.

Antes de and **después de** take an infinitive when there is not a change of subject:

Ven después de terminarlo. (both **venir** and **terminar** refer to the same person)
Come after you finish it.

Ven después de que lo termine. (**venir** and **terminar** refer to different people)
Come after s/he finishes it.

Exercise 9

Choose the correct form of the verb:

1 Antes de que vayas / vas llámame por teléfono.
2 Antes de ir / que vaya voy a comer algo.
3 Antes de que se me olvida / olvide, compra también leche cuando vayas a la tienda.
4 Hice todo antes de llamarte / te llamé.
5 Después de terminarlo / que lo termine iré al cine.
6 Antes de que lo termines / terminas, ven a verme.
7 Después de que lo haces / hagas mándamelo por correo electrónico.

Cuando is followed by a subjunctive when the event has not yet occurred:

Cuando vayas a Cádiz, pásate por Sanlúcar de Barrameda.
When you go to Cadiz go to Sanlucar de Barrameda.

Cuando estés en Sanlúcar, ten cuidado con lo que pides.
When you are in Sanlucar, be careful what you ask for.

The other verb in the sentence normally takes the imperative or the future tense:

Cuando compres productos de limpieza, ten cuidado con lo que compras.
When you buy cleaning products, be careful what you buy.

Cuando esté en Galicia, comeré un montón de marisco.
When I am in Galicia, I will eat lots of sea food.

Cuando vayas a Barcelona, ¿irás al Museo de Picasso?
When you go to Barcelona, will you go to the Picasso Museum?

But when it expresses a habitual action, the verb goes in the indicative:

Cuando llego a Bilbao lo primero que hago es comerme un pincho.
When I arrive in Bilbao the first thing I do is to eat a pincho.
(*I normally do this so it has happened many times*)

Cuando me levanto no tengo ganas de hablar.
When I get up I do not feel like talking. (*I always feel like this*)

Exercise 10

Fill in the gaps with the appropriate form of the verb, present tense indicative or subjunctive:

1 Cuando _____ bebo uno o dos vasos de vino (yo, comer).
2 Cuando _____ dinero me compraré una casa en el campo (yo, tener).
3 Cuando _____ en Madrid vete a ver el Museo Sofía (tú, estar).
4 Cuando _____ con sus amigos no quiere saber nada de nadie (ella, salir).
5 Podemos empezar cuando _____ a tu casa (ellos, llegar).
6 Cuando _____ las entradas te paso el dinero (tú, comprar).
7 Siempre voy a casa cuando mi madre _____ enferma (estar).
8 Iré cuando _____ (yo, poder).

En cuanto is followed by a subjunctive when the event has not yet occurred:

En cuanto lleguen las aves migratorias, vamos al parque.
As soon as the migratory birds arrive, we will go to the park.

En cuanto pongan un contenedor amarillo en el pueblo, podremos reciclar todo.
As soon as they place a yellow container in the village, we will be able to recycle everything.

But if the event has already occurred, the verb goes in the indicative, in the past simple:

En cuanto se supo lo que había pasado, la gente desapareció.
As soon as it was known what had happened, the people disappeared.

Una vez que plus the subjunctive:

Una vez que estés allí pide unas tortillas de camarones.
Once you are there, ask for the shrimp fritters.

Una vez que lo sepas llámame.
Once you know it, call me.

But if the event has already occurred, the verb goes in the indicative:

Una vez que terminó se fue.
Once s/he finished s/he left.

Tan pronto como plus subjunctive:

Pero mira, tan pronto como termine las clases . . .
Look, as soon as I finish the classes . . .

Tan pronto como cierren la central nuclear, tendremos una fiesta.
As soon as they close the nuclear power station, we will have a party.

But if the event has already occurred, the verb goes in the indicative:

Tan pronto como lo hizo se fue.
As soon as s/he did it s/he left.

Exercise 11

Choose the correct form of the verb:

1 En cuanto oyó / oiga lo del accidente se fue a casa.
2 Tan pronto como lo sepa / sabe, seguro que coge el primer avión que haya.
3 Una vez que llegas / llegues, no tendrás ningún problema.
4 Tan pronto como se fue / se vaya empezó a llover.
5 En cuanto se da cuenta / dé cuenta del problema, nos llamará.
6 Una vez que lo hizo / haga, no tuvo ningún problema.

How to make a complaint

There are two common expressions used to make a complaint:

Parece mentira que plus the subjunctive:

Pero parece mentira que haya minas tan cerca de un parque tan especial, ¿no?
But it is unbelievable there are mines so near such a special park, isn't it?

Parece mentira que la gente no recicle más.
It is unbelievable people do not recycle more.

Parece mentira que no te acuerdes de eso.
It is unbelievable you don't remember that.

Parece mentira que no esté todavía aquí.
It is unbelievable that s/he is not here yet.

Es increíble que plus the subjunctive:

Es increíble que lo haya hecho tan mal.
It's unbelievable s/he has done it so badly.

Es increíble que no lo sepas.
It's unbelievable you don't know about it.

Exercise 12

Match the place with the expression:

1	Parece mentira que no haya socorristas.	a	en un banco
2	Parece mentira que los servicios estén cerrados.	b	durante un examen
3	Parece mentira que ese camión vaya tan rápido.	c	en una playa
4	Parece mentira que no venga con tiempo.	d	en un bar
5	Parece mentira que no tengan dólares.	e	en una autopista

12 La política / La economía

In this unit you can learn about:

▶ how to wish or hope that something will happen: **ojalá (i)**
▶ how to express a good or a bad wish
▶ how to express 'hope'
▶ **creer** versus **no creer**
▶ how to express the idea of being fed up
▶ how to express how the action has developed: **dejar de, llegar a, acabar por**
▶ how to end a conversation: **bueno, pues nada, en fin**
▶ living standards in Spain

Exercise 1

Here are the main Spanish political parties: some of these are Catalan, Galician and Basque:

PP	Partido Popular
PSOE	Partido Socialista Obrero Español
IU	Izquierda Unida
PCE	Partido Comunista Español
PNV	Partido Nacionalista Vasco
EA	Eusko Alkartasuna
CiU	Convergencia i Union
ERC	Esquerra Republicana de Catalunya
BNG	Bloque Nacionalista Gallego

Some of these parties are from specific **Comunidades Autónomas**. Which of the political parties mentioned above are from the following **Comunidades Autónomas**?

1 País Vasco:

2 Cataluña:

3 Galicia:

Exercise 2

Match the verbs or nouns in the left-hand column with the appropriate nouns to form expressions, e.g. **convocar elecciones** (to call elections):

1	convocar	a	escaños
2	presentar	b	de impuestos
3	confrontar	c	tensiones sociales
4	el programa	d	electoral
5	reducciones	e	un acuerdo
6	gobierno	f	listas de candidatos
7	elecciones	g	generales / autonómicas / europeas
8	conseguir	h	elecciones / comicios
9	hacer	i	minoritario / mayoritario
10	alcanzar	j	campaña

Dialogue 1

*Lorna is in Spain and it appears that elections are about to be called. She is talking to Isabel, a Spanish friend from **Sevilla**, about the elections and the different parties involved.*

Vocabulary ◆

ojalá	I wish
elecciones (fpl) / **comicios** (mpl)	elections
campañas electorales (fpl)	electoral campaigns
estar harto de	to be fed up
encuestas (fpl) / **sondeos** (mpl)	opinion polls
fomento (m)	promotion, development
desilusionar	to disappoint
para colmo	to top it all
encarcelar	to imprison

ISABEL   Ojalá gane el partido socialista las próximas elecciones.

LORNA   ¿Tú crees que tiene alguna posibilidad de ganar?

ISABEL   No, de momento no creo que tenga ninguna pero la vida está llena de sorpresas. Nunca se sabe lo que puede pasar desde ahora hasta los comicios. Puede que salga algún escándalo y cambie todo.

LORNA   Espero que las campañas electorales no sean tan aburridas como en el Reino Unido. Para cuando llegan las elecciones todo el mundo está harto de leer encuestas, de leer artículos en los que un partido critica al otro. Al final la gente llega a desear que se terminen cuanto antes, gane quien gane. ¿Cómo son las campañas aquí?

ISABEL   No creo que sean muy diferentes a las del Reino Unido. La campaña dura 15 días y todos los días aparecen sondeos en la prensa así que al final la gente acaba por votar a quien sea.

LORNA   ¿Y cuándo dejan de aparecer los sondeos?

ISABEL   Los sondeos están prohibidos durante los cinco días anteriores a la fecha de las elecciones.

LORNA   ¿Y no se forman pactos electorales para intentar ganar más votos?

ISABEL   A veces sí. Por ejemplo en las elecciones del 2000 el PSOE formó un pacto electoral con IU, una coalición de disidentes del PSOE, liberales, nacionalistas, ex-radicales y verdes, dirigida por el Partido Comunista Español.

LORNA   ¿Y ganaron?

ISABEL   ¡Qué va! El PP ganó otra vez.

LORNA   Es difícil imaginar que después de tantos años de dictadura un partido derechista gane varias elecciones seguidas.

ISABEL   No te extrañe. El PSOE de Felipe González gobernó durante catorce años a partir de la conclusión de la llamada 'transición pacífica' del fascismo a la democracia al final de la dictadura de Franco. La política del PSOE de privatizaciones y del fomento de empleos casuales a tiempo parcial entre otras cosas desilusionó a muchos de sus partidiarios y para colmo encarcelaron a altos oficiales y ministros del PSOE por corrupción. En Inglaterra no hay tantos escándalos ¿no?

LORNA   ¡Ojalá fuera cierto! No sólo tenemos muchos escándalos políticos sino que también altos oficiales han terminado en la cárcel.

ISABEL   Parece mentira que en Inglaterra ocurra lo mismo.

LORNA   Bueno ¡que este año las elecciones sean más interesantes!

ISABEL   Esperemos que sí. Bueno, pues nada. Ya te contaré lo que pasa.

De acuerdo con la información recibida en esta Oficina, le comunicamos los datos de su inscripción en el censo electoral

Apellido 1:   AGUIRRE

Apellido 2:   LÓPEZ

Nombre: NEREA

Domicilio: 30, PRIORY RD.
              LONDON W4 5JB

País: REINO UNIDO

Sexo: Hombre ☐   Mujer ☒

Fecha de nacimiento: 04/12/1958

Lugar de nacimiento: AMURRIO
                            ALAVA

Provincia de inscripción: ALAVA

Municipio de inscripción: AMURRIO

Consulado: LONDRES

Si considera que alguno de los datos anteriores no es correcto, deberá communicarlo a su consulado

                         Madrid, Diciembre de 2002
                         OFICINA DEL CENSO ELECTORAL

Exercise 3

Listen to the dialogue again and answer the following questions:

1 What reasons does Isabel give for still hoping that the Socialist Party may win?
2 What details are given on the Spanish electoral campaign?
3 What parties were involved in the electoral pact and what was the success of the pact?
4 Why was the electorate disappointed with PSOE?

Language points ◆

How to wish or hope that something will happen

Ojalá plus subjunctive

The tense you will use with ojalá depends on whether you think it is probable the event will take place. You need to use the present subjunctive if you think it is probable.

Ojalá gane el partido socialista las próximas elecciones.
I hope (wish) the Socialist party will win the elections.

Ojalá Patricia apruebe el examen.
I hope (wish) Patricia passes her exam.

Ojalá Luis no llegue tarde.
I hope (wish) Luis does not arrive late.

You need to use the imperfect subjunctive if you think it is not likely. You will study the imperfect subjunctive in Unit 14.

Exercise 4

Translate into Spanish:

1 I hope (wish) my mum would come soon. (*she is planning to come*)
2 I hope Pete remembers to tape the film.
3 I hope we win the game tomorrow.

How to express a good or a bad wish

You use **que** plus a subjunctive to express a good or bad wish:

Bueno ¡que este año las elecciones sean más interesantes!
(I hope) the elections are more interesting this year!

¡Que tengas buen viaje!
Have a good journey! (**tú**)

¡Que tenga buen viaje!
Have a good journey! (**usted** or **él / ella**)

¡Que tengas suerte!
Good luck! (**tú**)

¡Que cumplas muchos más!
I hope you celebrate many (years) more. (**tú**)

¡Que (te) lo pases bien!
Have a good time! (**tú**)

¡Que se lo pase bien!
Have a good time! (**usted** or **él / ella**)

¡Que te mejores pronto!
Get better soon! (**tú**)

¡Que te vayas bien en Madrid!
I hope everything goes well in Madrid! (**tú**)

¡Que le vaya bien en Madrid!
I hope everything goes well in Madrid! (**usted** or **él / ella**)

¡Que sea leve!
I hope it is nothing serious.

¡Que te parta un rayo!
Go to hell! (**tú**)

Exercise 5

What would you wish the person who tells you the following?

1 Hoy hago cuarenta años.
2 María está en el hospital.
3 Mañana me voy a vivir a Málaga.

4 La semana próxima tengo exámenes.
5 Mañana me voy de vacaciones a Buenos Aires.
6 No quiero hablar nunca más contigo.

How to express hope

You have seen in previous chapters that you use the subjunctive after **esperar que**:

Espero que las campañas electorales no sean tan aburridas como en Inglaterra.
I hope the electoral campaigns are not as boring as in England.

Espero que no haya más problemas en Oriente Medio.
I hope there are no more problems in the Middle East.

Esperar que may also be followed by the future indicative or by the conditional:

Espero que vendrán.   I hope they come.
Espero que lo haría bien.   I hope s/he did well.

However, the subjunctive is the most common form:

Mi madre espera que estemos todos juntos en Navidad.
My mum hopes we are all together at Christmas.

Remember that when the subject of the main verb and the subordinate verb refer to the same person, the subjunctive is not used. The verb **esperar** is not followed by **que**:

Espero poder votar mañana.
I hope to be able to vote tomorrow.

Juan espera volver pronto.
Juan hopes to come back soon.

When verbs such as **aconsejar, necesitar, pedir, preferir, querer, permitir**, etc., are used with **que**, they always require the subjunctive:

Prefiero que vengas más tarde.   I prefer you come later.
Necesita que lo hagas pronto.   S/he needs you to do it soon.

Exercise 6

A friend has received the following email from a Spanish friend. He is not sure about the meaning so he has asked you to translate it for him.

Querido John

Espero que puedas venir a España el 23 de junio. Es la Primera Comunión de mi hija y queremos que vengas a celebrarla con nosotros. No creo que Lewis pueda venir pero si quieres puedes venir con algún amigo. Mi hija espera que vengas así que no la decepciones. Cuando sepas si puedes venir mándame un correo electrónico.

Un abrazo

Carmen

¡Ojalá puedas venir!

Creer versus *no creer*

No creer plus the subjunctive

When you use the negative form of the verb **creer,** you need to use the subjunctive:

De momento no creo que tengan ninguna posibilidad.
I don't think they have any chance (of winning) at present.

No creo que sean muy diferentes a las de Inglaterra.
I doubt the elections are any different from those in England.

No creo que el Partido Comunista gane las elecciones.
I don't think the Communist Party will win the elections.

No creo que los verdes ganen muchos escaños.
I don't think the Green Party will win many seats.

Creer que plus the indicative

When you use the affirmative form of **creer que,** you need to use the indicative form in the appropriate tense:

Creo que van a ganar los verdes.
I think the Green Party will win.

Creo que habrá muchos problemas.
I think there will be many problems.

Creo que ha habido elecciones en Ecuador.
I think there have been elections in Ecuador.

Exercise 7

Fill in the gaps with the appropriate form of the verb:

> Example: **Creo que _____ un acuerdo pero no creo que _____ más votos (ellos, alcanzar, atraer).**
>
> **Creo que alcanzarán un acuerdo pero no creo que atraigan más votos.**

1 Creo que _____ en las elecciones locales pero no creo que _____ las generales (él, perder).
2 Creo que _____ algún escaño pero no creo que _____ más de diez (el partido, ganar).
3 Creo que _____ un pacto electoral pero no creo que _____ las elecciones (haber, ganar).
4 Cree que IU _____ su candidatura pero no creo que el PSOE lo _____ (retirar, hacer).
5 Creo que el PSOE _____ al poder pero no creo que _____ pronto (volver, ser).
6 Cree que _____ muchos conflictos laborales pero no creo que _____ huelgas (haber).

How to express the idea of being fed up

Estar harto / a de plus an infinitive

Para cuando llegan las elecciones todo el mundo está harto de leer encuestas.
By the time the elections arrive everybody is fed up of reading polls.

Estoy harta de oir siempre lo mismo.
I am fed up of always reading the same.

Los españoles están hartos de la política exterior del gobierno.
The Spanish people are fed up with the foreign policy of the government.

Note that **estar harto** can also mean 'to be full':

No quiero más, gracias, estoy harta.
I don't want any more thanks, I'm full. (*a woman speaking*)

Estar harto / a de que plus a subjunctive

As with many verbs, you need to use the subjunctive with **estar harto de que** when there is a change in the subject:

Estoy harta de que cierta gente sólo sepa hablar de fútbol.
I am fed up with certain people who only know how to talk about football.

Estoy harto de que muchos políticos no hagan nada.
I am fed up with so many politicians who do not do anything.

Estar hasta la coronilla de / Estar hasta las narices de

coronilla	crown of the head
la nariz / narices	nose

These two expressions mean exactly the same and are two colloquial ways of expressing the idea of having had enough:

Lola está hasta las narices de oir a los políticos.
Lola is fed up of listening to politicians.

Estoy hasta la coronilla de oir hablar de él.
I'm fed up of hearing about him.

José está hasta la coronilla de que los políticos prometan siempre lo mismo.
José is fed up with politicians always making the same promises (*always promising the same*).

Exercise 8

Fill in the gaps with the appropriate words:

Example: **Los ingleses _____ _____ de que la gente _____ el fútbol con los hooligans (relacionar).**

Los ingleses están hartos de que la gente relacione el fútbol con los hooligans.

1 Mi madre _____ _____ de _____ siempre al mismo partido (votar).

2 Los españoles _____ _____ de que la gente sólo
   _____ de Franco (hablar).
3 ¡ _____ _____ la coronilla de ti! (yo)
4 Juan _____ _____ la coronilla de que la gente le
   _____ (insultar).
5 María _____ _____ de _____ que leer tantos correos
   electrónicos (tener).
6 Lola _____ _____ de tantos chismes.
7 Carlos _____ _____ las narices de tantas bromas.
8 Los verdes _____ _____ de _____ las elecciones
   (perder).

To express how the action has developed

Dejar de plus an infinitive is used to convey the interruption of a process:

¿Y cuándo dejan de aparecer los sondeos?
And when do the polls stop appearing?

Los políticos dejan de pensar en el electorado.
Politicians stop thinking about the electorate.

Llegar a plus an infinitive is normally used to convey the idea that something has been achieved after a slow process. It is normally translated by 'to eventually become':

Santiago llegó a ser el alcalde del pueblo.
Santiago eventually became the village mayor.

However, sometimes the end of the process can be negative:

Al final, la gente llega a desear que se terminen cuanto antes, gane quien gane.
By the end, the people end up wishing that the elections would finish quickly, whoever wins.

Llegó a desear su muerte.
S/he ended up wishing for her/his death.

Acabar por plus an infinitive / **acabar** plus a gerund are used to express the idea that something has finished after a long process:

Luisa acabó perdiendo todo.
Luisa ended up losing everything.

Acabar por has the same meaning as **llegar a** when the end of the process is negative:

Así que al final la gente acaba por votar a quien sea.
So in the end people end up voting for whoever.

Acabó por dejarme en paz.
S/he finally left me in peace.

Exercise 9

Fill in the gaps with the appropriate preposition if needed:

1 IU acabó _____ perdiendo muchísimos escaños.
2 PCE dejó _____ presentarse a las elecciones.
3 Felipe González llegó _____ ser presidente.
4 HB acabó _____ cambiando de nombre.
5 La gente acabó _____ votar al grupo minoritario.
6 El presidente dejó _____ hablar en la televisión.

How to end a conversation

Bueno, pues nada is a very common expression used to end a conversation. **Pues nada** can be used on its own or with **bueno**:

pues nada	right then
bueno, pues nada	right then

Bueno on its own can be used to start or to finish a conversation:

Bueno, me voy.	OK, I'm leaving.

En fin is used to conclude or summarise what has been discussed:

En fin, que no puedo ir.
Well / In short, I cannot go.

En fin, que me voy.
Well / In short, I'm leaving.

En fin, que es el mejor escritor de España.
Well / In short, he's the best writer in Spain.

Text 1 ⁙⑨

Barcelona supera a Madrid en nivel de vida y desarrollo económico

Tres provincias catalanas, entre las cinco más ricas, según La Caixa

La rivalidad entre Barcelona y Madrid se resuelve a favor de la capital catalana, según el estudio de La Caixa. Tanto el nivel de renta disponible por habitante como su evolución en los últimos años, es superior en Barcelona y su provincia. El estudio se limita a exponer los datos y no valora las causas. Según el director del servicio de estudios de la entidad financiera catalana, Josep M. Carrau, 'lo fundamental es que son dos provincias muy ricas y que están en la cabecera de España'.

De hecho, tanto Madrid como Barcelona se encuentran en un intervalo de renta por habitante de entre 11.400 y 12.000 euros al año. A ese nivel se encuentran también Álava, Baleares y Guipúzcoa. Les superan las provincias de Girona y Lleida, con una renta media entre 12.000 y 13.000 euros. Este nivel de vida representa casi el doble respecto de las dos provincias más pobres, Badajoz y Cádiz, cuya renta oscila entre 6.400 y 6.975 euros. Las provincias andaluzas y las extremeñas ocupan los lugares de cola. Según los autores del estudio, 'el abanico se está cerrando en los últimos años'.

En unas provincias el desarrollo es más rápido que en otras. Barcelona, con el puesto ocho, supera otra vez a Madrid, en el lugar 32, en cuanto a dinamismo económico durante el periodo 1995–2000. En el total de provincias españolas, Málaga, Álava y Badajoz están a la cabeza en evolución, mientras que los últimos lugares los ocupan Zaragoza, Lugo y Ourense.

Entre los municipios de más de 50.000 habitantes, el más rico sería Donostia-San Sebastián, seguido de Getxo, Girona, Lleida, Pozuelo de Alarcón, Las Rozas y Sant Cugat del Vallés. En todos ellos, la renta media por habitante supera los 13.000 euros. La Línea de la Concepción y Sanlúcar de Barrameda son los de más bajo nivel de renta, entre 6.400 y 6.975 euros. El municipio más dinámico es el madrileño de Parla, seguido de Badajoz y Fuengirola. Lugo, Melilla y Pamplona / Iruña están a la cola.

La Caixa ofrece también datos sobre la disposición que cada uno de los municipios españoles tiene de determinados bienes o servicios y su evolución en los últimos años. La media nacional es de 423 automóviles por cada 1.000 habitantes, 414 teléfonos fijos, una oficina bancaria, 16 actividades industriales, 21 comercios minoristas y 7 restaurantes, bares, cafeterías o quioscos. Entre los años 1996 y 2001 el número de oficinas de los bancos ha caído un 11,6%, mientras que las de las cajas de ahorro ha aumentado un 24,3%. Los autores del estudio lo explican porque la liberalización ha sido posterior en las cajas.

Source: Article from El País (Internet) 6 June 2002

Exercise 10

Read the following headings and choose one for each paragraph:

1 Levels of income
2 Rate of development
3 Barcelona comes top
4 The richest and the poorest provinces
5 More bars than banks

Exercise 11

Find the equivalents in the text above of the following words / expressions:

1st paragraph
income
data, facts
to be at the head of

2nd paragraph
standard of living
bottom places
the gap / the range (literally the fan)

3rd paragraph
development
the position

4th paragraph
the average income

5th paragraph
goods
retail shops
savings banks

Exercise 12

An English friend has asked you to send him information on the standard of living in Spain. Read the article again and make notes for him on:

1 In which areas does Barcelona come above Madrid?
2 Which regions have the highest and the lowest average income?
3 Which are the richest and the poorest municipalities?
4 What is the national average regarding cars and telephones?

13 La cultura y las artes

In this unit you can learn about:

▶ subjunctive: verbs of influence such as **querer que**
▶ how to express doubt
▶ using indirect speech (iv)
▶ how to express resignation
▶ how to introduce concessions (although, etc.)
▶ using subjunctives with subordinators of purpose (in order to)
▶ famous artists

Dialogue 1

*Andrea is going to **Bilbao** and wants to know where to go. She is talking to Nerea who is from Bilbao.*

ANDREA   Tengo un vuelo muy barato para Bilbao, tú eres de allí ¿no?

NEREA   Sí, ¿quieres que te recomiende un sitio donde quedarte?

ANDREA   No creo que me haga falta pero gracias de todos modos. Quizás me quede en casa de una amiga de Pete que vive en un pueblo en las afueras. Quiere que me quede con ella porque quiere practicar el inglés, creo que tiene un examen oral de inglés muy pronto. Pete me ha dicho que vaya también a Vitoria. Pero tú ¿qué me recomiendas que visite?

NEREA   Me imagino que no vas a perderte el Museo Guggenheim, ¿no?

ANDREA   ¡Ni loca! Es una de las razones por las que voy. Posiblemente sea uno de los edificios más impresionantes del mundo, ¿no crees?

NEREA   Sí, el edificio de Gehry es como una gran escultura. Lo he visto un montón de veces pero nunca me canso de él. Cada vez que lo veo encuentro alguna cosa diferente. Pero, aparte del edificio, la colección permanente incluye obras de los artistas más prominentes del siglo XX, hay ejemplos de arte pop, minimalismo, arte conceptual, expresionismo abstracto . . .

ANDREA   ¿No estará el Guernica de Picasso en el museo?

NEREA   ¡Ojalá fuera verdad! Cuando construyeron el museo se pensó que se podría traer el cuadro a Bilbao porque ahora teníamos un lugar idóneo para albergarlo, pero por desgracia el Museo Sofía no está dispuesto a entregarlo.

ANDREA   ¿Por qué no?

NEREA   Dicen que el cuadro es muy frágil, que no es una buena idea moverlo, que podría estropearse . . .

ANDREA   Es una pena que no esté en Bilbao, ¿no?

NEREA   Sí claro. Pero, bueno ¡qué le vamos a hacer! Además del Museo ahora hay muchos edificios interesantes aunque no sean tan espectaculares como el Guggi. Además te aconsejo que te des una vuelta por los pueblos pesqueros entre

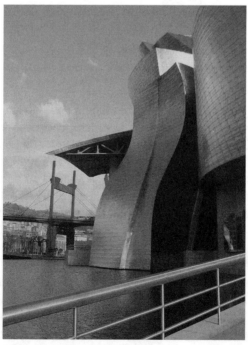

Guggenheim Museum, Bilbao.

Bermeo y San Sebastián. No es necesario que visites todos pero no puedes perderte Getaria, Lekeitio, Elantxobe, Ondarroa. ¡Ah! por poco se me olvida, y Hondarribia que está un poco más allá de San Sebastián, muy cerca de la frontera con Francia. Por cierto, te voy a dar unos euros para que me compres unas latas de anchoas que venden en Ondarroa.

Exercise 1

Listen to the dialogue again and answer the following questions:

1 Where is Andrea staying and why?
2 What does Andrea think of the Guggenheim Museum?
3 How does Nerea describe the Museum?
4 Is Picasso's painting, Guernica, in the Museum?
5 What does Nerea advise Andrea to do besides visiting the Museum?
6 What does Nerea give Andrea and why?

Language points ♦

How to use the subjunctive with verbs of influence

Querer que plus subjunctive

¿Quieres que te recomiende un sitio donde quedarte?
Do you want me to recommend a place to stay?

Quiere que me quede con ella porque quiere practicar el inglés.
She wants me to stay with her because she wants to practise her English.

Pero ¿qué me recomiendas que visite?
But, what do you recommend I visit?

Te aconsejo además que te des una vuelta por los pueblos pesqueros entre Bermeo y San Sebastián.
I advise you also to visit the fishing villages between Bermeo and San Sebastian.

Other common verbs that come in the same category are: exigir que, insistir en que, hacer falta que, necesitar que, pedir que, suplicar que, permitir que, ser necesario que, desear que, conseguir que.

Insisto en que lo hagas hoy.
I insist you do it today.

Necesita que lo traigas sin falta mañana.
S/he needs you to bring it without delay tomorrow.

Te pido / suplico que no vengas tarde.
I ask / beg you not to come late.

Es necesario que la llames por teléfono.
It is necessary for you to phone her.

¿Me permites que use tus libros?
Will you let me use your books?

¿Vas a conseguir que lo haga a tiempo?
Will you make him do it on time?

Te deseo que tengas un buen viaje.
I wish you a good journey.

Querer plus the indicative

Note that when there is no change of subject the subjunctive is not used:

Quiero comprar ese cuadro pero no tengo suficiente dinero.
I want to buy that picture but I don't have enough money.

¿Quieres venir conmigo a la exposición de Muñoz?
Do you want to come with me to the Muñoz exhibition?

Exercise 2

Write sentences with the following prompts:

Example: **Quiero / tú pintar / un cuadro**
Quiero que pintes un cuadro

1 Quiero / tú comprar / una escultura pequeña para Lorena
2 Necesito / tú vender / ese cuadro
3 Es necesario / vosotros llegar / pronto
4 Quiero / tú terminar / esta acuarela antes de que sea de noche
5 Quiero / ellos hablar / con ese pintor tan famoso
6 Quiero / él ver / todas sus obras
7 Necesito / ella diseñar / un edificio moderno

How to express doubt

There are many common words used in Spanish to express doubt: **quizá(s)**, **tal vez**, **acaso**, **a lo mejor**, **igual**, **lo mismo**, **posiblemente**. Some of them do not need the subjunctive.

A lo mejor, igual, lo mismo plus indicative are normally restricted to the spoken language:

A lo mejor voy al Museo del Prado el miércoles.
Perhaps I'll go to the Prado Museum on Wednesday.

Igual me quedo en casa esta noche, no me encuentro muy bien.
Perhaps I'll stay at home tonight, I don't feel very well.

Vete ahora mismo. Lo mismo llegas a tiempo.
Go straight away. Perhaps you'll arrive on time.

Quizá(s) / tal vez / acaso / posiblemente normally take the subjunctive when they are used with future events:

Quizás me quede en casa de una amiga.
Perhaps I will stay with a friend.

Tal vez compre uno de los muñecos Puppy inspirado en la obra de Jeff Koons.
Perhaps I'll buy one of the Puppy toys inspired by Jeff Koons' work.

Posiblemente sea uno de los edificios más impresionantes del mundo.
It is possibly one of the most impressive buildings in the world.

The use of the imperfect subjunctive is optional when the following expressions are used to describe past events:

Tal vez fue / fuera solo porque no quería estar con nadie.
Perhaps he went on his own because he did not want to be with anybody.

You may also hear people using **quizás** and **tal vez** with the indicative even if talking about future events. The use of the subjunctive indicates more uncertainty:

Quizás voy mañana.
Perhaps I'll go tomorrow.

Exercise 3

Choose the correct form of the verb:

1 A lo mejor fue / fuera sola porque no tenía con quien ir.
2 Quizás sabe / sepa todo aunque lo dudo.
3 Tal vez llega / llegue en tren.
4 Igual viene / venga con sus hermanos.
5 Quizás lo hace / haga el domingo pero no nos ha dicho nada.
6 A lo mejor no esté / está en casa.
7 Tal vez me lo dice / diga mañana.
8 Posiblemente no voy / vaya el sábado.

Text 1

Exercise 4

A friend of yours wants to know about Eduardo Chillida, a renowned Basque artist, whose sculptures have been exhibited all over the world. You have come across the following information about him. Read it and make notes for your friend on:

1 Chillida's stay in France
2 Chillida's studies
3 Type of materials used by Chillida

Eduardo Chillida nació el 10 de enero de 1924 en San Sebastián y murió el 19 de agosto de 2002. Pasó tres meses en Francia para aprender el idioma en 1936 antes de que empezara la Guerra Civil española. A los 19 años, después de haber finalizado los estudios escolares en un colegio en San Sebastián, se trasladó a Madrid para comenzar la carrera universitaria de Arquitectura, estudios que su padre alentó. Aunque adquirió una gran reputación como portero de fútbol de la Real Sociedad, tuvo que abandonar el fútbol debido a una lesión. Al mismo tiempo interrumpió sus estudios de Arquitectura. Empezó a acudir a clases de dibujo en una academia privada y comenzó a hacer esculturas. En 1948 volvió a París para estudiar donde vivió hasta 1951 cuando regresó definitivamente a su ciudad natal. Se estableció en Hernani, donde comenzó a trabajar en una fragua y donde realizó su primera escultura abstracta en hierro, 'Ilarik'. Chillida tiene obras en hierro forjado, en acero, en alabastro, en granito, en hormigón, piezas de madera, relieves en mármol. En su larga carrera ha recibido un sinnúmero de premios y sus obras han sido expuestas en todas las galerías y museos de renombre del mundo.

El peine de los vientos, by Eduardo Chillida, San Sebastian.

Indirect speech (iv)

When the main clause (**dice que**) is in the present or the present perfect (**ha dicho que**), the imperative in direct speech changes to the present subjunctive when the message is reproduced in indirect speech:

Direct speech	Indirect speech
Imperative	Present subjunctive

Pete me ha dicho que vaya también a Vitoria.
Pete has told me to go to Vitoria also.

'Llámame si tienes algún problema.'
'Call me if you have any problems.'

Me dice que le llame si tengo algún problema.
S/he says to call her/him if I have any problems.

'Sal de la oficina un poco antes.'
'Leave the office a bit earlier.'

Me dice que salga de la oficina un poco antes.
S/he tells me to leave the office a bit earlier.

'Pon los libros en el despacho.'
'Put the books in the study.'

Me dice que ponga los libros en el despacho.
S/he tells me to put the books in the study.

This can be useful when, if you are asking for something to be done, the person cannot hear you well and you need to repeat it:

A	**Trae una botella de vino tinto.**	Bring a bottle of red wine.
B	**¿Qué dices?**	What did you say?
A	**Que traigas una botella de vino tinto.**	Bring a bottle of red wine.

Remember that if the imperative is affirmative, the pronoun is attached to the verb. If the imperative is negative, the pronoun precedes the verb:

A	**Dame un cigarrillo.**	Give me a cigarette.
B	**¿Qué dices?**	What did you say?
A	**Que me des un cigarrillo.**	Give me a cigarette

A	**No me des más.**	Don't give me any more.
B	**¿Qué dices?**	What did you say?
A	**Que no me des más.**	Don't give me any more.

Exercise 5

You have asked a friend for a number of things but she cannot hear you well so you need to repeat the statements:

Example: **Escribe toda la información aquí.**
    ¿Qué dices?
    Que escribas toda la información aquí.

1 Manda toda la información que puedas.
   ¿Qué dices?

   _____

2 Haz todo lo que puedas antes de irte.
   ¿Qué dices?

   _____

3 Tráeme otra botella.
   ¿Qué dices?

   _____

4 No te preocupes.
   ¿Qué dices?

   _____

5 Ven cuando puedas.
   ¿Qué dices?

   _____

How to express resignation

¿Qué le vamos a hacer?   What can one do?

A   **¿No te van a devolver el dinero?**   Aren't they going to give
                                          you the money back?
B   **No, ¡qué le vamos a hacer!**   No. What can one do?
A   **¿Te han robado todo?**   Have they taken
                               everything?
B   **Sí, ¡qué le vamos a hacer!**   Yes. What can one do?

No (me, te, etc.) quedar más remedio que ... There is nothing we
can do but ...

   No nos queda más remedio que conformarnos con lo que nos den.
   All we can do is to make do with what they give us.

   No me queda más remedio que estudiar más.
   There is nothing I can do but to study more.

Exercise 6

Match the following statements with the correct expression of resignation:

1 Tengo el examen final el   a Si lo quieres de verdad, no te
   viernes   queda más remedio que
                                        soltar el dinero

2 Sólo me han dado
cuatrocientos euros

b Si es tu amigo no te
queda más remedio que
visitarlo

3 Le han suspendido el examen

c Si quieres aprobar no te
queda más remedio que
estudiar todo lo que puedas

4 No me apetece ir al hospital

d Si quiere aprobar no le
queda más remedio que
presentarse de nuevo

5 No me apetece gastar tanto
dinero

e No te queda más remedio
que conformarte con lo que
te han dado

How to introduce concessions (although, etc.)

Aunque plus subjunctive   even if

You need to use the subjunctive with **aunque** when you are talking about events that you have no experience of, events you are uncertain about or unknown events:

Además del Museo hay muchos edificios interesantes aunque no sean tan espectaculares como el Guggi. (*the speaker does not want to use the indicative because it is a very subjective opinion*)
There are other interesting buildings besides the Museum even if they are not as spectacular as the Guggenheim.

Aunque no sea el mejor pintor de España, a mí es el que más me gusta.
Even if he is not the best painter in Spain, he is the one I like most.

Aunque llueva, iremos al concierto.
Even if it rains, we will go to the concert.

Aunque tenga mucho dinero, no podrá comprar ese cuadro.
Even if s/he has a lot of money, s/he will not able to buy that picture.

Aunque plus indicative   although

Aunque is followed by the indicative when you are talking about events that you are certain about:

Aunque llueve salimos ahora mismo. (*it is raining*)
Although it is raining we are leaving right now.

Aunque sólo tiene 21 años, es uno de los mejores escultores de España.
Although he is only 21 years old, he is one of the best sculptors in Spain.

Aunque Julio es rico, no creo que pueda comprar esa escultura.
Although Julio is rich, I don't think he can buy that sculpture.

The following expressions can also be used with the subjunctive or the indicative: **a pesar de que, pese a que, por más que:**

A pesar de que llueva, iremos al concierto en el parque.
Even if it rains, we will go to the concert in the park.

A pesar de que llueve, iremos al concierto en el parque.
Although it is raining, we will go to the concert in the park.

Pese a que haga viento, iremos en bicicleta.
Even if it is windy, we will go by bicycle.

Pese a que hace viento, iremos en bicicleta.
Although it is windy, we will go by bicycle.

Por más que estudies, no aprobarás.
Even if you study a lot, you will not pass.

Por más que estudia, no aprende nada.
Although s/he studies a lot, s/he does not learn anything.

Exercise 7

Fill in the gaps with the appropriate form of the verb indicated. Some of them may take both, subjunctive and indicative, options:

1 Aunque _____ tarde iremos al restaurante (él, llegar).
2 Aunque _____ tarde todos los días, nunca pide disculpas (él, llegar).
3 A pesar de que sólo _____ 3 años, habla bastante bien los dos idiomas (ella, tener).
4 Aunque _____ rico no creo que pueda vivir sin trabajar (él, ser). (*You don't know how much money he has*)
5 Aunque _____ rico no es feliz (él, ser).
6 Por más que lo _____ no te voy a creer (tú, repetir).
7 Pese a que _____ joven, siempre está enfermo (él, ser).
8 Aunque no _____ la mejor cantante, va a ganar el festival (ella, ser).

Subjunctives with subordinators of purpose (in order to)

Para que plus subjunctive

Por cierto, te voy a dar unos euros para que me compres unas latas de anchoas que venden en Ondarroa.
By the way, I'm going to give you some euros so that you can buy me some tins of anchovy that are sold in Ondarroa.

Voy el domingo a tu casa para que me cuentes todo.
I am going to your house on Sunday so that you can tell me everything.

Iré para que no haya problemas.
I'll go so that there are no problems.

The following are also followed by a subjunctive: **con el objeto de que, a que, con la intención de que, no sea que:**

Sonia ha ido al colegio a que le den las notas.
Sonia has gone to the school to get her grades.

Alberto ha venido con la intención de que le demos dinero.
Alberto has come to get money from us.

The expression **no sea que** expresses the idea of 'avoidance':

Iré yo sola no sea que se enfade.
I'll go on my own so that s/he does not get angry.

Le pagaré la cena no sea que se quede sin dinero.
I'll pay her/his dinner so that s/he is not left without money.

Exercise 8

Match the following questions with the correct answers:

1 ¿Para qué me diste ese cuadro?
2 ¿Para qué me llamas a estas horas?
3 ¿Para qué vas a venir el sábado?

a Para que la gente no se olvide de mí.
b Para que mi madre esté contenta.
c Para que pueda pagar lo que debe.

4 ¿Para qué le cuentas todo?   d   Para que no te pierdas el programa que están dando en la tele.

5 ¿Para qué le das dinero todos los meses?   e   Para que me digas la verdad.

6 ¿Para qué vas a España tanto?   f   Para que no lo oiga de otra gente.

7 ¿Para qué escribes tantas cartas?   g   Para que lo pongas en la pared del salón.

Exercise 9

Match the statements:

1 Me voy ahora mismo   a   no sea que se ofenda.
2 Se lo digo ahora mismo   b   no sea que pierda el último tren.
3 Sal ya   c   no sea que esté enfermo.
4 Explícale todo   d   no sea que pierdas el autobús.
5 Llámale a casa   e   no sea que se lo diga Manuel.

Exercise 10

A friend has just read a book in English by Almudena Grandes. She has written to you asking for information on the writer. Listen to the following extract of a recording about the writer and make notes for your friend on:

1 Other books written by Almudena Grandes and their popularity in Spain
2 Her reason for becoming a writer
3 Her thoughts on Spanish literature

Almudena Grandes nació en Madrid en 1960. Su primera obra publicada fue *Las edades de Lulú* con la que ganó el premio La Sonrisa Vertical de narrativa erótica que otorga anualmente Tusquets editores. Es uno de los libros más vendidos de los últimos 25 años. Otra novela suya muy leída en España, especialmente entre los jóvenes es *Malena es un nombre de tango*. En las novelas de Almudena las protagonistas son siempre mujeres. Almudena dice que se hizo escritora por equivocación, porque terminó estudiando geografía e historia en vez de latín. También dice que no escribe como se supone que escriben los novelistas que lo cambian todo cuando terminan la novela, ella sólo hace una versión. Según ella, la literatura nacional tiene buena salud, hay diez escritores buenos y se lee ahora más que antes aunque es un país de poca lectura si se compara con el resto de Europa.

Exercise 11

A friend has just seen the film *Lucía y el sexo* in London. She has asked you for some information on the director. Read the following article and make notes for her on:

1 His studies
2 His jobs
3 His prizes

Julio Medem nació en San Sebastián en 1958. Estudió Medicina y Cirugía General en la Universidad del País Vasco. Hizo crítica de cine en el diario *La Voz de Euskadi* y colaboró en una serie de publicaciones como Cinema 2002. Realizó varios cortos en formato súper-8. En 1987 decidió dedicarse al cine de forma profesional, desempeñando diversos cometidos: ayudante de dirección, guionista, montador profesional, etc. En 1988 escribió y dirigió el mediometraje *Martín* para TVE. Dirigió su primer largometraje *Vacas* en 1992 con el que ganó el premio Goya a la mejor dirección novel. Su segundo largometraje *La ardilla roja* también fue galardonado en la Quincena de Realizadores del festival de Cannes obteniendo el premio a la mejor película extranjera. Una de sus últimas películas ha sido *Lucía y el sexo*, filmada en Formentera.

14 Las quejas

In this unit you can learn about:

▶ past tenses of the subjunctive: imperfect and perfect
▶ how to wish or hope that something will happen: **ojalá (ii)**
▶ indirect speech (v)
▶ how to express the conditional
▶ using the pluperfect subjunctive
▶ writing a letter of complaint

Dialogue 1 ⑴👂

John, who booked his holiday through a Spanish travel agent, has just had a really bad holiday in **Murcia.** *Next to his hotel room they were building an extension and the noise and distraction were unacceptable. He is now talking to a Spanish friend about how to present a claim.*

Vocabulary ◆

reclamar	to claim
por escrito	in writing
estar de vuelta	to be back
un formulario	a form
denuncia (presentar una denuncia)	to lodge a complaint
un impreso	a form
exponer	to explain
remitir	to send
adjunto / a	enclosed

JOHN	¿Qué crees que debo hacer para reclamar?
CARLOS	¿Hiciste una queja por escrito en el hotel?

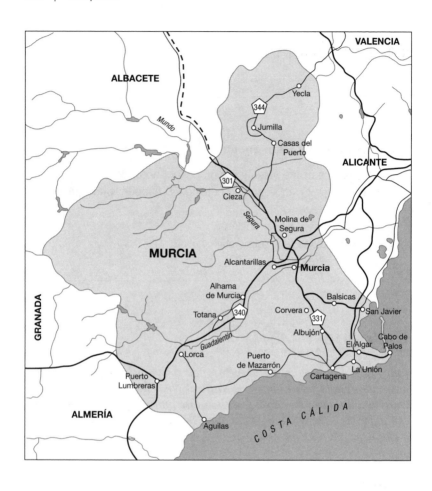

JOHN	No, sólo hablé con el representante del tour ¿debería haberlo hecho por escrito?
CARLOS	Si lo hubieras hecho sería más fácil. Pero tranquilo, no quiere decir que no puedas presentar una reclamación. ¿Qué te dijo el representante cuando te quejaste?
JOHN	Me dijo que fuera a la agencia una vez estuviera de vuelta aquí porque él no podía hacer nada.
CARLOS	¿Sacaste fotos de las obras?
JOHN	Sí, pero no estoy seguro de que sean muy buenas, compré una cámara de esas de tirar.
CARLOS	No te preocupes. No tienen que ser profesionales siempre que se vea bien el problema.

JOHN	¿Qué debo hacer ahora?
CARLOS	Bueno, en primer lugar tienes que rellenar una hoja de reclamaciones que es un formulario oficial que la agencia debe poseer. Si te lo negaran, lo cual dudo, podrías efectuar la denuncia al Servicio Territorial de Turismo.
JOHN	¿Y dónde está este servicio?
CARLOS	Normalmente está en la oficina del consumidor de tu ayuntamiento. En tu denuncia debes hacer constar tu nombre, nacionalidad, domicilio, número de pasaporte además de los demás datos que aparezcan en el impreso. Expón claramente los hechos que te motivan a quejarte. En cuanto lo tengas todo, debes remitir el original de esta hoja a la Delegación Provincial del Ministerio de Comercio y Turismo. La copia rosa que adjunta el impreso se quedará en poder del encargado de la agencia. Tú debes hacer una fotocopia del original por si acaso.
JOHN	¿Les mando las fotos también?
CARLOS	Sí, pero quédate con alguna, no vaya a ser que se pierdan. De todas formas si tienes algún problema llámame, ¿vale?
JOHN	No sabes cómo te agradezco toda esta información. No estoy acostumbrado a este tipo de gestión así que a lo mejor recibes una llamada mía muy pronto . . .

Exercise 1

Listen to the dialogue again and tick the statements that are true:

☐ John had made a complaint in writing.
☐ John was told by the representative to go to the agency when he returned from his holidays.
☐ John took photographs of the building work.
☐ The first thing John has to do is to fill in a 'complaints form'.
☐ John needs to give the following information: name, nationality, address, passport number and other details.
☐ John needs to keep the pink copy.
☐ John does not need to send his photographs but needs to keep them.
☐ John may phone Carlos.

Language points ♦

The past subjunctive

In previous chapters you have studied the present subjunctive. The tense (present, imperfect or perfect, pluperfect and continuous tenses) you need to use depends on the context of the message and on the tense of the main clause. There are more combinations but for the moment the following are the most common ones:

Main clause	Subordinate clause
Present indicative	Present subjunctive
	Perfect subjunctive
Espero que	**lo pases bien**
I hope	you have a good time
	lo hayas pasado bien
	you have had a good time

Main clause	Subordinate clause
Conditional	Imperfect subjunctive
Me gustaría que	**vinieras de vacaciones**
	conmigo I would like you
	to come with me on holidays

Main clause	Subordinate clause
Perfect indicative	Present subjunctive
Te he dicho que	**vengas**
I have told you	to come

Main clause	Subordinate clause
Imperfect indicative	Imperfect subjunctive
Preterite indicative	Pluperfect subjunctive
Quería que	**vinieras**
I wanted you	to come
Quiso que	**lo hubieras hecho ya**
He wanted you	to have done it already

Perfect subjunctive

In order to form the perfect subjunctive, you need to use the present subjunctive of the auxiliary **haber: haya, hayas, haya, hayamos, hayáis, hayan,** plus the past participle (**hecho, trabajado**) of the verb.

Carlos espera que haya sacado fotos.
Carlos hopes I have taken photos.

Espero que lo hayas hecho bien.
I hope you have done it well.

Espero que no se haya puesto enferma.
I hope she hasn't become ill.

Mi madre espera que hayamos comprado ya los billetes.
My mum hopes we have already bought the tickets.

Espero que no hayáis tenido problemas.
I hope you (*plural*) haven't had any problems.

Espero que ya hayan llegado.
I hope they have already arrived.

It is mainly used to express a past action when the main clause is in the present indicative:

Espero que hayan llegado a tiempo.
I hope they have arrived on time.

Carlos espera que ya lo hayas terminado.
Carlos hopes you have already finished it.

Exercise 2

Fill in the gaps with the perfect subjunctive:

Example: **Ojalá no _____ _____ (ella, suspender).**
Ojalá no haya suspendido.

1 Espero que _____ _____ ya (ellos, llegar).
2 No creo que lo _____ _____ ya (él, hacer).
3 Ojalá _____ _____ (ella, aprobar).
4 Cuando lo _____ _____ (tú, terminar).
5 Parece mentira que no le _____ _____ todavía (tú, llamar).

6 Espero que no _____ _____ el avión (ellos, perder).
7 Cuando _____ _____ todos los papeles, llámame (tú, recibir).
8 Espero que no _____ _____ sola (ella, ir).

Imperfect subjunctive

In order to conjugate the imperfect subjunctive of -ar verbs, you need to add the following endings -ara, -aras, -ara, áramos, -arais, -aran, to the third person singular of the preterite indicative:

Infinitive	Third person preterite stem	Imperfect subjunctive
trabajar	trabaj(ó)	trabajara
hablar	habl(ó)	hablara

Carlos esperaba que yo <u>trabajara</u> más.
Carlos hoped I worked more.

(Yo) esperaba que <u>trabajaras</u> más.
I hoped you worked more.

(Yo) esperaba que <u>trabajara</u> más.
I hoped s/he worked more.

Carlos esperaba que <u>trabajáramos</u> más.
Carlos hoped we worked more.

(Yo) esperaba que <u>trabajarais</u> más.
I hoped you (*plural*) worked more.

¿Esperabas que <u>trabajaran</u> más?
Did you hope they worked more?

Be careful with some irregular verbs:

Raúl quería que le diera más dinero.
Raúl wanted me to give him more money.

(Ella) No quería que anduviera tanto.
She did not want me to walk so much.

(Yo) No quería que estuviera allí.
I did not want her/him to be there.

In order to conjugate the imperfect subjunctive of -er and -ir verbs, you need to add the following endings -iera, -ieras, -iera, -iéramos, -ierais, -ieran, to the third person singular of the preterite indicative:

Infinitive	Third person preterite stem	Imperfect subjunctive
comer	com(ió)	comiera
escribir	escrib(ió)	escribiera

Tu madre quería que yo comiera más.
Your mum wanted me to eat more.

Quería que bebieras menos.
I wanted you to drink less.

Mi madre quería que le escribiera.
My mum wanted me to write to her/him.

Juan quería que bebiéramos más vino.
Juan wanted us to drink more wine.

Juan quería que bebierais menos.
Juan wanted you (*plural*) to drink less.

Mi madre quería que sus hijos le escribieran.
My mum wanted her children to write to her.

Be careful with those verbs that are irregular in the preterite. Here are some of the most frequently used ones.

Infinitive	Third person preterite stem	Imperfect subjunctive
dormir	durm(ió)	durmiera
pedir	pid(ió)	pidiera
poder	pud(o)	pudiera
poner	pus(o)	pusiera
querer	quis(o)	quisiera
saber	sup(o)	supiera
tener	tuv(o)	tuviera
venir	vin(o)	viniera

María quería que <u>durmiera</u> en su casa.
María wanted me to sleep in her house.

Luis quería que le <u>pidiera</u> el coche a José.
Luis wanted me to ask José for his car.

No creía que <u>pudiera</u> hacerlo.
I didn't believe s/he could do it.

Carmen quería que lo <u>pusiera</u> en su casa.
Carmen wanted me to put it in her house.

No creía que lo <u>quisieras</u>.
I didn't believe you wanted it.

Quería que lo <u>supieras</u>.
I wanted you to know it.

No creía que <u>tuviera</u> tantos problemas.
I didn't know s/he had so many problems.

Quería que <u>vinieras</u> antes.
I wanted you to come earlier.

The following irregular verbs drop the **i** in **-iera**. All the verbs whose infinitive ends in **-ducir** (**traducir, producir,** etc.) follow the same pattern.

Infinitive	Third person preterite stem	Imperfect subjunctive
construir	construy(ó)	construyera
ser / ir	fu(e)	fuera
decir	dij(o)	dijera
conducir	conduj(o)	condujera
traer	traj(o)	trajera
oir	oy(ó)	oyera

Quería que <u>construyera</u> una casa.
S/he wanted me to build a house.

Quería que <u>fuera</u> más activa.
S/he wanted me to be more active.

Quería que te <u>dijera</u> la verdad.
S/he wanted me to tell you the truth.

No quería que <u>condujera</u>.
S/he did not want me to drive.

Quería que <u>trajeras</u> el otro libro.
S/he wanted you to bring another book.

Quería que <u>oyera</u> las noticias.
S/he wanted me to hear the news.

You have probably noticed that all the verbs in the main clauses in the examples given above are in the past tense. Although there are no fixed rules, the verb in the subordinate clause is in the imperfect subjunctive when the tense used in the main clause is in the past tense (imperfect, preterite, pluperfect).

Esperaba que viniera hoy.
I was hoping s/he would come today.

Te dije que lo hicieras para hoy.
I told you to do it by today.

Te había dicho que vinieras.
I had told you to come.

If the present perfect is used in the main clause, the present subjunctive is used in the subordinate clause:

Te he dicho que vengas ahora mismo.
I've told you to come right now.

Le he pedido que lo traiga hoy.
I've asked her/him to bring it today.

All the different uses of the present subjunctive you have looked at in previous units apply to the imperfect subjunctive:

Estoy harta de que siempre llegue tarde.
I am fed up with her/him always arriving late.

Estaba harta de que siempre llegara tarde.
I was fed up that s/he always arrived late.

Me dice que me queje al director.
S/he tells me to complain to the director.

Me dijo que me quejara al director.
S/he told me to complain to the director.

No creo que lo haga bien.
I don't believe s/he will do it well.

No creía que lo hiciera bien.
I didn't believe s/he would do it well.

You will also see and hear other endings for the imperfect subjunctive: **-ase, -ases, -ase, -ásemos, -aseis, -asen,** for **-ar** verbs, and **-iese, -ieses, -iese, -iésemos, -ieseis, -iesen,** for **-er** and **-ir** verbs. Both **-ara** and **-ase** endings are used but I would advise you to use just one, at least to start with. The **-ara** endings are used in this book as they are the more frequent form.

Exercise 3

Choose the correct form of the verb:

Example: **Quería que hagas / hicieras esto para mañana.**
Quería que hicieras esto para mañana.

1 Esperaba que escribas / escribieras a la agencia.
2 Espero que te quejes / te quejaras por escrito.
3 Necesito que me ayudaras / ayudes a rellenar este formulario.
4 No creía que pueda / pudiera hacerlo tan bien.
5 Quería que efectue / efectuara la denuncia pero no lo hizo.
6 Quiero que remitas / remitieras el original.
7 Esperaba que rellene / rellenara la hoja de reclamaciones.
8 Queríamos que te quedaras / te quedes con una copia del original.

How to wish or hope that something will happen

Ojalá plus imperfect subjunctive

You learnt in Unit 12 that you could use **ojalá** plus the present subjunctive to express a wish that you think is probable:

Ojalá Santi me compre ese vestido.
I hope Santi buys me that dress.

You need to use the imperfect subjunctive if you think it is not likely:

Ojalá fuera cierto.	I wish it were true.
Ojalá fuera ya verano.	I wish it were summer.
Ojalá no tuviera que trabajar.	I wish I did not have to work.

Exercise 4

Translate into Spanish:

1 I wish tomorrow were Sunday (*today it's Monday*).
2 I hope Sandra comes soon.
3 I wish it was not true (*unfortunately it is*).
4 I wish I did not have to go (*unfortunately you have to*).
5 I hope it is sunny tomorrow (*it's summer so it is possible*).

Text 1

Tourism has been growing in Spain steadily and it is a major source of income. However, the number of tourists visiting Spain in 2002 did not increase.

Besalú, province of Girona.

Exercise 5

Read the accompanying article that appeared in the newspaper *El Mundo* and answer the following questions:

1 Why does Juan Costa believe that the figures are positive?
2 Which areas of Spain suffered the most? Why?
3 Which areas of Spain have seen an increase in the number of tourists?
4 Why will the income from tourism be lower than other years?

Vocabulary ♦

estancarse	to come to a standstill
aportar	to contribute
desaceleración (f)	deceleration, slowing down
mostrar	to show
cabe destacar	it is worth highlighting
pernoctar	to spend the night
ecotasa	green tax (the government of the Balearic Islands introduced a tax to protect the environment)
previsiones (fpl)	forecast

El turismo español se estanca por primera vez en ocho años

Durante el primer semestre, entraron en España más de 21,7 millones de visitantes – Baleares, una de las regiones más afectadas por la crisis

MADRID, – Tras ocho años de crecimiento ininterrumpido, el número de turistas que ha pasado por nuestro país en el primer semestre del año se ha estancado con respecto a los que lo hicieron en 2001. Entre enero y junio del presente año, 21.745.117 turistas han entrado en España, prácticamente la misma cifra que en igual periodo de 2001 (21.754.153), según datos aportados por el secretario de Estado de Comercio y Turismo, Juan Costa.

A pesar de la desaceleración del mercado mundial, Costa afirmó que estos datos muestran 'la consolidación del mercado turístico español', por lo que calificó el resultado como 'positivo', aunque esté lejos del aumento del 3,7% de 2001.

'España lo está haciendo bien en materia turística, y aunque es cierto que a todos nos gustaría que fuera mejor, lo cierto es que lo estamos haciendo mucho mejor que los mercados competitivos del sector', indicó.

Por comunidades, cabe destacar la caída de turistas en Baleares, que acumula desde enero un 9% menos de pernoctaciones que el año pasado. Costa no consideró la ecotasa como causante de este descenso, aunque reconoció que 'influye', e hizo un llamamiento a las autoridades de las islas para que revisen su política, 'porque Baleares es el principal destino español en verano y proyecta una parte importante de la imagen turística de España al exterior'.

En el polo opuesto se encuentran Cataluña, la Comunidad Valenciana y Andalucía, que han visto incrementado su número de turistas en un 15,8%, 9,3% y un 2,9%, respectivamente, con respecto al primer semestre de 2001.

Cataluña se ha visto beneficiada del aumento de viajeros que han accedido a nuestro país por carretera (17,5% más que el año pasado), así como del incremento en un 25% de los visitantes franceses.

El británico, con 1,6 millones de turistas en lo que va de año, es el mercado exterior que más visita nuestro país, mientras que 540.000 alemanes han cambiado España por otros destinos, lo que 'debe hacernos reflexionar' . . .

Finalmente, el secretario de Comercio y Turismo consideró que los ingresos por este apartado en este año serán 'moderados', debido al 'gran esfuerzo que está realizando el sector turístico por ofrecer precios competitivos'. Por su parte, la Asociación Empresarial de Agencias de Viajes se mostró preocupada debido a la caída en un 12% en los ingresos que calculan.

Indirect speech (v)

The imperative in direct speech changes to the imperfect subjunctive when the message is reproduced in indirect speech and the main clause is in the preterite (**dijo que**).

Direct speech	Indirect speech
Imperative	Imperfect subjunctive

'**Llámame si tienes algún problema.**'
'Call me if you have any problems.'

Me dijo que lo llamara si tenía algún problema.
S/he told me to call him if I had any problems.

'**Sal de la oficina un poco antes.**'
'Leave the office a bit earlier.'

Me dijo que saliera de la oficina un poco antes.
S/he told me to leave the office a bit earlier.

'**Pon los libros en el despacho.**'
'Put the books in the study.'

Me dijo que pusiera los libros en el despacho.
S/he told me to put the books in the study.

'**Escríbeles una carta explicando todo.**'
'Write them a letter explaining everything.'

Me dijo que les escribiera una carta explicando todo.
S/he told me to write a letter to them explaining everything.

Exercise 6

Here are some of the things that Carlos told John in the dialogue at the beginning of the unit. Fill in the gaps with the imperfect subjunctive:

Example: **Me dijo que _____ la queja por escrito (realizar).**
          Me dijo que realizara la queja por escrito.

1 Me dijo que _____ a la agencia (ir).
2 Me dijo que les _____ las fotos (mandar).
3 Me dijo que me _____ con algunas fotos por si acaso (quedar).
4 Me dijo que _____ una hoja de reclamaciones (rellenar).
5 Me dijo que _____ mi nombre, nacionalidad y domicilio (escribir).
6 Me dijo que _____ el original de esa hoja a la Delegación Provincial del Ministerio de Comercio y Turismo (remitir).
7 Me dijo que _____ una fotocopia del original (hacer).
8 Me dijo que le _____ si tenía algún problema (llamar).

Pluperfect subjunctive

In order to form the pluperfect subjunctive, you need to use the imperfect subjunctive of the auxiliary haber: **hubiera, hubieras, hubiera, hubiéramos, hubierais, hubieran,** plus the past participle (**hecho, trabajado**) of the verb:

Esperaba que lo hubieras hecho para hoy.
I was hoping you would have done it by today.

Quería que hubieras venido antes.
I wanted you to have come earlier.

Si hubieras llegado a tiempo habrías podido hacerlo.
If you had arrived on time you would have been able to do it.

Exercise 7

Match the following statements:

1 Si hubiera tenido dinero	a no tendrías dolor de estómago.
2 Si hubiera aprobado	b para ahora sabría todo.
3 Si no hubieras bebido tanto	c habría comprado esa casa.
4 Si hubiera salido antes	d ahora podría irme de vacaciones en vez de tener que estudiar.
5 Si lo hubieras hecho antes	e podrías coger mi coche.
6 Si le hubiera llamado	f no habría perdido el último tren.
7 Si hubieras comido menos	g ahora no tendrías que trabajar.

Conditional

Si plus the present tense of the indicative

Remember that **si** is followed by the present tense of the indicative when there is a possibility that the condition will be fulfilled:

> **De todas formas si tienes algún problema, llámame.**
> Anyway, if you have any problem, call me.

> **Si tienes fotos, puedes mandarlas con la hoja de reclamación.**
> If you have photographs, you can send them with the claim form.

Si plus the imperfect subjunctive . . . plus conditional or imperative

This conditional tense is used when there is very little chance that the condition will be fulfilled:

> **Si te lo negaran . . . podrías efectuar la denuncia.**
> If they were to refuse . . . you could carry out the claim.

> **Si tuviera más dinero compraría una casa en España.**
> If I had more money I would buy a house in Spain.

> **Si mi madre fuera más joven, podría visitarme más a menudo.**
> If my mother were younger, she could visit me more often.

> **Si no te lo dieran, dímelo.**
> If they do not give it to you, tell me.

Exercise 8

Write down five things you would do if you had more money. Once you have written them down, compare them with the author's selection of things she would do. Listen to what she would do if she had more money.

Si plus the pluperfect subjunctive . . . plus the perfect conditional, the pluperfect subjunctive or the conditional

These conditional tenses are used to describe past events in which the condition was not fulfilled:

> **Si hubieras ido antes lo habrías visto / lo hubieras visto.**
> If you had gone earlier, you'd have seen him.

> **Si hubiera estudiado más habría aprobado / hubiera aprobado.**
> If I had studied more, I'd have passed.

**Si nos hubiéramos levantado antes no habríamos perdido /
hubiéramos perdido el avión.**
If we had got up earlier, we would not have missed the plane.

**Si te hubieras quejado antes habrías podido / hubieras podido
resolver el asunto, pero ya es demasiado tarde.**
If you had complained earlier, you would have been able to
resolve the matter, but it is too late now.

Si lo hubieras hecho antes sería más fácil hacerlo ahora.
If you had done it earlier, it would be easier to do it now.

Exercise 9

Change the following sentences into the past tense:

Example: **Si pudiera hacerlo lo haría.**
If I could do it, I would (do it).

Si hubiera podido hacerlo lo habría hecho.
If I had been able to do it, I would have done it.

1 Si tuviera tiempo iría contigo.
2 Si pudiera hablar con él lo haría.
3 Si estuviera en España no vería los partidos de fútbol.
4 Si hubiera problemas hablaría con él.
5 Si trabajara más lo terminaría pronto.
6 Si Manuel trajera más vino habría suficiente.
7 Si tuviera suficiente dinero compraría ese reloj.
8 Si pudiera venir vendría.

Text 2

Exercise 10

A friend, unhappy about the service he received in a restaurant, has
asked you for information on how to lodge a complaint. You have
come across the following information on the **hojas de reclamaciones**.
Read it and make notes for him on:

1 What **hojas de reclamaciones** are
2 Whether the forms are the same in the different **Comunidades
   Autónomas**
3 What to do if the restaurant refuses to give him the form

Hojas de reclamaciones

Las hojas de reclamaciones son impresos que disponen de tres copias, una para el reclamante, otra para remitir y otra para el reclamado. Estas hojas son obligatorias en muchos establecimientos comerciales, en talleres de reparaciones, en restaurantes y hoteles, en las empresas de transportes públicos, etc. El modelo de hoja de reclamaciones es uniforme en toda España aunque cada Comunidad Autónoma puede cambiar lo que crea oportuno. Es posible que algunos lugares, dependiendo también de la Comunidad Autónoma, no dispongan de las hojas así que infórmese antes de pedir el impreso. En el caso de que no le dieran la hoja o el libro de reclamaciones, acuda a la policía local. La policía puede levantar acta de la negativa que en sí misma es una infracción. Si no puede presentar personalmente la reclamación, puede mandarla por correo certificado administrativo. Si quiere que el servicio de correos ponga el sello de certificación el sobre debe estar abierto para que el funcionario pueda comprobar la identidad entre original y copia.

Exercise 11

Fill in the gaps with the most appropriate word from the list below:

Estimados Señores:

Siento tener que 1 _____ a ustedes para presentar una 2 _____ contra el mal servicio de uno de los hoteles de su cadena.

Mi marido y yo fuimos al Hotel Barcelona de la localidad malagueña de Marbella para realizar la 3 _____ de una habitación doble para 4 noches. Tras realizar la reserva a las 13:00 horas y hablar con el personal de la recepción del hotel, quien nos informó que no era necesario entregar una cantidad en concepto de 4 _____ para realizar la reserva, decidimos ir a almorzar.

Cuando regresamos al hotel, nos llevamos la desagradable sorpresa de que la habitación 5 _____ por otra pareja. Solicitamos una 6 _____ pero el hotel 7 _____ alegando que no estaba obligado a dárnosla aunque había un cartel que informaba de la existencia de las mismas.

El hotel no dio ningún tipo de 8 _____ ni solución y nos vimos obligados a pasar la noche en un hotel de diferente categoría.

Esperamos que 9 _____ las medidas necesarias para que este tipo de problema no vuelva a ocurrir en sus hoteles. Esperando una pronta 10 _____.

Les saluda atentamente

1 contactarme / dirigirme / hablar
2 carta / queja / solución
3 reclamación / reserva / queja
4 reserva / entrada / señal
5 había sido dada / había sido ocupada / había sido entregada
6 hoja de reclamaciones / otra habitación / otro hotel
7 se negó / se enfadó / se disculpó
8 ayuda / justificación / notificación
9 tomen / toman / hayan tomado
10 carta / solución / respuesta

¡Enhorabuena! You have finished this book. I am sure it has not been easy and at times it must have felt like a struggle but I hope it has been worth it. Learning languages is not easy but it is rewarding. Not only will you be able to talk to people in Spain and Latin America, but you will also be able to read newspapers and books written in Spanish, and see the increasingly popular Spanish and Latin American films in their original language.

Having said that, don't stop now. You have now a very good base to continue learning. Thanks to the Internet, you have access to a vast variety of materials, from Spanish newspapers to government policies. Find out about things that interest you whether it is football, films, literature. Your vocabulary will increase without hardly noticing it, your knowledge of the country and its culture will become almost intuitive. Here are some useful sites:

www.yahoo.es

Spanish newspapers:
www.elpais.es
www.elmundo.es
http://www.abc.es

Government:
www.la-moncloa.es

Language:
www.el-castellano.com
http://perso.wanadoo.es/gramatica.home.htm
http://cvc.cervantes.es/aula/

Grammar reference

Pronouns

Personal	object	(direct and indirect)	prepo-sitional	reflex-ive	possessive
First person singular					
	yo	me	mí (conmigo)	me	mi / mis
Second person (*informal***) singular**					
	tú	te	ti (contigo)	te	tu / tus
Second person (*formal***) singular**					
	usted	lo / la / le	usted	se	su / sus
Third person singular					
	él	lo / la / le	él	se	su / sus
	ella	la / le	ella	se	su / sus
First person plural					
	nosotros/as	nos	nosotros/as	nos	nuestro / a / os / as
Second person plural (*informal***)**					
	vosotros/as	os	vosotros/as	os	vuestro / a / os / as
Second person plural (*formal***)**					
	ustedes	los / les	ustedes	se	su / sus

Prepositions

Para

- to express the idea of 'in order to', 'for the purpose of'
- to express a deadline
- to express a specific period of time
- to express direction
- to express the idea of 'to be about to'
- to express 'in my opinion'

Por

- to express the cause of or reason for something
- to express a period of time
- to express who has done the action in a passive sentence
- to express the idea of 'on the part of'
- to express apology and gratitude
- to express the idea that there are still things to do

Verbs

Present

Regular verbs

	hablar	**beber**	**vivir**
yo	habl**o**	beb**o**	viv**o**
tú	habl**as**	beb**es**	viv**es**
él / ella / usted	habl**a**	beb**e**	viv**e**
nosotros / nosotras	habl**amos**	beb**emos**	viv**imos**
vosotros / vosotras	habl**áis**	beb**éis**	viv**ís**
ellos / ellas / ustedes	habl**an**	beb**en**	viv**en**

Stem-changing verbs

Conjugated like **contar** (to tell): **aprobar** (to pass an exam), **comprobar** (to check), **acordarse** de (to remember), **acostarse** (to go to bed), **encontrar** (to find), **mostrar** (to show), **probar** (to prove / to try), **recordar** (to remember), **soñar** (to dream), **volar** (to fly):

contar	cuento	contamos
	cuentas	contáis
	cuenta	cuentan

Conjugated like **comenzar** (to start): **atravesar** (to cross), **calentar** (to heat), **despertarse** (to wake up), **encerrar** (to shut in), **gobernar** (to govern), **negar** (to deny), **pensar** (to think), **recomendar** (to recommend), **sentarse** (to sit down), **nevar** (to snow):

comenzar	comienzo	comenzamos
	comienzas	comenzáis
	comienza	comienzan

Conjugated like **soler** (to be in the habit of): **devolver** (to give back), **doler** (to hurt), **llover** (to rain), **oler** (to smell), **resolver** (to resolve), **volver** (to return):

soler	suelo	solemos
	sueles	soléis
	suele	suelen

Conjugated like **preferir** (to prefer): **divertirse** (to enjoy oneself), **mentir** (to lie), **sugerir** (to suggest), **herir** (to wound), **arrepentirse** (to repent), **sentir** (to feel):

preferir	prefiero	preferimos
	prefieres	preferís
	prefiere	prefieren

Conjugated like **repetir** (to repeat): **corregir** (to correct), **elegir** (to choose), **impedir** (to impede), **seguir** (to follow), **servir** (to serve), **pedir** (to ask for):

repetir	repito	repetimos
	repites	repetís
	repite	repiten

Conjugated like **entender** (to understand): **defender** (to defend), **encender** (to light), **perder** (to lose):

entender	entiendo	entendemos
	entiendes	entendéis
	entiende	entienden

Some irregular verbs:

dar	decir	estar	hacer	ir	poder	poner	ser
doy	digo	estoy	hago	voy	puedo	pongo	soy
das	dices	estás	haces	vas	puedes	pones	eres
da	dice	está	hace	va	puede	pone	es
damos	decimos	estamos	hacemos	vamos	podemos	ponemos	somos
dais	decís	estáis	hacéis	vais	podéis	ponéis	sois
dan	dicen	están	hacen	van	pueden	ponen	son

querer	salir	saber	tener	valer	venir	ver
quiero	salgo	sé	tengo	valgo	vengo	veo
quieres	sales	sabes	tienes	vales	vienes	ves
quiere	sale	sabe	tiene	vale	viene	ve
queremos	salimos	sabemos	tenemos	valemos	venimos	vemos
queréis	salís	sabéis	tenéis	valéis	venís	veis
quieren	salen	saben	tienen	valen	vienen	ven

Preterite

The simple past or preterite (**indefinido**) is used to express an action completed at a definite period in the past. This tense is normally used with time expressions such as **ayer, anoche, la semana pasada, el otro día, en 1997, en octubre, hace un año,** etc.

Regular verbs

	hablar	**beber**	**vivir**
yo	habl**é**	beb**í**	viv**í**
tú	habl**aste**	beb**iste**	viv**iste**
él / ella / usted	habl**ó**	beb**ió**	viv**ió**
nosotros / nosotras	habl**amos**	beb**imos**	viv**imos**
vosotros / vosotras	habl**asteis**	beb**isteis**	viv**isteis**
ellos / ellas / ustedes	habl**aron**	beb**ieron**	viv**ieron**

Irregular verbs

ir		dar	
fui	fuimos	di	dimos
fuiste	fuisteis	diste	disteis
fue	fueron	dio	dieron

Irregular verbs that can be grouped together: **estar, tener, andar, poder, saber, poner, venir, querer.**

Infinitive	root
estar	estuv-
tener	tuv-
andar	anduv-
poder	pud-
saber	sup-
poner	pus-
venir	vin-
querer	quis-

estar	endings
estuve	-e
estuviste	-iste
estuvo	-o
estuvimos	-imos
estuvisteis	-isteis
estuvieron	-ieron

Another group: **decir, traer, traducir, conducir, atraer, producir, maldecir:**

decir	dije	dijimos
	dijiste	dijisteis
	dijo	dijeron

Another group: **pedir, repetir, despedir, sentir, reír, reñir, advertir, mentir, preferir, sugerir:**

pedir	pedí	pedimos
	pediste	pedisteis
	pidió	pidieron

Another group: **construir, caer, oir, leer, excluir, influir:**

construir	construí	construimos
	construiste	construisteis
	construyó	construyeron

Another group: **dormir, morir:**

dormir	dormí	dormimos
	dormiste	dormisteis
	durmió	durmieron

Imperfect

The imperfect tense (**imperfecto**) is used mainly to talk about events that used to happen repeatedly, for descriptions in the past, and to express continuance and duration (in English normally the continuous form, e.g., I was working in restaurants, is used). This tense is normally used with time expressions such as: **cada día, con frecuencia, a menudo, siempre,** etc.

Regular verbs

	hablar	**beber**	**vivir**
yo	habl**aba**	beb**ía**	viv**ía**
tú	habl**abas**	beb**ías**	viv**ías**
él / ella / usted	habl**aba**	beb**ía**	viv**ía**
nosotros / nosotras	habl**ábamos**	beb**íamos**	viv**íamos**
vosotros / vosotras	habl**abais**	beb**íais**	viv**íais**
ellos / ellas / ustedes	habl**aban**	beb**ían**	viv**ían**

Irregular verbs

ir		ser		ver	
iba	íbamos	era	éramos	veía	veíamos
ibas	ibais	eras	erais	veías	veíais
iba	iban	era	eran	veía	veían

Present perfect

The present perfect tense (**pretérito perfecto**) is used when the action is finished but the period of time in which the action took place has not finished. You could almost say 'up to now' I've done this or that. This tense is normally used with the following time expressions: **esta semana, este mes, este año, hoy,** etc.

Regular verbs

	hablar	**beber**	**vivir**
yo	he hablado	he bebido	he vivido
tú	has hablado	has bebido	has vivido
él / ella / usted	ha hablado	ha bebido	ha vivido
nosotros / nosotras	hemos hablado	hemos bebido	hemos vivido
vosotros / vosotras	habéis hablado	habéis bebido	habéis vivido
ellos / ellas / ustedes	han hablado	han bebido	han vivido

Common irregular past participles:

volver	vuelto	poner	puesto
devolver	devuelto	escribir	escrito
hacer	hecho	decir	dicho
abrir	abierto	cubrir	cubierto
morir	muerto	romper	roto
ver	visto		

Pluperfect

	hablar	beber	vivir
yo	había hablado	había bebido	había vivido
tú	habías hablado	habías bebido	habías vivido
él / ella / usted	había hablado	había bebido	había vivido
nosotros / nosotras	habíamos hablado	habíamos bebido	habíamos vivido
vosotros / vosotras	habíais hablado	habíais bebido	habíais vivido
ellos / ellas / ustedes	habían hablado	habían bebido	habían vivido

Progressive tenses (i)

The progressive tenses in Spanish are used to express that an action is taking place. Although one of the most common auxiliaries used in the progressive tenses is the verb **estar**, you can use other verbs as auxiliaries: **ir, seguir, andar, salir.**

	hablar	beber	vivir
yo	estoy hablando	estoy bebiendo	estoy viviendo
tú	estás hablando	estás bebiendo	estás viviendo
él / ella / usted	está hablando	está bebiendo	está viviendo
nosotros / nosotras	estamos hablando	estamos bebiendo	estamos viviendo
vosotros / vosotras	estáis hablando	estáis bebiendo	estáis viviendo
ellos / ellas / ustedes	están hablando	están bebiendo	están viviendo

Some irregular verbs:

dormir	durmiendo	**construir**	construyendo
decir	diciendo	**leer**	leyendo
pedir	pidiendo	**oir**	oyendo
sentir	sintiendo	**ir**	yendo

Future

	hablar	beber	vivir
yo	hablaré	beberé	viviré
tú	hablarás	beberás	vivirás
él / ella / usted	hablará	beberá	vivirá
nosotros / nosotras	hablaremos	beberemos	viviremos
vosotros / vosotras	hablaréis	beberéis	viviréis
ellos / ellas / ustedes	hablarán	beberán	vivirán

Irregular verbs

Infinitive	Future stem
decir	dir-
hacer	har-
poder	podr-
poner	pondr-
haber	habr-
salir	saldr-
venir	vendr-
querer	querr-
saber	sabr-
valer	valdr-
tener	tendr-
salir	saldr-

decir
diré
dirás
dirá
diremos
diréis
dirán

- The future tense is used in Spanish the same way as it is in English to refer to an action in the future. It is more commonly used in the written language. The form **ir a** plus an infinitive is used in everyday conversation.
- to express probability / uncertainty / guesswork
- to express surprise or doubt
- to express indignation
- to express orders

Future perfect

	hablar	beber	vivir
yo	habré hablado	habré bebido	habré vivido
tú	habrás hablado	habrás bebido	habrás vivido
él / ella / usted	habrá hablado	habrá bebido	habrá vivido
nosotros / nosotras	habremos hablado	habremos bebido	habremos vivido
vosotros / vosotras	habréis hablado	habréis bebido	habréis vivido
ellos / ellas / ustedes	habrán hablado	habrán bebido	habrán vivido

Conditional

	hablar	beber	vivir
yo	hablaría	bebería	viviría
tú	hablarías	beberías	vivirías
él / ella / usted	hablaría	bebería	viviría
nosotros / nosotras	hablaríamos	beberíamos	viviríamos
vosotros / vosotras	hablaríais	beberíais	viviríais
ellos / ellas / ustedes	hablarían	beberían	vivirían

Irregular verbs

Infinitive	Future stem
decir	dir-
hacer	har-
poder	podr-
poner	pondr-
haber	habr-
salir	saldr-
venir	vendr-
querer	querr-
saber	sabr-
valer	valdr-
tener	tendr-
salir	saldr-

decir
diría
dirías
diría
diríamos
diríais
dirían

Conditional perfect

	hablar	beber	vivir
yo	habría hablado	habría bebido	habría vivido
tú	habrías hablado	habrías bebido	habrías vivido
él / ella / usted	habría hablado	habría bebido	habría vivido
nosotros / nosotras	habríamos hablado	habríamos bebido	habríamos vivido
vosotros / vosotras	habríais hablado	habríais bebido	habríais vivido
ellos / ellas / ustedes	habrían hablado	habrían bebido	habrían vivido

This tense is used to express what would have taken place had something else not intervened.

Imperative

The affirmative imperative:

- **Tú**: third person of the present tense.
  Irregular verbs: **ten (tener)**, **pon (poner)**, **ven (venir)**, **di (decir)**, **ve (ir)**, **sal (salir)**, **haz (hacer)**, **sé (ser)**.
- **Usted**: third person singular of the present subjunctive.
- **Vosotros**: trabaj*ad*, beb*ed*, escrib*id*.
- **Ustedes**: third person plural of the present subjunctive.

The negative imperative:

- **Tú**: **no** plus second person singular of the present subjunctive.
- **Usted**: **no** plus third person singular of the present subjunctive.
- **Vosotros**: **no** plus second person plural of the present subjunctive.
- **Ustedes**: **no** plus third person plural of the present subjunctive.

Subjunctive: present tense

hablar	beber	vivir
hable	beba	viva
hables	bebas	vivas
hable	beba	viva
hablemos	bebamos	vivamos
habléis	bebáis	viváis
hablen	beban	vivan

Perfect subjunctive

hablar	beber	vivir
haya hablado	haya bebido	haya vivido
hayas hablado	hayas bebido	hayas vivido
haya hablado	haya bebido	haya vivido
hayamos hablado	hayamos bebido	hayamos vivido
hayáis hablado	hayáis bebido	hayáis vivido
hayan hablado	hayan bebido	hayan vivido

Pluperfect subjunctive

hablar	comer	vivir
hubiera hablado	hubiera comido	hubiera vivido
hubieras hablado	hubieras comido	hubieras vivido
hubiera hablado	hubiera comido	hubiera vivido
hubiéramos hablado	hubiéramos comido	hubiéramos vivido
hubierais hablado	hubierais comido	hubierais vivido
hubieran hablado	hubieran comido	hubieran vivido

Imperfect subjunctive

hablar	beber	vivir
hablara	bebiera	viviera
hablaras	bebieras	vivieras
hablara	bebiera	viviera
habláramos	bebiéramos	viviéramos
hablarais	bebierais	vivierais
hablaran	bebieran	vivieran

Irregular verbs

Infinitive	Third person preterite stem	Imperfect subjunctive
dormir	durm(ió)	durmiera
pedir	pid(ió)	pidiera
poder	pud(o)	pudiera
poner	pus(o)	pusiera
querer	quis(o)	quisiera
saber	sup(o)	supiera
tener	tuv(o)	tuviera
venir	vin(o)	viniera

Irregular

Infinitive	Third person preterite stem	Imperfect subjunctive
construir	construy(ó)	construyera
ser / ir	fu(e)	fuera
decir	dij(o)	dijera
conducir	conduj(o)	condujera
traer	traj(o)	trajera
oir	oy(ó)	oyera

Tense agreement:

Main clause	Subordinate clause
Present indicative	Present subjunctive
	Perfect subjunctive
Perfect indicative	Present subjunctive
Imperfect indicative	Imperfect subjunctive
Preterite indicative	Pluperfect subjunctive
Conditional	Imperfect subjunctive

Some uses of the subjunctive:

- **Antes de que / después de que** plus subjunctive. However, when the action has already happened the verb takes the indicative.
- **Cuando** plus the subjunctive when the event has not yet occurred.
- **En cuanto** plus a subjunctive when the event has not yet occurred.
- **Una vez que** plus the subjunctive when the event has not yet occurred.
- **Tan pronto como** plus subjunctive when the event has not yet occurred.
- **Parece mentira que** plus the subjunctive.
- **Ojalá** plus subjunctive. The tense you will use with **ojalá** will depend on whether you think it is probable the event will take place.
  - You need to use the present subjunctive if you think it is probable.
  - You need to use the imperfect subjunctive if you think it is not likely.
- **Que** plus the subjunctive to express a good or bad wish.
  ¡Que tengas suerte!   Good luck! (**tú**)
- **Esperar que** plus the subjunctive.
- **No creer** plus the subjunctive. However, **creer que** plus the indicative.
- **Estar harto / a de que** plus a subjunctive.
- **Querer que** plus subjunctive.

When verbs such as **aconsejar, necesitar, pedir, preferir, querer, permitir,** etc are used with **que,** they always require the subjunctive: Other common verbs that come under the same category are: **exigir que, insistir en que, hacer falta que, necesitar que, pedir que, suplicar que, permitir que, ser necesario que, desear que, conseguir que,** etc.

- **Quizá(s) / tal vez / acaso, posiblemente** plus subjunctive. These expressions normally take the subjunctive when they are used with future events. The use of the subjunctive is optional when these expressions are used to describe past events.
- **Aunque** plus subjunctive   even if
- **Aunque** plus indicative   although

The following expressions are used like **aunque: a pesar de que, pese a que, por más que.**

- **Para que** plus subjunctive.

The following are also followed by a subjunctive: **con el objeto de que, a que, con la intención de que, no sea que.**

Conditional

- **Si** plus the present tense of the indicative . . . plus the present, the imperative or the future.
- **Si** plus the imperfect subjunctive . . . plus conditional or imperative. This conditional tense is used when there is very little chance that the condition will be fulfilled.
- **Si** plus the pluperfect subjunctive . . . plus the perfect conditional, the pluperfect subjunctive or the conditional. This conditional tense is used to describe past events in which the condition was not fulfilled.

The pronoun *se*

- **Se** is the third person, singular and plural, reflexive pronoun
- The indirect object **le** changes to **se** when it is followed by a direct object: **lo, la, los, las.**
- Impersonal. **Se** plus a verb in the third person singular.
- Passive. **Se** plus a verb in the third person (singular or plural).

Passive and active sentences

When using verbs (**decir, robar, dar, decir**) which normally need an indirect object (**me, te, le, nos, os, les**) never use the passive; make the sentence active by using the third person plural of the verb with the appropriate indirect object.

Ser and *estar*

Ser

- to express identity or nature
- to express origin, nature
- to express possession
- to express 'to take place'
- to talk about the time
- to express a permanent quality
- to form the passive

Estar

- to express state as opposed to nature
- to express location
- **estar** plus an adverb

Here are some words that change their meaning

ser **listo/a**	to be clever	estar **listo/a**	to be ready
ser **católico/a**	to be catholic	no**estar católico/a**	to be unwell
ser **rico/a**	to be rich	estar **rico/a**	to be delicious
ser **malo/a**	to be bad	estar **malo/a**	to be ill / to be bad (food)
ser **verde**	to be green / smutty	estar **verde**	to be unripe
ser **orgulloso/a**	to be proud	estar **orgulloso/a**	to be proud of something
ser **aburrido/a**	to be boring	estar **aburrido/a**	to be bored

Direct and indirect speech

When reproducing a message in indirect speech you must remember to change all the necessary tenses and words (time, space). You do not need, however, to change the tenses when the main clause (**dice que**) is in the present.

Direct speech	Indirect speech
Present	Imperfect
Imperfect	Imperfect
Preterite	Pluperfect
Present Perfect	Pluperfect
Future	Conditional
Future Perfect	Conditional Perfect
Imperative	Imperfect Subjunctive

Direct speech	Indirect speech
hoy	ese día, aquel día
ayer	el día anterior
mañana	al día siguiente

Direct speech	Indirect speech
aquí	allí
este, esta, esto	ese, esa,eso, aquel, aquella, aquello

Key to exercises

Unit 1

Exercise 1

1 Otaola Alday are her Spanish family names and Sale is her husband's name. **2** She is from Oquendo, a small village near Bilbao. **3** She doesn't miss Spain very much, but she misses her family, her friends and being able to go to a bar at any time of the day. **4** The weather is very similar. **5** She likes the fact that London is very cosmopolitan.

Exercise 2

Se llama Antonio Banderas
Nació en Málaga, en el sur de España.
En los Estados Unidos.
Está casado.
Su esposa se llama Melanie Griffiths.
Stella del Carmen.
Le gusta mucho ir a Málaga, le gusta navegar, le gusta jugar con su hija.

Exercise 3

1 Verdadero **2** Falso **3** Falso 4 Verdadero **5** Verdadero **6** Verdadero

Exercise 4

1 es (nationality), es (nationality) **2** está (location), está (location) **3** Hay **4** está location), es (description, fact) **5** está (location), Está (location) **6** es (fact), es (origin) **7** Hay **8** es (fact) **9** es (fact) **10** Hay

Exercise 5

1 A **2** en **3** De **4** al **5** de **6** con **7** en / por **8** a

Exercise 6

1 Me levanto a la / las ... **2** Me levanto a la / las ... **3** Me baño / me ducho. **4** Prefiero ducharme por la noche / prefiero ducharme por la mañana. **5** No tardo mucho / tardo bastante / sí, tardo mucho.

Exercise 7

1 b **2** a **3** c **4** b **5** a

Exercise 8

1 ha venido **2** he estado **3** has llegado **4** han leído **5** ha preparado **6** hemos hablado

Exercise 9

1 fui **2** vimos **3** cocinó **4** estudiaste **5** visitaron **6** hablasteis

Exercise 10

1 vivía, andaba **2** tenía **3** eras, eras **4** querías, tenías **5** estábamos **6** venían

Exercise 11

1 Son (fact) **2** es (nationality) **3** es (nationality) **4** está (location) **5** es (description, fact) **6** hay **7** es (description, fact) **8** es (fact) **9** es (fact) **10** es (description, fact) **11** está (state) **12** están (location) **13** estar (location) **14** hay **15** está (state) **16** está (state) **17** está (state) **18** es (fact, description) **19** es (fact, description) **20** es (origin) **21** es (fact, profession) **22** es (origin) **23** es (fact, profession) **24** es (fact, description) **25** está (state) **26** es (fact, description).

Unit 2

Exercise 1

1 She wants to go out because a friend is waiting for her but she cannot do it. **2** Her suitcases are in Morocco. **3** She has a wedding to go to and her dress is in the suitcase.

Exercise 2

1 c **2** d **3** b **4** e **5** a

Exercise 3

1 se siente **2** Siente **3** siente **4** siento **5** Me siento

Exercise 4

1 d **2** f **3** g **4** b **5** a **6** c **7** e

Exercise 5

1 Lo leo por la tarde / noche. **2** La quiero ver el sábado. **3** Va a visitarme el mes que viene / próximo / Me va a visitar el mes que viene / próximo. **4** Los voy a ver mañana / Voy a verlos mañana. **5** Lo voy a terminar la semana próxima / que viene / Voy a terminarlo la semana próxima / que viene. **6** Sí, los estoy haciendo / Sí, estoy haciéndolos, no te preocupes. **7** Las quiere para el domingo.

Exercise 6

1 Tienes **2** Puede **3** vamos / volvemos **4** volver / ir **5** Acabo **6** Van

Exercise 7

1 Hace su trabajo con rapidez. **2** Por desgracia no se siente bien / no se encuentra bien. **3** Por suerte se siente mejor / se encuentra mejor. **4** Escribió el documento con facilidad.

Exercise 8

1 Approximately 55 minutes, around 45 flights a day, each way, 4 an hour. **2** The majority of passengers are business people. **3** It is advisable to book a ticket if you need to be in a place at a certain time. **4** It is quite difficult to park at the airport. You can go by taxi but it is more expensive. You can also go on the underground from the centre of Madrid.

Exercise 9

1 ¿Cuántos vuelos diarios hay? **2** Este periódico es un periódico semanal. **3** Hay trenes cada media hora. **4** Hay dos vuelos a la semana.

Exercise 10

1 Flight number: IB425
   Message: There will be an hour's delay.
   Reason: Heathrow airport is busy.
2 Flight number: IB384
   Message: The flight has been cancelled.
   Reason: technical failure
   Action to be taken: Passengers to go to the Information desk to find out about the next flight.
3 Flight number: BA831
   Message: To embark through gate number 4.
4 Names: Mrs Gónzalez Martín and Mrs López Isla
   Message: To go to gate number seven, it is the last call.
   Reason: This is the last call.

Exercise 11

1 Age and driving experience needed: over 21 years old, one year **2** Type of insurance included in the price: obligatory car insurance and third party insurance **3** It is worth paying extra for full insurance. **4** What to do regarding the petrol: fill up the tank before returning the car. **5** You are responsible for the fines unless they are due to the state of the car. **6** It is better to book in advance because there is much demand.

Exercise 12

1 peor, que **2** menos, que **3** menos, que **4** el mayor de **5** más, que **6** mejor, que **7** mayor, que **8** más, que

Exercise 13

E Me gustaría alquilar un coche pequeño por una semana, sin límite de kilometraje.

B Muy bien, ¿un Ford Fiesta está bien?

E Bien, aquí tiene mi carné de conducir.

B Bien, ¿me puede dejar su tarjeta de crédito?

E Aquí tiene la tarjeta de crédito. ¿Qué tipo de seguro está incluído?

B La tarifa incluye el seguro obligatorio del vehículo y el de responsabilidad civil a terceros.

E ¿Cuánto tengo que pagar para tener más protección?

B 24 euros al día.

E Está bien. ¿Está el depósito lleno?

B Sí, llene el depósito antes de devolverlo.

E Vale. ¿Tiene un mapa de la región?

B Sí, aquí tiene uno.

Unit 3

Exercise 1

1 It is a very popular festival and it lasts for a week. **2** The pressing of the grapes, the offering of the first grape juice to the patron of La Rioja, the parade of floats, food and drink and bull fighting.

Exercise 2

1 Qué **2** Cuál **3** cuál **4** Cuál **5** cuál **6** Qué

Exercise 3

El espectacular / bonito festival de los patios fue reconocido en 1960 por el entonces Ministerio de Información y Turismo como fiesta de interés internacional aunque no se trata de un concurso nuevo pues empezó en 1918. Este bonito / espectacular festival representa a Córdoba como las Fallas a Valencia y los Sanfermines a Pamplona. Dura todo el mes de mayo. La maceta es uno de los elementos fundamentales de los patios junto con el pozo.

Exercise 4

1 empecé **2** murió **3** Hablaste **4** hubo **5** bebimos **6** dormí

Exercise 5

1 Sí **2** No, celebran el 24 y el 25. **3** Sí, su madre prepara una gran cena. **4** No, reciben los regalos el 23 de diciembre. **5** Sólo sale su hermana. **6** Sí, comen muchos dulces.

Exercise 6

1 Humour and satire. **2** They join different groups. **3** They compose songs about the local polititians and they sing them during the parades. **4** The 'coros' have around 30 people, the 'cuartetos' have 4 people, and the 'comparsas' have no more than 12 people.

Exercise 7

1 True **2** False **3** True **4** True **5** True **6** False **7** True **8** False

Exercise 8

1 Nunca llego a casa antes de las seis / No llego nunca a casa antes de las seis. **2** ¿No hay nadie en tu casa? **3** No lo sabe nadie / Nadie lo sabe. **4** ¿No tienes nada de beber en tu casa? **5** ¿Por qué no hablas con nadie? **6** Manolo nunca va a Italia de vacaciones / Manolo nunca va de vacaciones. **7** ¿No tienes ninguna esperanza de aprobar? **8** Mis padres no viven con ningún amigo.

Unit 4

Exercise 1

1 There was no hot water, the flat was dirty and there was hardly any cutlery or cups. **2** The office was closed because it was late.

Exercise 2

1 c **2** f **3** a **4** e **5** b **6** d

Exercise 3

1 llegué, estaba **2** había **3** fui, estaba **4** Eran, llamó **5** estabas, llamé **6** estuvo, compró **7** dijo, era **8** salí, llovía **9** tenían, se casaron **10** nos bañamos, hacía

Exercise 4

1 ¿Cúando se fueron los otros inquilinos? **2** ¿Por qué no hay agua caliente?
3 ¿Por qué no hay toallas? **4** ¿Por qué no contestó al teléfono cuando llamé?
They left Monday morning.
I did not know there was no hot water.
We don't supply towels; the tenant has to bring them.
There has been a lot of work and I haven't been in the office much.

Exercise 5

Estaba, estaba, había, estaba, había, estaba, era, eran, era, estaba, había

Exercise 6

1 c **2** a **3** e **4** b **5** d

Exercise 7

1 They had not been used for more than 40 years. **2** The location, the architecture of the area, plus the idea of accommodation they had in mind. **3** Traditional materials. **4** Help from the European Union through the Programme Leader.

Exercise 8

1 voy **2** veía **3** quería **4** saben **5** sabíamos **6** estás **7** salía **8** conocías

Exercise 9

1 estaba (state, temporary) **2** era, era (description, permanent for both) **3** estaba (state, temporary) **4** era / estaba (description, general, permanent) estar (to describe tasty food)

Exercise 10

1 No sólo es guapo sino que (también) tiene mucho dinero también. **2** No sólo viene tarde sino que trae una botella de vino malísima también. **3** No sólo ocurre aquí sino en el norte también. **4** No sólo ha muerto su mujer sino que ha perdido su casa también. **5** No sólo escribe libros sino que pinta cuadros también. **6** No sólo me ha mandado una carta sino dinero también.

Unit 5

Exercise 1

1 Travelled through Latin America. **2** Because a friend invited her to Chile. **3** She hasn't got any yet.

Exercise 2

1 f **2** d **3** a **4** e **5** b **6** c

Exercise 3

1 Nosotros ya habíamos hablado con él cuando su madre llegó. **2** ¿Ya te habías levantado cuando te llamé? **3** Yo ya había comido cuando Lola apareció. **4** Nerea ya había cocinado cuando le expliqué que éramos cinco. **5** Ya había limpiado cuando mi padre llamó a la puerta. **6** Antonio ya había terminado el informe cuando llegó su jefe.

Exercise 4

1 La conocía bien. **2** Lo supe ayer. **3** Andrés no quiso ir al teatro. **4** Laura no pudo hacerlo. **5** ¿Qué pensaste de ella? **6** La conocí ayer. **7** No sabía qué hacía en España. **8** No quería hacerlo.

Exercise 5

1 f **2** e **3** b **4** a **5** c **6** d

Exercise 6

Datos personales:
Nombre: Sonia Rodríguez Martín
Lugar de nacimiento: Burgos
Fecha de nacimiento: 4 de diciembre de 1969
Educación:

1976–1984	Santa María	EGB
1974–1988	Instituto San Vicente	BUP y COU
1988–1993	Universidad de Deusto	Filología inglesa
1994–1995	Escuela Oficial de Idiomas	francés

Experience:

1993–1994	Londres	profesora de español
1995–1999	Escuela 'Lucas Rey'	profesora de inglés
2000–	Universidad de Granada	profesora de literatura inglesa
IT:	conocimientos de Internet, data base	

Exercise 7

'Good communication skills'
Capacidad de relaciones interpersonales
Capacidad para la comunicación
Altas dotes de comunicación, fluidez verbal
Excelentes dotes de comunicación
'Personnel / management skills'
con capacidad para motivar y dirigir a un equipo joven
Buen manejo de recursos humanos
dotes para la supervisión de personal
con dotes de mando

Exercise 8

dinámico dynamic   **adaptable** adaptable   **ambicioso/a** ambitious
analítico/a analytical   **creativo/a** creative   **fiable** trustworthy   **responsable**
responsible   **dispuesto/a** willing   **eficiente** efficient   **trabajador/a** hard-
working   **entusiasta** enthusiastic   **estable** balanced / stable   **independiente**
independent   **objetivo/a** objective   **optimista** optimistic   **voluntarioso/a**
willing / helpful

Exercise 9

This could be one of the many different letters you could have written:

Según su anuncio publicado en el periódico EL PAÍS, el 4 de mayo, me es grato adjuntarles mi currículum vitae, para que tengan buen conocimiento, tanto de mis aptitudes como de mi experiencia profesional. Mi experiencia profesional demuestra mi capacidad para la dirección de equipo y una elevada iniciativa. Me considero una persona entusiasta, y tengo un gran sentido de la responsabilidad, por eso creo que podría encajar satisfactoriamente en el equipo de la empresa que Ud. dirige.

Esperando recibir noticias suyas, a fin de concertar una entrevista personal, reciba un cordial saludo. Atentamente

Exercise 10

1 a tiempo parcial **2** a tiempo completo **3** salario mínimo **4** prorrogable **5** seguridad social **6** abonar / cotizar **7** gratificaciones

Unit 6

Exercise 1

el árbitro, el colegial; el técnico, el entrenador; el hincha, el aficionado; la tarjeta, la cartulina; el portero, el guardameta; el estadio, el campo.

Exercise 2

1 People: el defensa, el hincha, el delantero, el arbitro, el centrocampista, la plantilla, los suplentes, los titulares, el entrenador, el lateral izquierdo / derecho, el portero **2** Stadium: las gradas, el banquillo, el estadio / campo, el césped **3** Actions: empatar, marcar goles, cometer una falta, perder, ganar

Exercise 3

1 He is satisfied with the attitude of the players. **2** Because they have not used the system for very long. **3** The other teams were playing for the championship. **4** He hasn't got any problems.

Exercise 4

1 Está saliendo con un futbolista de Manchester. **2** Luis está jugando en un equipo japonés. **3** Nosotros estamos entrenando para los Juegos Olímpicos. **4** Estoy preparando la cena para un grupo de hinchas del Arsenal que acaba de llegar de Londres. **5** Estoy leyendo el periódico porque estoy buscando un artículo del portero Cabanillas. **6** ¿Quiénes están jugando?

Exercise 5

1 c **2** e **3** d **4** a **5** f **6** b

Exercise 6

1 La verdad es que no estoy contento con el portero / el guardameta. **2** Si bien es verdad que tenemos buenos jugadores en el equipo, todavía necesitamos un lateral izquierdo. **3** Si te / le he de decir la verdad, creo que Jaime no está en forma. **4** Si bien es verdad que el árbitro / el colegial no nos ayudó, perdimos porque no jugamos bien. **5** Para decirte / le la verdad necesitamos otro portero / guardameta.

Exercise 7

Andrés spoke to Luis. Luis had been trying to phone Andrés the whole afternoon

Exercise 8

1 Estaba **2** estuviste **3** estaban **4** estaba **5** estuvieron **6** estaba **7** estuvieron

Exercise 9

1 Me dijo que quería marcar tres goles. **2** Me dijo que necesitaba hablar con el técnico. **3** Me dijo que Raúl se había ido a otro equipo. **4** Me dijo que el césped estaba muy mal. **5** Me dijo que toda la plantilla estaba de mal humor. **6** Me dijo que habíamos perdido porque habíamos jugado muy mal. **7** Me dijo que habían ganado porque Sánchez había jugado muy bien. **8** Me dijo que Ángel estaba lesionado.

Exercise 10

1 Me dijo que no quería hablar conmigo de eso otra vez. **2** Me dijo que me llamaba hoy al día siguiente. **3** Me dijo que no había podido jugar ayer / el día anterior. **4** Me contó que no quería hablar con ella de eso otra vez. **5** Me contó que había ido al teatro la semana pasada / la semana anterior. **6** Me dijo que había estado allí todo el día.

Exercise 11

1 Me preguntó si quería dormir en su casa. **2** Me preguntó (que) dónde vivían mis padres. **3** Me preguntó si iba a ver la última película de Almodóvar. **4** Me preguntó (que) por qué no hablaba con ella. **5** Me preguntó si me gustaba ese vestido.

Exercise 12

1 Me dijo que *estaba* cansada de esperar *tus* llamadas. **2** Me dijo que *llevaba* mucho tiempo esperando un emilio con detalles del estado del piso. **3** Me dijo que *hacía* mucho tiempo que no *recibía* el alquiler. **4** Me dijo que esperaba recibir un cheque *la semana anterior*. **5** Me dijo que *quería* saber si *podías* pagar o no.

Exercise 13

1 Because they took coal to Vizcaya. **2** Because they wanted to study. **3** They have always been in the Premier league. **4** All the players are Basque.

Unit 7

Exercise 1

resaca (hangover): malestar general, dolor de cabeza, mareos, vómitos, dolor de estómago
gripe (flu): malestar general, fiebre alta, tos, dolor de cabeza, molestias musculares, dolor de garganta, escalofríos, ronquera
resfriado (cold): malestar general, estornudos, tos, dolor de cabeza, ronquera
migraña (migraine): malestar general, dolor de cabeza, mareos, vómitos

Exercise 2

1 He is in the hospital because he has had an operation. **2** Because her brother works in the hospital 'Clínico'. **3** Because she does not get on with them.

Exercise 3

1 d **2** e **3** f **4** g **5** b **6** c **7** h **8** a

Exercise 4

1 No, pero iré luego. **2** No, pero vendrá luego. **3** No, pero lo sabré luego. **4** No, pero los tendremos luego. **5** No, pero saldrá luego. **6** No, pero se lo diré luego. **7** No, pero se lo mandaré luego. **8** No, pero comeremos luego.

Exercise 5

1 ¿En qué estará pensando? **2** ¿Quiénes serán esos hombres? **3** ¿Será posible que todavía esté aquí? **4** Tú dirás lo que quieras pero yo no me voy de aquí. **5** ¡Si estarás de acuerdo con ella! **6** ¿De qué vivirá la vecina? No trabaja en ningún sitio. **7** ¿Será tu hermano el que llama? **8** Tú irás allí ahora mismo.

Exercise 6

Here are some possible ways of translating those sentences:

1 Antes de que se me olvide, ¿sabes si Juan está mejor? **2** Eso me recuerda, ¿Tienes ya hora / cita con el médico? **3** Por cierto, ¿cómo tienes el estómago ahora? **4** Perdona / e que te / le interrumpa pero ¿has / ha visitado a Andrés? ¿has / ha ido a ver a Andrés? **5** Antes de que se me olvide, ¿sabes si estas pastillas son buenas? **6** Por cierto, ¿has recibido ya los resultados del análisis de sangre?

Exercise 7

1 c **2** e **3** a **4** f **5** b **6** d

Exercise 8

1 Comería más pero estoy llena. **2** Estoy segura de que lo haría si se lo pides. **3** Me iría contigo ahora mismo pero no puedo. **4** La visitaría pero no me gustan los hospitales. **5** ¿Te quedarías mañana con ella? **6** Mis padres vendrían pero cuestan mucho los billetes. **7** ¿Le escribirías si te doy la dirección electrónica? **8** Cuando él llegó, serían las cinco.

Exercise 9

Querida Susana

El mes que viene iré a Madrid a pasar dos semanas. Llegaré al aeropuerto de Barajas a las 11 de la noche, ¿podrías / te importaría venir a recogerme? Si no puedes, ¿podría Juan venir a recogerme? No sé si alquilaré un coche, pero si no tengo suficiente dinero, ¿podrías / te importaría dejarme tu coche unos días? No sé tampoco dónde quedarme, ya sabes que no ando bien de dinero,

¿Podría quedarme las dos semanas en tu casa? Cuando esté en Madrid, tengo que ir a ver a un amigo que está muy enfermo en el hospital pero no quiero ir solo, ¿vendrías conmigo? También me gustaría pasar unos días en la Sierra, ¿podrías coger unos días de vacaciones? Por último, necesito encontrar información del último libro de Rosa Montero ¿te importaría / podrías ir a alguna librería y preguntar por él?

Perdona por pedirte tantos favores pero es que tengo muchos problemas.

Exercise 10

1 Me dijo que vendría el lunes sin falta. **2** Me dijo que iría sola si no quería venir. **3** Me preguntó que cuándo llegaría. **4** Me preguntó si pintaría su casa. **5** Me preguntó si le ayudaría luego. **6** Me dijo que saldría más tarde.

Exercise 11

1 Yo que tú me quedaría en hoteles. **2** Yo en tu lugar iría en Navidad. **3** Yo que tú sólo comería cosas calientes. **4** Yo que tú me pondría la de la polio y la de hepatitis. **5** Yo en tu lugar tomaría las pastillas. **6** Yo que tú no me pondría la vacuna contra el cólera. **7** Yo en tu lugar viajaría en tren. **8** Yo en tu lugar sólo bebería agua mineral.

Exercise 12

- Areas to avoid: the south, the centre and the east, the Mediterranean coast.
- Keep the windows closed during the night.
- Use air conditioning with filters.
- Not to do too many activities outside between 5 and 10 in the morning and 6 and 10 in the evening.
- Keep the car windows closed when travelling.
- Place filters in the car air conditioning.
- Stay at home as much as possible during the days with a high level of pollen concentration.
- Avoid going out during windy days.
- Spend your holidays in places such as the beach.
- Not to cut the grass.
- Not to lie down on the grass.
- Not to dry the clothes outside during the days with a high pollen level.
- Wear sunglasses when going out.

Exercise 13

1 d 2 e 3 b 4 f 5 c 6 a 7 g

Exercise 14

	Doctor	Dialysis	Specific treatments
Documents / forms needed	E.111 form, original and copy Passport or ID	E.111-D1 form	E.112 form
Organisation / people responsible for obtaining the documents	Yourself / or INSS	The corresponding organisation of the country of origin	Social Security department of the country of origin

Unit 8

Exercise 1

1 las notas   los resultados de los exámenes **2** la matrícula   la inscripción **3** reembolsar   devolver el dinero que ya has pagado **4** la anulación   la cancelación **5** antelación   con anticipación, con cierto espacio de tiempo **6** convocatoria   cita o llamada a un examen / concurso

Exercise 2

	True	False
Sara has just done her exams.		X
Sara had the flu.	X	
Sara has been given her enrolment fee back.		X
Sara is sure she is is going to continue her studies.		X
Sara wants to stay in Madrid.		X
Sara has not talked to her tutor.	X	

Exercise 3

1 ¿Habrá ido a matricularse? **2** ¿Habrá aprobado todas las asignaturas? **3** ¿Habrán repetido el curso? **4** ¿Se habrá puesto nerviosa en el examen? **5** ¿Habrán sabido todas las preguntas? **6** ¿Le habrán dado la licenciatura? **7** ¿Habrá venido a tiempo? **8** ¿Habrá reconocido las tres novelas?

Exercise 4

1 Habríamos terminado ya pero no había luz. **2** Ellos se habrían ido de vacaciones pero no tenían dinero. **3** Habría estudiado inglés pero no había profesores. **4** Me habría matriculado pero no tenía los papeles. **5** Habría aprobado el examen pero no se encontraba bien. **6** Habrían estudiado más pero su madre estaba enferma.

Exercise 5

1 f **2** d **3** c **4** a **5** e **6** b

Exercise 6

1 Ella dijo que suponía que habría llegado. Ella dice que supone que habrá llegado. **2** Él me preguntó si no habría visto a Luis. **3** Me preguntó si lo habría terminado para el verano. **4** Dijo que creía que ya habría terminado. Dice que cree que ya habrá terminado. **5** Dijo que suponía que ya habría terminado la licenciatura. Dice que supone que ya habrá terminado la licenciatura. **6** Dijo que suponía que habría suspendido.

Exercise 7

1 ✓ Habrás visto a tu madre, ¿no? **4** ✓ Te habrás matriculado, ¿no?

Exercise 8

1st part: Itinerarios desde los 14 años 2nd part: Repeticiones 3rd part: Reválida 4th part: Grupos de refuerzo 5th part: Idioma extranjero

Exercise 9

1 actualmente **2** suspender, prueba, convocatoria, adelantar **3** superar, la nota, el expediente de Bachillerato **4** aprendizaje **5** potenciar

Exercise 10

1 True **2** False **3** True **4** True **5** False

Exercise 11

1 Tienes que <u>optar entre</u> las seis asignaturas, no puedes estudiar todas. **2** No sabía qué estudiar pero al final él <u>optó por</u> humanidades. **3** No <u>contaban con</u> la nieve y llegaron tarde. **4** Ellos <u>optaron por</u> hacer el examen en septiembre. **5** La reválida <u>cuenta con</u> dos pruebas. **6** No puedes <u>contar con</u> él, ya sabes que está muy enfermo. **7** <u>Contaba con</u> terminar hoy.

Exercise 12

1 Se construyó en 1968. **2** Se encontraron en su habitación. **3** Se descubrieron muchos errores. **4** Se resolvió el error. **5** Se hizo el año pasado. **6** Se firmó la semana pasada. **7** Se anuló la reunión. **8** Se creó un nuevo curso.

Exercise 13

1 Se puede pasar el examen sin estudiar. **2** No se puede beber. **3** No se puede comer carne de vaca en la India. **4** Se vive bien en Barcelona.

Unit 9

Exercise 1

1 False **2** False **3** True **4** True **5** False

Exercise 2

1 Algeciras and Milán. **2** Of having committed a crime against the rights of foreigners. **3** One person is under age. **4** All the people who have been arrested except for the one person who is under age.

Exercise 3

1 c **2** d **3** b **4** e **5** a

Exercise 4

1 trasladados, detenidos, interrogados **2** localizados **3** devueltos **4** rescatada, detenida, interrogada **5** interrogado

Exercise 5

1 Los turistas fueron trasladados al hotel. **2** El hotel fue construido hace muchos años. **3** La piscina será limpiada mañana. **4** La autopista será cerrada la semana próxima / que viene. **5** El grupo fue detenido ayer.

Exercise 6

1 fueron / son / han sido / serán. **2** fue **3** está **4** fue / es / ha sido / será **5** estaba

Exercise 7

1 El marroquí se quedó en el sur de España. **2** Los menús son muy baratos. **3** Este poster es fantástico. **4** Los jóvenes israelíes se fueron a Estados Unidos. **5** Estos rubíes son muy caros. **6** El iraquí está muy sorprendido. **7** Esos esquís son de tu hermano. **8** Me gustan estos films.

Exercise 8

	Time limitations	Geographical limitations	Activity limitations	Renewal
Type A	9 months		seasonal	no
Type B	1 year	specific place	specific	yes
Type C	3 years	anywhere in Spain	any activity	no
Type D	1 year		self-employed	yes

Exercise 9

1 con puntos y comas **2** en su punto **3** a la altura de las circunstancias **4** a punto **5** no veo ni gota **6** a punto **a** Debes llegar en punto. **b** Has dado en el punto. **c** Tienes razón pero hasta cierto punto. **d** Estaba a punto de decirle la verdad cuando entraste.

Exercise 10

> Reason for journey: to travel
>
> Money: 500 euros
>
> Friends in Spain: a female friend who lives in Seville
>
> Problem with her clothes: she has winter clothes although it's summer

Exercise 11

1 b **2** e **3** d **4** c **5** a

Exercise 12

1 a group of 59 immigrants **2** picking fruit **3** Nigeria, Sierra Leone, Bangladesh and Algeria. 'Han sido contratados como jornaleros.'

Unit 10

Exercise 1

1 She would like to work for an Internet company. **2** She was told on the telephone. **3** Her bag was stolen. **4** She cannot obtain it at the moment.

Exercise 2

1 Suspendieron la exposición. **2** Destrozaron los cuadros. **3** Trasladaron a las personas a la comisaría. **4** Detuvieron y trasladaron a dos estudiantes a la comisaría también. **5** Interrogaron a los dos estudiantes. **6** Golpearon a uno de los estudiantes.

Exercise 3

1 Me robaron en El Rastro. **2** Me lo dijeron ayer por la mañana. **3** Le ofrecerán un contrato. **4** Me dieron sólo la mitad del dinero. **5** Le dijeron una mentira. **6** No me dijeron nada. **7** Me ofrecieron un trabajo ayer. **8** Le dirán la verdad.

Exercise 4

1 b **2** e **3** a **4** c **5** f **6** d **7** g

Exercise 5

- Have you got many cash machines? (6)
- Have you thought of paying your bills by direct debit? (1)
- How much do you charge for the Cuenta 2000? (2)
- Which cards could I have? (3)
- How much is the fee for the credit card? (5)
- Could you give me the brochures related to the account? (7)
- How much credit would I have? (4)

Exercise 6

1 b **2** a **3** b **4** c **5** b

Exercise 7

1 leídas **2** pensado **3** cerrada **4** pensado **5** preparado **6** vista **7** reservadas

Exercise 8

1 c **2** e **3** g **4** h **5** b **6** j **7** i **8** a **9** f **10** d

Exercise 9

✓ Every country applies sanctions to the unemployed who reject a 'reasonable employment'.
✓ In Spain, in order to receive benefits, it does not matter how the unemployed has lost his / her job.

Exercise 10

1 para (in order to) **2** por (reason) **3** por (passive) **4** para (destination) **5** por (period of time) **6** para (in order to) **7** por (reason) **8** para (in order to) **9** por (reason) **10** para (deadline) **11** por (apology) **12** para (to be about to)

Exercise 11

1 En primer lugar voy a hablar sobre la nueva ley del paro, en segundo sobre los objetivos del gobierno y por último sobre las medidas que se van a tomar. **2** En primer lugar voy a hablar (me gustaría hablar) sobre el problema actual del paro, en segundo sobre las causas y por último sobre las posibles soluciones. **3** En primer lugar voy a hablar sobre el problema del SIDA en África, en segundo sobre la ayuda de la Unión Europea y por último sobre la ayuda internacional.

Unit 11

Exercise 1

✓ Liz has not heard about the Parque Doñana.
✓ Rosa has been in the park many times.
✓ Rosa advises Liz to have shrimp fritters and camomile tea.

Exercise 2

1 Espero que no vengas tarde. **2** Espero que salgas pronto. **3** Espero ir mañana. **4** Espero que comas toda la tortilla. **5** Espero que no valga mucho. **6** Espero que esté bien. **7** Espero tener suerte. **8** Espero que lo pases bien en Barcelona. **9** Espero que apruebes los exámenes. **10** Espero que no lo sepa.

Exercise 3

1 fumes **2** vengas **3** sepa **4** estén **5** llegue **6** trabajes **7** tengas **8** haya **9** vayamos

Exercise 4

✓ No utilices pilas recargables.   Utiliza pilas recargables.
✓ Tira las pilas en cualquier sitio.   No tires las pilas en cualquier sitio.
✓ Compra animales de especies protegidas.   No compres animales de especies protegidas.
✓ Cambia el agua de la piscina todos los días.   No cambies el agua de la piscina todos los días.
✓ No recicles los periódicos.   Recicla los periódicos.

Exercise 5

• Reserva el hotel para la primera noche en India.
• No cojas cualquier taxi en el aeropuerto, coge un taxi oficial.
• No bebas agua del grifo, compra siempre agua mineral.
• Come con la mano derecha, no comas con la mano izquierda.
• Viaja en tren, es muy cómodo.
• No te quedes en hoteles muy baratos, pueden ser peligrosos.
• Ten cuidado en las estaciones.
• Quítate los zapatos antes de entrar en los templos.
• No conduzcas por la noche, es peligroso.
• Si te invitan a cenar come algo antes de ir, normalmente cenan muy tarde.

Exercise 6

convivir	vivir con una persona
heredar	recibir dinero / posesiones después de la muerte de alguien
prueba	la demostración
albergar	alojar, dar protección
frenar	parar
talas	es la acción de talar, cortar los árboles
pastoreo	el cuidado del ganado (animales como las vacas)
implicar	envolver
compromiso	cuando estás dispuesto a hacer algo
acudir a	asistir a, ir a
tubo de escape	es el tubo en el coche por donde sale humo

Exercise 7

✓ Nature and mankind can live together in harmony.

✓ Forests purify the air and stop the development of erosion and deserts.

✓ Forests also offer many resources.

✓ The programme 'Look after your forests' tries to involve everybody in Andalucia.

✓ It is only possible to recover the natural resources through the commitment and participation of the citizens.

Exercise 8

- Don't light fires in the forests.
- Don't leave rubbish behind.
- Go to the forest on foot or by bicycle.
- Camp in suitable places.

Exercise 9

1 vayas **2** ir **3** olvide **4** llamarte **5** terminarlo (de que lo termine if it refers to somebody else) **6** termines **7** hagas

Exercise 10

1 como **2** tenga **3** estés **4** sale **5** lleguen **6** compres **7** está **8** pueda

Exercise 11

1 oyó **2** sepa **3** llegues **4** se fue **5** dé cuenta **6** hizo

Exercise 12

1 c **2** d **3** e **4** b **5** a

Unit 12

Exercise 1

1 País Vasco: PNV, EA **2** Cataluña: CiU, ERC **3** Galicia: BNG

Exercise 2

1 h **2** f **3** c **4** d **5** b **6** i **7** g **8** a **9** j **10** e

Exercise 3

1 There could be a scandal. **2** The campaign lasts for fifteen days, everyday there are opinion polls. **3** PSOE and IU but it wasn't successful. **4** People became disappointed with PSOE because of their privatisation policy and their encouragement of part-time jobs.

Exercise 4

1 Ojalá venga pronto mi madre. **2** Ojalá Pete recuerde grabar la película. **3** Ojalá ganemos mañana.

Exercise 5

1 ¡Qué cumplas muchos más! **2** ¡Que se mejore pronto! **3** ¡Qué te vaya bien en Málaga! **4** ¡Qué tengas suerte! **5** ¡Qué te lo pases bien! **6** ¡Qué te parta un rayo!

Exercise 6

Dear John

I hope you can come to Spain on the 23rd of June. It is my daughter's First Communion and we would like you to come to celebrate it with us. I don't think Lewis can make it but if you want, you can bring a friend with you. My daughter hopes you can come so do not disappoint her. When you know if you can come, send me an email.

Hugs

Carmen

I do hope you can come.

Exercise 7

1 Creo que perderá en las elecciones locales pero no creo que pierda las generales. **2** Creo que ganará algún escaño pero no creo que gane más de diez. **3** Creo que habrá un pacto electoral pero no creo que ganen las elecciones. **4** Cree que IU retirará su candidatura pero no creo que PSOE lo haga. **5** Creo que PSOE volverá al poder pero no creo que sea pronto. **6** Cree que habrá muchos conflictos laborales pero no creo que haya huelgas.

Exercise 8

1 Mi madre está harta de votar siempre al mismo partido. **2** Los españoles están hartos de que la gente sólo hable de Franco. **3** ¡Estoy hasta la coronilla de ti! **4** Juan está hasta la coronilla de que la gente le insulte. **5** María está harta de tener que leer tantos correos electrónicos. **6** Lola está harta de tantos chismes. **7** Carlos está hasta las narices de tantas bromas. **8** Los verdes están hartos de perder las elecciones.

Exercise 9

1 IU acabó perdiendo muchísimos escaños. **2** PCE dejó de presentarse a las elecciones. **3** Felipe González llegó a ser presidente. **4** HB acabó cambiando de nombre. **5** La gente acabó por votar al grupo minoritario. **6** El presidente dejó de hablar en la televisión.

Exercise 10

1 Levels of income, Paragraph 2 **2** Rate of development, Paragraph 3 **3** Barcelona comes top, Paragraph 1 **4** The richest and the poorest provinces, Paragraph 4

Exercise 11

1st paragraph		*2nd paragraph*	
income	renta	standard of living	nivel de vida
data, facts	datos	bottom places	los lugares de cola
to be at the head of	estar en la cabeza de	the gap / the range	el abanico

3rd paragraph		*4th paragraph*	
development	desarrollo	the average income	la renta media
the position	puesto		

5th paragraph	
goods	bienes
retail shops	comercios minoristas
savings banks	cajas de ahorro

Exercise 12

1 Income per capita and its development. **2** Girona and Lleida have the highest income and Badajoz and Cádiz have the lowest. **3** Donostia / San Sebastián is the richest and La Linea de la Concepción and Sanlúcar de Barrameda are the poorest. **4** 423 cars per 1000 people. 414 telephones per 1000 people.

Unit 13

Exercise 1

1 She is staying with Pete's friend because she wants to practise her English. **2** She thinks the building is one of the most impressive in the world. **3** It is like a large sculpture. **4** No, it isn't, it is in Madrid. **5** To visit other interesting buildings in Bilbao, and to visit the fishing villages between Bermeo and San Sebastian. **6** Nerea gives Andrea money and wants her to buy some tins of anchovy from Ondarroa.

Exercise 2

1 Quiero que compres una escultura pequeña para Lorena. **2** Necesito que vendas ese cuadro. **3** Es necesario que lo empaquetéis bien. **4** Quiero que termines esta acuarela antes de que sea de noche. **5** Quiero que hablen con ese pintor tan famoso. **6** Quiero que vea todas sus obras. **7** Necesito que diseñe un edificio moderno.

Exercise 3

1 fue **2** sepa **3** llegue **4** viene **5** haga **6** está **7** diga **8** vaya

Exercise 4

1 He spent three months in France learning the language in 1936. He was also in Paris from 1948 to 1951. **2** He studied Architecture at college but did not finish the degree. He also studied painting at a private school. He also studied in Paris. **3** He used iron, steel, alabaster, granite, cement, wood and marble.

Exercise 5

1 Que mandes toda la información que puedas. **2** Que hagas todo lo que puedas antes de irte. **3** Que traigas otra botella. **4** Que no te preocupes. **5** Que vengas cuando puedas.

Exercise 6

1 c **2** e **3** d **4** b **5** a

Exercise 7

1 Aunque llegue tarde iremos al restaurante. **2** Aunque llega tarde todos los días, nunca pide disculpas. **3** A pesar de que sólo tiene 3 años, habla bastante bien los dos idiomas. **4** Aunque sea rico no creo que pueda vivir sin trabajar. **5** Aunque es rico no es feliz. **6** Por más que lo repitas no te voy a creer. **7** Pese a que es joven, siempre está enfermo. **8** Aunque no sea / es la mejor cantante, va a ganar el festival.

Exercise 8

1 g **2** d **3** e **4** f **5** c **6** b **7** a

Exercise 9

1 b **2** e **3** d **4** a **5** c

Exercise 10

1 *Las edades de Lulu* is one of the most popular books in the last 25 years and *Malena es un nombre de tango* is read a lot, especially by young people. **2** She became a writer by mistake, she ended up studying Geography and History instead of Latin. **3** She thinks that the Spanish literature is in a good state; that there are about ten good writers and that Spanish people read more than before.

Exercise 11

1 He studied medicine. **2** journalist, assistant film director, scriptwriter, professional producer. **3** The Goya prize with his film *Vacas*, also a prize for the best foreign film at Cannes with *La ardilla roja*.

Unit 14

Exercise 1

✓ John was told by the representative to go to the agency when he returned from his holidays.
✓ John took photographs of the building work.
✓ The first thing John has to do is to fill in a complaints form.
✓ John needs to give the following information: name, nationality, address, passport number and other details.
✓ John may phone Carlos.

Exercise 2

1 hayan llegado **2** haya hecho **3** haya aprobado **4** hayas terminado **5** hayas llamado **6** hayan perdido **7** hayas recibido **8** haya ido

Exercise 3

1 escribieras **2** te quejes **3** ayudes **4** pudiera **5** efectuara **6** remitas **7** rellenara **8** quedaras

Exercise 4

1 Ojalá fuera domingo mañana / Ojalá fuera mañana domingo. **2** Ojalá Sandra venga pronto. **3** Ojalá no fuera verdad. **4** Ojalá no tuviera que ir. **5** Ojalá haga sol mañana.

Exercise 5

1 Juan Costa thinks the figures are positive because the number of tourists remains the same and Spain is doing better than their competitors. **2** The Balearic Islands have suffered the most and although Juan Costa does not blame the green tax, he has asked the Balearic government to revise their policy. **3** Cataluña, Valencia and Andalucia. **4** The income will be lower because they had to reduce their prices in order to be competitive.

Exercise 6

1 Me dijo que fuera a la agencia. **2** Me dijo que les mandara las fotos. **3** Me dijo que me quedara con algunas fotos por si acaso. **4** Me dijo que rellenara una hoja de reclamaciones. **5** Me dijo que escribiera mi nombre, nacionalidad y domicilio. **6** Me dijo que remitiera el original de esa hoja a la Delegación Provincial del Ministerio de Comercio y Turismo. **7** Me dijo que hiciera una fotocopia del original. **8** Me dijo que le llamara si tenía algún problema.

Exercise 7

1 c **2** d **3** e **4** f **5** g **6** b **7** a

Exercise 8

1 Si tuviera más dinero compraría una casa en España. **2** Si tuviera más dinero trabajaría menos. **3** Si tuviera más dinero ayudaría a mi familia. **4** Si tuviera más dinero cogería más vacaciones. **5** Si tuviera más dinero viajaría más a menudo a España.

Exercise 9

1 Si hubiera tenido tiempo habría ido contigo. **2** Si hubiera podido hablar con él lo habría hecho. **3** Si hubiera estado en España no habría visto los partidos de fútbol. **4** Si hubiera habido problemas habría hablado con él. **5** Si hubiera trabajado más habría terminado pronto. **6** Si Manuel hubiera traído más vino habría habido suficiente. **7** Si hubiera tenido suficiente dinero, habría comprado ese reloj. **8** Si hubiera podido venir habría venido.

Exercise 10

1 They are forms that shops, restaurants, etc., must have so that a client can make a complaint in writing about the service offered. **2** The forms are normally the same across Spain but the Comunidades Autónomas may change some areas. **3** You may go to the local police station.

Exercise 11

Estimados Señores:

Siento tener que <u>dirigirme</u> a ustedes para presentar una <u>queja</u> contra el mal servicio de uno de los hoteles de su cadena.

Mi marido y yo fuimos al Hotel Barcelona de la localidad malagueña de Marbella para realizar <u>la reserva</u> de una habitación doble para 4 noches. Tras realizar la reserva a las 13:00 horas y hablar con el personal de la recepción del hotel, quien nos informó que no era necesario entregar una cantidad en concepto de <u>señal</u> para realizar la reserva, decidimos almorzar antes.

Cuando regresamos al hotel, nos llevamos la desagradable sorpresa de que la habitación <u>había sido ocupada</u> por otra pareja. Solicitamos <u>una hoja de reclamaciones</u> pero el hotel <u>se negó</u> alegando que no estaba obligado a dárnosla aunque había un cartel que informaba de la existencia de las mismas.

El hotel no dio ningún tipo de <u>justificación</u> ni solución y nos vimos obligados a pasar la noche en un hotel de diferente calidad.

Esperamos que <u>tomen</u> las medidas necesarias para que este tipo de problema no vuelva a ocurrir en sus hoteles. Esperando una pronta <u>respuesta</u>.

Les saluda atentamente

Topic index